The

Great Governing Families

of

England

THE

GREAT GOVERNING FAMILIES

OF

ENGLAND

BY

JOHN LANGTON SANFORD

AND

MEREDITH TOWNSEND

IN TWO VOLUMES

VOL. I.

Essay Index Reprint Series

 BOOKS FOR LIBRARIES PRESS
FREEPORT, NEW YORK

First Published 1865
Reprinted 1972

Library of Congress Cataloging in Publication Data

Sanford, John Langton, 1824-1877.
  The great governing families of England.

  (Essay index reprint series)
  Reprint of the 1865 ed.
  1. Gt. Brit.--Nobility. I. Townsend, Meredith
White, 1831-1911, joint author. II. Title.
DA305.S2 1972   929.72   77-37862
ISBN 0-8369-2623-4

PRINTED IN THE UNITED STATES OF AMERICA
BY
NEW WORLD BOOK MANUFACTURING CO., INC.
HALLANDALE, FLORIDA 33009

Preface.

In the compilation of these histories, the object has not been to produce a work of original research, or one based on unpublished or exclusive materials, but (while not neglecting to make use of any facts of this description which the Authors' own reading occasionally supplied) to subject rather the matter already existing in a more or less scattered form in printed books to the test of the accepted rules of historical evidence, and (with the limitations imposed by selection and condensation) to place before the general reader, in a popular form, the leading ascertained facts in the history of our Great Families in connection with the results of the latest researches into our national history.

Such being the plan of the book, references to authorities, and acknowledgments of obligations to particular writers, were (except in rare cases) out of the question. For the justification of their judgment on facts and persons, the Authors must appeal to those who have studied the subject for themselves, merely observing that they have endeavoured to steer a just course between the extremes of scepticism and credulity—to reject absolutely only manifest errors and fabrications—to admit, under the reserve of a suspended judgment, possible facts and probable hypotheses, and to carefully distinguish these from statements resting on positive and satisfactory evidence.

The papers have now been revised throughout, and matter has been occasionally added which had been previously omitted through want of space.

Contents of the First Volume.

GREAT GOVERNING FAMILIES

OF

ENGLAND.

Introduction.

ENGLAND is governed in times of excitement by its
people; in quiet times by its property. That is, I
believe, a true as well as a brief description of that
"aristocratic" element in the constitution which alike
in its habitual force and in its occasional failures so
often perplexes the critics of the Continent. The
ultimate sovereignty rests, and, under more or less
cumbrous forms, always has rested, with the tax-pay-
ing body, and, whenever fairly aroused by a great
danger, a widespread desire, or a novel conviction,
they have exercised their authority with a force before which class resistance has become almost imper-
ceptible. That resistance has regulated the tide, but
from the Reformation to the Crimean war it has never
succeeded in arresting or seriously retarding its flow.
In quiet times, however, when the people has no

A

angry grievance or immediate want, is unstirred by
any strong current of emotion, and not impelled by
any appeal to its imagination, this country has always
been governed by a limited class, whom, with our
usual adherence to words after their meaning has
passed away, we continue to term the aristocracy.
Their organised power, it is true, is in appearance a
thing of the past. The country is not, as it was under
the Conqueror's sons and the Plantagenets, ruled by
a small number of families, combining all political
privileges with all the rights of ownership. The land-
holders are not, as they were under the Tudors—when
their individual power had become illegal, and their
collective sway was impaired by the reverence paid to
the reigning house—the effective depositaries of all
military strength. Nor can they now, as they could
in all quiet times from the Great Rebellion to 1831,
nominate a clear working majority of apparently independent legislators, with rights greater than those
ever yet legally exercised by a European sovereign.
But their influence on ordinary occasions, and within
the limits specified, is still almost irresistible, and
could they ever agree to unite to use their strength
as a body—as they very nearly do, for example, in
defence of the Established Church—might be danger-
ously strong. It is difficult to over-estimate, for example, the direct power of the two or three hundred
individuals whose names are recorded upon the map
which faces the title-page of this volume. They could
not, it is admitted on all sides, arrest a popular religious reform, or refuse to commence an ardently
longed-for war, or drive the country into a course of
policy to which the commercial and working classes

were, either from instinct or conviction, definitively opposed. They could not, for example, send an army to reseat the Pope, or abolish trial by jury, or drive the nation back into a protective tariff. But they could, without doubt, so completely control provincial opinion, as, with the aid of the classes who habitually follow them, to select a majority of the Legislature. They could, if united, render the existence of any Cabinet of which they did not approve impossible for long periods, and they could and do impose on every political administration, every political party, and most political manifestations, certain strict tradition-ary rules of action, certain limits within which the whole play of the forces created by the constitution must be carried on or be arrested. It is their influ-ence, partly direct and used through their property, partly and chiefly indirect and exerted through social position, which keeps the popular force from spending itself on ideals, as in France, or in vague and purpose-less efforts equally marvellous for strength and steri-lity, as for the hour in America.

The direct power of this class, best defined as that of the larger Landowners, through their property, is, we conceive, habitually under-estimated. Unlike the Prussian nobility or the Austrian, they are, fortunately for the State, so disunited that their immense legal authority is, though not unfelt, still unresented. If the nation ever believes itself to be fighting a caste, as it believed in the matter of the Reform Bill, it still fights it with members of the same caste, using the same means and wielding the same powers, marching at its head. Had *all* the landowners overtly resisted that measure, the first step of the nation after its inevi-

table success would have been to abolish primogeniture
—the key to modern English society—and so render
the existence of a landlord power in the State in a few
years impossible. This is what the Dutch, who live
in a great measure under social conditions identical
with our own, have actually done, and the measure is
just beginning to pulverise their aristocracy. It is
only when united by some attack on a vital privilege
like this that the direct power would be painfully
visible, or that we should fully realise that the landlords could, by simply threatening to use the property-
right of changing tenants without reason assigned,
nominate, at least, one clear half of the reformed
House of Commons—viz., most of the county members,
many of the medium borough members, and all the
members for those boroughs which, like East Retford,
though nominally towns, are really strips carved out
of the surrounding county. We simply mention the
fact, however, to show that "aristocracy," or, in other
words, landlord influence, has in England a legal basis,
for the postulate assumed is the most extreme expression of the truth. No union is possible, nor is any
occasion conceivable, on which it would be worth
many landlords' while to call up from the soil an
entirely new body of tenantry. The power, however,
exists, and, as applied to individual elections, has been
repeatedly and effectively employed, and only seems
endurable or natural because if Blenheim seats a Tory
for Woodstock, Woburn Abbey can seat an extreme
Liberal for Tavistock. The extent of the direct sway
may be illustrated, to quote only one example, from
the Act passed a session or two ago, for strengthening
the Game Laws. The towns had no manner of wish

to increase the stringency of those laws—rather, if anything, disliked the measure, as at once unjust and superfluous. The tenant-farmers felt the innovation as one more attack on their rights, and the agricultural labourers viewed the enlarged powers conceded by it to the police as undisguised oppression. Still the law was swept through by a majority far greater than any which usually secures the gravest measures when proposed by the most popular administration.

It is, however, through indirect means that the landlords usually exercise their power. The million of voters who are in England the legal trustees of the people, partly from traditionary respect, partly in the counties from fear of consequences, and partly from habitual and rooted self-distrust, turn, on the occurrence of any event, to the educated few for guidance. Those few in their turn are swayed—naturally, as Englishmen think, though the fact is almost peculiar to Great Britain—by the men whose property has for generations enabled them to stand close to the political centre, and whom, therefore, they think, on the whole, the best informed. Why they should be so swayed is a point which an entire history of England might be written to explain. Nobody dreams of such a reference in Germany, or Sweden, or any of the many countries of Europe which still recognise a privileged class. Mr Disraeli explains the practice as growing out of the imaginative influence secured by "the sustained splendour of their stately lives;" but we conceive, though that has its effect, its root is to be sought in the confidence that the great landlords will care first of all for the interests and honour of England, that the great families may be relied on for

B

freedom from personal motive—that, in short, the "stake in the country" idea is a reality. History certainly does not suggest that that confidence is misplaced. A house, for example—it is not, strictly speaking, a family—which, like that of Percy, has six times staked its grand position and the heads of its members upon political objects having no political bearing, has earned its claim to be heard when the public weal is in question. The majority of those it advises do not, perhaps, know its history; but they do know that it has been their habit to take that advice, and till full cause has been shown Englishmen do not abandon habits. The advice so given spreads from castle to grange, grange to mansion, thence through the limited but powerful society which lives in habitual contact with the great, and in a few weeks three or four hundred individuals have laid down the ideas on which Parliament and the Cabinet alike will act. The Upper House feels them at once, and the Lower stands directly *en rapport* with the great proprietors. They, as we have said, return an enormous proportion of county members. Their social weight brings the class which has wealth but not distinction to their feet, and they have besides all these a link to the House of Commons known elsewhere in Italy alone. Whether from innate flunkeyism, as Mr Bright would assert, or from the effect of historical associations, as the compilers of Peerages would affirm, or from the influence of property supported by both these feelings, as we should be apt to believe, the act is certain. In the most Radical borough in the most Radical county of England, the chance of the eldest son of a great landed proprietor is, *cæteris pari-*

bus, better than that of any conceivable opponent, except a recognised statesman or orator of the very first stamp. Earl Grosvenor unknown will, unless a very outrageous Tory, beat any local notability in a place like Marylebone, and, if an outrageous Tory, will have a thousand or two more votes than any merchant or banker who might for party purposes venture to stand a contest on the same side. The sons of the landlords do habitually so come forward; and the consequence of this feeling, combined with their direct power, is, that there were, in the session of Parliament of 1864, 1 Marquess, 5 Earls, 15 Viscounts, 34 Lords, 72 Baronets, 58 Honourables, and 100 palpably belonging to the historic names of the land, seated in the House of Commons. In other words, the members in direct and constant communication with the great landlords, who habitually defer to them, and who, above all, take from them their political *tone*, control the whole of the Upper House, and, with their allies among the *nouveaux riches*, a majority in the Lower. As we have before said, this influence *seems* less, because it is so divided, but it is clearly apparent in matters of Church government, and the present position of ecclesiastical questions exactly indicates both its extent and its limits. The aristocracy are, on the whole, more liberal in theological opinion than the middle class, and probably would, if the matter were left to them, completely remodel the whole arrangement of subscriptions, tests, and articles of belief. They are utterly powerless to do anything of the kind, afraid almost to open their lips, lest their liberality should be mistaken by the ignorant for infidelity. Here they are in conflict with the nation, and therefore without even the semblance of active leadership. But they can, and do, marshal an almost impregnable array in defence of an abuse at which the nation looks askance, but which it is not yet prepared vehemently to assail—viz., the territorial *status* of the Irish Church. Who doubts that but for their shield that Church would at once go down, or that they could, if united, protract its existence, perhaps for centuries more ; or that, were the nation resolved—as resolved as on the Corn Laws—the irresistible opposition would silently melt away, till men wondered how they ever believed reform so hopeless or so distant ?

The existence of a real and permanent aristocratic power in English politics, wielded by men whose numbers are by no means very great, is, I conceive, as certain as that of the people or the throne. With its merits or demerits I have at present nothing whatever to do. My own belief is that its habitual action, if limited by severe restraints and co-existent with the essentially democratic influence of a free press, is decidedly beneficial. The pressure from above anneals the governing class below, hardens all " ideas " till they become plans, narrows all floods of emotion till they can work as regulated motive powers. Above all, the class serves, as it were, to *strain* the popular sentiment, relieving the torrent of its impurities, eliminating that element of vulgarity which, in politics as in social life, has its root in a contempt for the feelings and rights of others. The present purpose is analysis, and not argument,—to point out that even now, whatever a few thinkers may assert, the power of the aristocracy is still the most direct and constant of the five influences—the landlords, commerce, the priesthood, the press, and the population—which in quiet times direct the internal and external policy of Great Britain. It is, then, perhaps, worth while to define what the English "aristocracy" really means. It is, I conceive, only another word for the greater owners of land. It has little to do with office, though that in England has been, and is, rarely held by very poor men. Still less has it to do with pedigree, though ancient birth may increase the influence which primarily belongs to property. The possession of estates by one house through a long series of years indefinitely increases the authority of that house, but it is from the influence of habit, not from any reverence paid to blood. No one cares as a political point whether the Stanleys are Smiths or no; but the loss of their estates would at once destroy their local power. The Percies have from the Conquest always held their present position, though the family has been absorbed once in the Lovains, then in the Seymours, and finally in the Smithsons, a race, though by no means plebeian, comparatively without a pedigree, but, nevertheless, exercising the hereditary influence as fully and with as little resistance as if they had descended unbroken from the first man who robbed the Saxons. There is no pedigree in England, and very few in Europe, which can vie with that of the Earls of Devon—and, unlike most, it is not of heralds' manufacture—but an additional five thousand acres would represent five times the political influence derived from that descent. It is doubtful whether the pedigree of the Sovereign in the least exalts her rank in the eyes of her people, for the infinite majority of the middle class trace it back to the Electress Sophia, and there stop. It is true that in the centre of the group of landlords occur some great historic names, and that the most prominent — Percies and Stanleys, Russells and Howards, Lowthers and Grenvilles —are intertwined with the whole history of Great Britain; but a family now of vast influence — the Gowers—is but faintly linked into the national annals, and of those we have mentioned not one can show what Continental heralds call unbroken descent. Historic associations convey influence, but they cling to the property rather than the race, and the " aristocratic element" of the English constitution is, in fact, simply the class which owns the soil.

It was with these views that I suggested the publication, in a popular form, through the columns of the 'Spectator,' of a series of histories of the greater English families—those few whose influence being still great has from age to age been perceptible in our annals, who form, as it were, the backbone of the aristocratic system. Consulting Mr Langton Sanford, a gentleman whose studies had led him to a minute investigation of several periods of English history, he was struck with the idea, and agreed to carry it out to the end. The bulk of this work is therefore his, and it is only in deference to his generous dislike to assume the credit of any labour however trifling, or any idea however inchoate, which was not his own, that my name is attached to it at all. All that I have contributed is the original suggestion, this introduction, a few notes, and a general supervision—very real as regards the Percies, Stanleys, Lowthers, Gowers, and one or two others—quite illusory as regards the

remaining histories. The patient and thorough investigation which has marked each narrative is no
credit of mine, nor have I anything whatever to do
with the most original portion of the whole, the personal sketches, which amount in some cases—notably
in that of the Protector Somerset—to new biographies.

It remains only to explain, with something more of
detail, the strict, and, as it appeared to many, somewhat capricious limits of selection. The object of the
series was *not* the history of aristocratic influence in
Great Britain. That immense subject, which would
be worthy of a Hallam, was altogether beyond the
range of any newspaper, even of one which dares
think that educated men care nearly as much to read
of the origin of political powers as to watch their
daily operation. The purpose was simply to remind
the readers of the 'Spectator' of a fact always forgotten, the permanence given to English policy by the
influence continuing through centuries of a limited
group of families. That group contains only the
houses which, while now in the front rank, have been
for generations distinguished by holding high office
in the field or civil administration, who have advised
cabinets or won victories. The lesser aristocracy,
however wealthy or however old, had in the plan no
place whatever. Under any scheme, no family, however old, was included unless it was now also great;
no family, however great, could be reckoned unless
it had also a great political history. The first rule
struck out, as to my own surprise it proved, every
commoner, with the doubtful exception of the Wynns
of Wynnstay; the second left us dubious only as
to the claims of the clergyman-peer who now repre-

sents the mighty family of the King-maker, and whose descendants, if they continue to manage their wide but poor estates as he is doing, may yet claim a place among the most powerful in the land. My object was to elucidate the half-forgotten but cardinal fact of British constitutional history, the existence in the empire of a few great families who have exercised from age to age an unbroken influence upon its policy, who have occasionally been powerful enough to govern the country as if it were their property, and who even now, when the feudal *régime* has disappeared, when opinion has become an executive force, when ultimate power has been legally transferred to the whole middle class, are stronger than any other single interest, and, if united, could resist almost any combination of interests. The origin of these families has been various—conquest, service, Court favour, or high business ability—the single uniform fact being that they can survive everything except the loss of their lands ; but from the time of the Reformation they have been leading influences in the State, the fixed data with which every Government and party and political genius has had sooner or later to reckon. They wrested from the people the spoils of the monasteries, and they defended the people against the policy of the Stuarts ; they built up the constitutional throne under William the Dutchman, and saved it under George the German ; they fought Europe through the great struggle which lasted our fathers' lives, defied the people in 1831, were beaten by them in 1832, and have, as will be speedily shown, in the succeeding thirty-two years, once more rebuilt their power. That power, as the series shows, has rested on many circum-

stances ; but it has always been connected inseparably
with the possession of land. During the feudal times
the class ruled naturally, for the great owners of land
were by the feudal system the only men in command of
military force. When the Wars of the Roses, the cruelly
subtle policy of the House of York, and the extraordinary personal qualities of the House of Tudor, appeared
to have shattered their strength, they and their depen-
dants contrived to seize the third of England which
belonged to the Church, and when the last Tudor died
they retained under the Stuart dynasty the only consistent power. Could Cromwell but have conciliated
them we should still in all human probability be living
under the shadow of a national dynasty, English in
lineage and speech and habit of thought, English, too,
in all likelihood, in its narrow insularity. As it was,
the steady abstinence of the nobles prevented the
necessary enthronement, gave time for the reaction,
and enabled the people once more to recall the evil
Scotch House who in England never entertained a
policy their people approved—who never built aught,
or founded aught, or reformed aught—to whom power
brought nothing so sweet as the opportunity of tyranny,
and adversity no lesson so keenly felt as the value of
dissimulation. When the reaction had become intolerable the great families called in a Stuart, who was also
a Dutchman ; and when the curse which in all ages
has, fortunately for Englishmen, rested on the race,
had spoiled even that experiment, when half-Stuart
William, and Stuart Mary, and Stuart Anne, had died
childless, they summoned the German House, under
whose reign we and they alike have flourished beyond
historic precedent.

From the Act of Settlement to 1831, English history is but the record of the intrigues of the governing families ; and when in 1832 the people deprived them of the legal autocracy they and their cousins possessed through their majority in Parliament, they bided their time, secure that in " the long-run the influence of property was sure to tell." It did tell. During the long peace which followed 1832 their property increased enormously; the ability the class has always displayed led them to take the lead in all productive enterprise; they reformed agriculture, opened mines, built great harbours, planted forests, cut canals, accepted and profited by the railway system, and built the faubourgs of the great cities. Able and audacious, still regarded with curious liking by the people, and full of that individuality, that sense of personal right, which is the strength of an aristocracy, they again threw themselves into politics, and speedily regained nearly their ancient monopoly of power. They alone could afford to follow politics from boyhood as a profession, and that fact gave and gives them a twenty years' start of all competitors. They alone have as a class that instinct of control given to able individuals in all classes, and they therefore speedily monopolised high offices. Above all, they alone had as a class not to be made known to the people. Smith must serve before a constituency knows who Smith is, but a Seymour's name tells the same constituency all about him, his antecedents and his connections, his fortune and his tone. Hence a preference on the hustings almost ludicrously strong—so strong that in the counties a bad specimen of the class, some red-eyed, knock-kneed, gawky lad of twenty-one, has often a better chance of public favour

than the man who has all his life been the guiding
mind of the locality. So powerful has been the action
of these circumstances, so engrained is in England the
preference for these houses, that the thirty-one families
whose histories we have related supply at this moment
one clear fourth of the English House of Commons,
the ultimate power in the State. A careful analysis
shows that the thirty-one families at this moment supply one hundred and ten members, or a clear working
fourth of the English section of the representation—
have, in fact, as great a direct power as the whole kingdom of Ireland, double that of Scotland, five times
that of London, as much as that of London and the
forty next greatest cities. I believe it to be beyond
all shadow of doubt that when we have added the
great Irish and the great Scotch proprietors, it will be
found that sixty families supply, and for generations
have supplied, one-third of the House of Commons,
one-third of the ultimate governing power for an
Empire which includes a fourth of the human race.

The political signification of a fact like this needs
little exposition, but I may in a few words just point
to the main advantage and disadvantage which the
Empire has derived from its existence. The great
houses have been, and to a large extent still are, to
our political system what bones are to the body. Un-
seen, they have given strength and firmness to what
might else have been a gelatinous mass. No king,
or demagogue, or soldier has been able to mould the
mass according to his own fancies because of these
hard substances. They have frequently resisted even
the apparently irresistible current of events; once, in
the great Continental war, decidedly and very un-

wisely they turned it back. Slow, like all oligarchies, to admit the necessity of change, tenacious of ideas once received, daring in experiment when a need has once become patent to them, they have given to our policy consistency, courage, and, above all, that faculty which all democracies without exception lack—an almost asinine patience. Seymours or Percies, Russells or Herberts expect to be great next century as now, plan for next century as well as this, reckon immediate advantage light when compared with the great objects, the permanent grandeur and rank and power which they desire England to hold, because with the greatness of England their own is indissolubly bound up. It is the element of resistance, the breeze in the brick, the hair in the mortar, the fibre in the wood, the bone in the body, which they contribute to our social fabric, the quality of permanence which they add to our institutions. They are the trees in the hedge ; and that simile also expresses the one great disadvantage of their existence. They shade the field too much. Corn must be very good and the sunshine very bright for it to ripen under them. Or to quit metaphor, it is the disadvantage of aristocracy that all political ability not immediately connected with rank has a double task to perform—first to rise to the aristocratic level, then to persuade the people. It takes an able man twenty years to obtain from the nation the consideration these families obtain from birth, to put Jones at forty-five on a level with Cavendish at twenty-one. This is true not only of Parliament but of the services; and the consequence is, that three-fourths of the ability and courage and genius of the people is lost to the service of the State. A

Wellesley is a general at thirty, a Havelock or Campbell wastes his life in rising to the point at which
men think of making him a general. The consequence is, that unless England happens at any one
moment to find a genius in the highest rank, she
must either do without one, or content herself with
one who comes from the mass, and has wasted half
his power in raising himself above them. But for the
fact that the great families sometimes adopt a man of
striking ability, as they adopted Burke, Pitt, Peel in
part, Sir Cornewall Lewis, and may yet adopt Mr
Gladstone, this evil would, in the long-run, outweigh
all the advantages of their power; for if, in the cloudy
lesson of history, there be one maxim clear, it is that
nations in their hour of trial are saved by men and
not by systems—that though a patriciat may govern
Rome, it is the individual dictator who must in
emergency preserve it. Even as it is, this mischief is
most marked, and will before long call for some strong
remedy, if we would not acknowledge to all the world
that England is becoming effete. Strength and exclusiveness are the good and the evil of the oligarchical element in the British Constitution. Fortunately
for the country the division into parties, while it
leaves the strength intact, diminishes the exclusiveness. Whigs and Tories maintain on all grand points,
such as the necessity of power at sea, the same tradi-
tional policy ; but as neither Whig nor Tory can rely
on the whole of the aristocratic strength, each is
thrown back on the people, and Lord Derby stands
surrounded by a Cabinet of commoners, and even
Whig magnates angrily doubt whether the son of a
West Indian merchant can be prevented from becom-

ing Premier. But for this, and the total inaptitude of
the class for journalism, the only political function
they have never attempted, the exclusiveness might
yet make our history resemble too nearly that of
Venice. The Republican oligarchy ruled ably a
thousand years and died, while the little dukedom
which was once its feeble rival has expanded into a
sixth Great Power.

Will the influence of these great families endure ?
The answer of most thinkers is that it will not—that
the steady growth of the democratic idea has pul-
verised influences greater than theirs, and must ultimately pulverise them. I cannot feel so certain—
cannot blind myself to the facts, that after Cæsarism
had crushed the Roman world to one uniform level
of slavery, the patriciat had still a monopoly of regular administration ; that in modern France the Fau-
bourg St Germain still rules society ; that in modern
America it is a real help to a man to be born Adams,
or Randolph, or Winthrop ; that in this England of
ours the abolition of the Upper House would instantly
fill the Lower one with great Peers. Let the suffrage
be universal, and Earl Derby stand for Lancashire,
does any one know any Hodgson who would have a
chance ? The re-division of property may ultimately
shatter their power, but short of that their dignity
and consideration will probably for a century steadily
increase. We are probably but on the threshold of
commercial success, and of that vast enterprise it is
they who always reap the first-fruits. No trade can
flourish that for every pound does not pour a shilling
into the treasury of a Grosvenor or a Bentinck, a Russell or a Stanley, a Neville or a Gower. They own

the soil, and rental rises with wealth, as the surface
of a field rises from successive deposits of guano.
Every year, too, the pedestal on which they stand,
the greatness of the Anglo-Saxon race, rises and
spreads wider. In another hundred years these
thirty-one families will be the marked and ticketed
families among two hundred millions of English-
speaking men, the only persons possessed of advantages to which ordinary men cannot attain, the only
figures higher than that increasing crowd. A Percy,
say, was great under the Tudors—that is, among two
millions of half-civilised men. He is less now comparatively, but positively he stands socially above
sixty millions of wholly civilised men, who are rack-
ing nature to find him means of gratification. His
political power may decline, but his social power
must increase. A Scott might once have taken the
field at the head of four thousand followers—the Duke
of Buccleuch could not rely on the swords of four;
but then 190 members of Parliament would not have
voted that a road should be turned lest the house of
Scott should be compelled to look on coaches. Every
year, too, adds to the number of the *nouveaux riches*,
precipitates into society some four or five men, each
with his million, with the power which belongs to a
million, and with a sovereign reverence for the few
families which have millions too, *and* something else
they themselves can neither pretend nor buy, a direct
connection with the past history of an imperial race.
Dukedoms may be abolished by the year 2000,—we
pretend to no opinion on that point—perhaps no man
save John Stuart Mill could give us even a reasonable
prophecy ; but of this we feel assured, that if they

are not abolished, an English dukedom will in that year be a prize beyond all social compare—a prize such as a throne is now—a position the ultimate goal of all that is great, or ambitious, or rich, among a race which will by that time be ruling directly or indirectly over half the world. The increase of intelligence, the new rapidity of intercommunication, the terrible publicity under which all our children will be doomed to live, will only increase this tendency, as telescopes make the boulders on a plain more and not less prominent to the eye. The political power may depart, though I do not think it will, for wealth grows stronger instead of weaker, and the great houses more conscious of their position, and therefore more careful for its maintenance; but the social power must increase; and, unless we greatly mistake, a hundred and thirty years hence a popular journalist will still find in this series materials which will interest a far larger and more widely-scattered audience. Mankind is more conservative than enthusiasts dream; and, remembering that after all the long and weary struggles of the nations the descendants of Henry the Fowler still move all the armies of Europe save the French, we cannot feel certain that our great-grandchildren will have lost the help or escaped the influence of the Great Governing Families.

MEREDITH TOWNSEND.

The Percies.

NGLISH family history dates from the Conquest,* two hundred years later than the appearance of the royal caste of Europe, who may be said generally to date from Charlemagne. There are a few families who claim a Saxon descent, but scarcely one of them has risen to the first rank, and, perhaps, only one of them, the reigning house, can show a root in the Heptarchy beyond all doubt or cavil. Not one even claims to be descended from a Roman settler, though the Romans held England four hundred years, and erected a civilised state,

* Pedigree is one of the permanent delusions of mankind, though the founder of a great race is always its greatest, and a plebeian; and there seems no *primâ facie* reason why some families should not be very much older—why, for instance, the Roman consular houses should have died out so completely. As a matter of fact, however, the tide which submerged the Empire washed out the record, and the modern patriciat starts from 800. The oldest provable succession is that of the Ranas of Oodeypore, who have reigned in one place 3000 years; but it is kept up by adoption. The man who died about 1036, as the last Prince of the Captivity, had *possibly* a pedigree stretching through all history. He was the descendant of a family which, in the time of Domitian, was accepted by all Jews and by the Emperor as descended from David; and if that belief were correct—as, from the similar history of Mohammed's family, it *may* have been—that would be a pedigree traceable name by name to Adam. There is no other instance that we know of a pedigree even possibly older than Rome.—(M. T.)

C

whose history may yet be recovered, and some of whose rulers must have retreated with the Britons into the hills. Not one is *certainly* Briton or Dane; the two or three said to be Saxon owe a great deal to heralds; and even of early Normans but few can be proved to survive. Among the very earliest is the great house of Percy, which represents directly, though somewhat imperfectly, a man who followed William the Bastard to the conquest and spoil of England, and which has a history to show of almost unique grandeur. At least, we know of no other uncrowned house in Europe which has seven times driven back the tide of foreign invasion, and for eight hundred years stood in the front of resistance to regal tyranny. Who the first Percy was no historian has discovered. The Duke of Northumberland very possibly believes that Manfred, a Danish pirate, ravaged Neustria in 886, that his son Geoffrey accompanied Rollo, and settled amidst the general pillage in "Percy," a village still existing near Villedieu. He may have warrant for his belief, which is just as likely as any other of the theories invented to account for a family name; only as he has first to prove the existence of Rollo, then of his follower, and then his relation to one of the miscellaneous scum of Europe who followed the Bastard, the inquirer may prefer to begin with a fact a little less legendary. It is quite certain that in 1066 one WILLIAM DE PERCY did land in England; it is also certain that he was the recognised leader of a number of more or less disciplined fighting persons; and it is highly probable that this number was considerable, and that he led them well, for William the Norman gave nothing for nothing, and Domesday

Book shows that he gave Percy much. He received
in Lincolnshire thirty-two lordships, among them
Immingham, Cabourne, and Ludford ; and in Yorkshire eighty-six lordships, among which Topcliffe in
the North Riding and Spofforth in the West Riding,
became the chief seats of the family in those parts for
many succeeding ages. The king, too, was not his
only benefactor. The Conqueror's nephew, Hugh
Lupus, the grim Earl of Chester, gave him, wherefore
we are not told, the whole lordship of Whitby, with
the large territory adjacent, in the North Riding, and
here William de Percy, to soothe his conscience, founded
anew the Abbey of St Hilda, ravaged, *he* said, by a
Danish and pagan ancestor, in whom he, perhaps,
believed. Still further to soothe his conscience, he is
said to have married Emma de Port, of whose lands
at Seamer, near Scarborough, he had taken possession
by the sword. Legend has it that she was the daughter of Earl Gospatrick, the great Saxon Earl of Northumberland, and that it was Lord William who saved his
father-in-law after the last Saxon rising. Be that as
it may, Lord William, nicknamed Percy Alsgernons—
i.e., Percy of the Whiskers—undoubtedly was a real
personage, who was great enough to coerce the hard-
fisted Conqueror into liberality, who founded a great
Yorkshire family, rebuilt the Abbey of St Hilda, acquired a reputation which made his subjects willing
to repeat stories of his Saxon rights and Saxon cle-
mency, and died a crusader with Robert Curthose in
the Holy Land in 1096. He was the true Founder
— the strong man who built himself a house and
stamped his name on the soil. The founder's son was
Lord Alan, of whom we know little save that he

married Emma Gaunt, granddaughter of Baldwin, Earl of Flanders, and had seven legitimate sons and one bastard, mother unknown. The eldest son, William, on that principle of inheritance by indivisible military tenure, which we now confound with the totally different Mosaic regulation of primogeniture, took all the properties, staked them by adopting Stephen's side—*i. e.*, the side of aristocratic against regal power —and performed the first of the endless services of his house by repelling a Scotch invasion in the terrible battle of the Standard, a duty which for four hundred years was never again absent from the thoughts or plans of the Percy. In that battle the bastard brother fought on the Scottish side. By his wife, Alice de Tonbridge, Lord William had several sons, who all died before him—it is a specialty of this family, as we shall see, to kill off collaterals—and two daughters, Maud and Agnes, the former of whom died without issue, while the latter carried the vast Percy estates into the house of Louvain. Here, then, in 1168, in the reign of Henry II., after a hundred and two years of splendour, ended the first male line of the Percies. Sea rovers or French adventurers, they had at all events done their part on earth. They belonged, it is true, as Mr Disraeli says, to the " limited class which had then a monopoly of action;" but the family which in a century invades a great country successfully, carves out therefrom a mighty lordship, so conciliates the conquered that its legends all bear trace of an effort to justify submission, fights a crusade, saves its adopted country from invasion, and so graves its name into the popular heart that all successors are compelled to adopt it, and leaves such a tradition that

after a lapse of seven hundred years the name is of
itself a patent of nobility, cannot be classed even by
Liberals with the *fainéant* eaters of beeves.

The new Percies were greater in the way of pedigree than those whom they superseded. Josceline de
Louvain, who married the heiress, was a younger son
of Godfrey with the Beard, Duke of Nether-Lorraine
and Count of Brabant and Louvain, who claimed descent from the pagan chiefs of Hainault, and from the
only line which might tempt a thinker to wish for
a pedigree—that of Charlemagne. Josceline's sister
Adelise had been second wife of Henry I., and
brought over her brother to marry the Percy under
condition of accepting either her name or her arms.
He chose the former, which was popular, substituting
only his own arms for those borne, and probably invented, by Lord William the founder. (From the
eldest brother of this Josceline are descended the
Electors of Hesse-Cassel and the mother of the Princess of Wales.) Queen Adelise had obtained a grant
of the honour and castle of Arundel, in Sussex, from
Henry I., and after his death she and her second
husband, William de Albeney, appointed Josceline
castellan of Arundel, and granted him the honour of
Petworth, in Sussex, which grant was confirmed by
Henry II., while still only Duke of Normandy, and
was the title of the Percies to the great Sussex possessions they held for so many years. He had four sons,
the eldest of whom seems to have been a nonentity,
for the sway of the house passed to the youngest,
Richard. He claimed and obtained—by a quaint
compromise between the Norman idea of succession
to eldest male, and the Saxon and Oriental idea of

succession to eldest *efficient* male—the great Whitby property for life, and while he lived was virtual head of the Percies. He deserved his position, for he calmly staked it and his head in resistance to John Lackland, was a leader among the framers of the organisation which extorted the Great Charter, and was one of the Five-and-twenty appointed armed guardians of that great pact—a pact, by the way, which anybody who takes the trouble to read it, will see was a national as well as a baronial scheme. His disobedience to the Pope's Legate earned him an excommunication, then as now irrefragable proof of nobility, then as now despised among strong Englishmen; and when the barons, in despair of the Plantagenets, resolved on the policy which, in 1688, their descendants carried out, and brought over Prince Louis, the Percy reduced all Yorkshire to obedience. He died in 1244 (being buried before the high altar in Fountains Abbey), and the estates reverted to his nephew, William, who ought to have had them on the Norman theory before, and who had acquired through his second wife the tract in Durham now known as Dalton-Percy, which descended to his younger son. Lord William, however, survived his great uncle but one year, and his son Henry de Percy commenced a less creditable and not very intelligible career. He seems to have been at heart a Constitutionalist, and stood up for the Great Charter; but King Henry III. seized his lands, and to save them he acted first against the barons, and afterwards as mediator between the King and Simon de Montfort. His son, also Henry, however, redeemed the family honour; was knighted by Edward I. before Berwick;

fought at Dunbar; was appointed governor of Galloway and Ayr; was invested with a vague authority or Lord-Lieutenancy over Westmoreland and Cumberland; and fortified his principal seats, Spofforth and Leckonfield in Yorkshire, and Petworth in Sussex. It is from him, too, that the family dates as a Northumbrian house. On November 19, 1309, Anthony Beck, "proud" Bishop of Durham, granted and sold to Lord Henry the Barony of ALNWICK in Northumberland; and from that day forward the family have been known as the Percies of Alnwick, and described as a house whose root is in Northumberland. He resisted Gaveston in the popular interest, and on the minion's fall received his office of Warden of all Forests north of the Trent. He died in 1315, leaving his wife Eleanor (a Fitzalan) guardian of the estates, and a son, Henry, who at seventeen obtained a grant of all the estates in Northumberland belonging to Dunbar, Earl of March, then in rebellion, and at twenty-one was acknowledged chief of his house. Like his father he detested the corrupt rule of the favourites; was one of Prince Edward's firmest supporters; and received from Edward III., on the throne, the title of Lord of the Marches and the castle and barony of Warkworth, with other magnificent gifts. According to the ethics of that day he earned them well, devoting his life to Edward's grand but premature idea of a united island. He fought and won at Halidon Hill, for which victory Edward Baliol gave him Annandale and Moffatdale, then held by Randolph, Earl of Murray; and he commenced that struggle of generations with the Douglas, around which ballad and legend have thrown such a romance.

His greatest exploit, however, was his command at
Nevill's Cross, in Durham, where, in 1346, he crushed
the great army with which David Bruce, tempted by
Edward's absence in France, had invaded England.
Next year we find him raising an army to the assistance of Edward Baliol, and in the next, transporting
it to France to the aid of the Black Prince. He died
in 1352, a soldier and statesman of the first rank.
His successor, still Henry de Percy, third Henry of
Alnwick, by a daughter of Lord Clifford—the great
old Cumberland race, whose territory is now ruled
from Lowther Castle—led a comparatively quiet life.
He only fought at Crecy, passed his life "regulating"
the Border—*i.e.*, hanging marauders and besieging ob-
streperous chieftains—and made a semi-royal alliance,
marrying the Lady Mary Plantagenet, granddaughter
of Edward of Lancaster, second son of Henry III.
His royal connection was well supported by his truly
regal estate, he being possessed at his death of the
manors of Leckonfield, Claytop, Settle, Giggleswick,
Nafferton, Chatton, Wharram-Percy, Walton, parcel of
the manor of Spofforth, Scarbothall in Craven Topcliffe, Seamer, Tadcester, and Pocklington, in Yorkshire; of the manor and castle of Alnwick, with the
appurtenances, in the county of Northumberland; as
also of the manor of Rock, the castle and manor of
Warkworth, the towns of Berling, Acklington, Roth-
biry, East Wetton, Threpston, Snitter, Over-Bothal-
ston, Teggisden, the manors of Corbridge, Newburne,
Thrasterton, with the hamlets of Botlaw, Walbothall,
and the fishing in the river Tyne; and of the inheritance of Joan, his wife, of the manor of Toft-juxta-
Witham, in Lincolnshire; as also part of the manor

of Old Bokenham, and hundred of Shropham (parcel of the barony of Tate-shale), in Norfolk, and the manor of Cratfield, in Suffolk.

The two sons of this third Lord Percy of Alnwick played most important parts in the reigns of Edward III., Richard II., and Henry IV., and both obtained the rank of Earl, Henry Percy, the elder, becoming (July 16, 1377) first Earl of Northumberland, and Thomas Percy, the younger, Earl of Worcester. These are the Percies whom Shakespeare has mentioned in his historical plays of Richard II. and Henry IV., and the former of them is the father of Harry Hotspur, first knight of that age. Henry (the fourth Lord Percy of Alnwick) was one of the few nobles whose power, aided by John of Gaunt, shielded Wycliff, and so fostered the germs of the Reformation. He quarrelled, however, with Lancaster, and, the Scots seizing Berwick, was adjudged by Parliament to forfeiture of all his estates—an early instance of that tremendous system of forfeiture which, during the Wars of the Roses, prostrated almost all barons. The King, however, refused to confirm the sentence. About the 8th of Richard II., the Earl, having married as his second wife Maud, sister and heiress of Anthony, Lord Lucy, joined with her in a settlement of the honour and castle of Cockermouth, in Cumberland, with a large proportion besides of her great inheritance, upon himself and her, and the heirs-male of their bodies; in default, to the heirs of her body; in default, to Henry, Lord Percy, his eldest son by his first wife, and the heirs-male of his body, on condition of bearing the arms of Percy; in default, to the Earl's brother Thomas, and the heirs-male of his body; in default,

to Sir Thomas Percy, second son of the Earl, and the
heirs-male of his body, with remainder to Sir Ralph
Percy, the third son of the Earl, and the heirs-male
of his body, remainder to the right heirs of the said
Maud. In 1398 Lord Henry, who had recovered
his influence, was one of the Twelve appointed to
control Richard II. The King did not forgive this
measure, and on the recovery of his power next year
he sentenced the Earl to perpetual banishment, and
so produced the well-known "Conspiracy of the Three
Henries"—Henry de Percy, Henry of Bolingbroke,
Duke of Lancaster (and kinsman of the Percy), and
Henry Hotspur, the Percies' heir-apparent. The conspiracy ended in the deposition and death of Richard
—as Harding, the Percy's servant, says, *against* his
master's will. That seems doubtful, and, at all events,
he accepted from the successful Henry IV. a gift of
the Isle of Man, and was made Lord High Constable
of England, Constable of the Castles of Chester,
Conway, Flint, and Carnarvon, General Warden of
the West Marches, and Governor of Carlisle. The
Border warfare continued; and on August 15, 1388,
Hotspur had fought Otterbourne, better known to
ballad-loving mankind as Chevy Chase,* in which
James, Earl of Douglas, was killed, and Hotspur and
his brother Ralph—whose portrait not having been
painted by Shakespeare seems comparatively indistinct—were taken prisoners. The ransom enabled

* " The Persé owt of Northombarlande,
　　And a vowe to God mayd he,
　　That he wolde hunte in the mountayns
　　Off Chyviat within dayes thre,
　　In the mauger of doughté Dogles,
　　And all that ever with him be."

Lord John Montgomery to build a castle, but the
Percies scarcely felt the blow, and on 14th September
1402, they, with an army raised by themselves,
fought the terrible battle of Homildon against Archi-
bald, Earl of Douglas, and 12,000 men. It was the
unluckiest achievement in the whole family record.
Henry, who, like every Plantagenet, understood kingcraft, and did not wish to divide his realm, rewarded
the magnificent service by a grant of a great section
of the Douglas estates in *Scotland*—a process like
giving Lord Clyde, for example, a lawsuit instead of
a pension—and demanded all the prisoners. The
Percy blood took fire at an act as distinctly unjust as
a seizure of all prize-money would be now, and, releasing the Douglas, Percy declared for the Earl of
March, head of the Clarence branch of the Plantagenets. The King, however, was no mean soldier ;
he had an army just levied for Wales, and in the
battle of Shrewsbury he overthrew the Earl, killed
Hotspur, resumed his grant of the Isle of Man—
which he gave to Sir John Stanley, whose descendant
now heads Her Majesty's Opposition—and tried hard
to impoverish Percy by a fine. He was baffled, however, by an incident perhaps more creditable to the
Percies than any in their history. Whether from his
brilliant personal character, the romantic popular feeling for his son, or the recollection of Homildon, all
England rose in protest against serious harm to the
Earl. The Peers acquitted him of treason, and the
Commons passed a formal vote of thanks to the King
for remitting his fine on the mighty Peer. Henry
could not, however, cease from hating him, and the
proud old noble, unable to bear the slights to which he

was exposed, again rebelled, fled first to Scotland, then to Owen Glendower—whence some of Shakespeare's finest scenes—then to France, and, re-entering his estates from Scotland, was, on 29th February 1408, surprised and killed on Bramham Moor. His head was set on a pole on London Bridge. Spofforth was given to Rokeby, the Sheriff of Yorkshire, who had defeated him, and the rest of his vast estates to the King's son, John, Duke of Bedford. His brother, the Earl of Worcester, taken prisoner at Shrewsbury, was shortly after that battle beheaded, and the house of Percy seemed—specially to John of Bedford—utterly swept from the land. Only one lad remained, a son of Harry Hotspur, and he had been placed by his father in Edinburgh, and grew up the favourite page and companion of Prince James.

Had Henry IV. lived, there is little doubt that the family, like hundreds of others, would have disappeared; but his successor was at once more generous and more deeply interested in the affairs of the Continent. He was statesman enough to see that the deep-rooted power of the Percies, sanctioned by the traditions of four hundred years and the attachment of the population north of the Trent, was the best counterpoise to the dangers always imminent from the alliance of Scotland and France. He restored the dignities of the family, and so backed the heir's petition to Parliament that in 1414 that body voted a restoration in blood, and the restitution of all the estates held in tail,—those only held in fee simple passing away to the King. Henry V. sent Sir John Neville and the Lord Grey to bring the young lord from Scotland. "On coming into England," as an old writer expresses it, the young Percy married the Lady Eleanor Neville, daughter of the Earl of Westmoreland, at Berwick-on-Tweed. There is a poem on their loves, called 'The Hermit of Warkworth.' On 16th March 1415 he did homage to Henry in presence of the Estates as second Earl of Northumberland. The Duke of Bedford, moved by the King, resigned the lands assigned to his share, in consideration of an annuity of 3000 marks a-year; and the house, once more invested with the Wardenship of the Border, was re-established in all its dignity. The family attributed this restoration to the personal grace of Henry, and for three generations following staked and lost their lives and liberties and possessions for the sake of the house of Lancaster. The restored Earl, after escorting the captive King of Scotland, his own fellow-pupil, back to Edinburgh, and endowing the three Divinity Fellowships in University College, Oxford, took up arms for the son of his benefactor, by whom he had been created Constable of England. He was slain fighting, on 20th May 1455, in the battle of St Alban's, along with the Duke of Somerset, and lies in the Abbey Church. He held the Northumbrian and Yorkshire and Petworth property, Crawley, and two other manors in Sussex; Wrentham in Suffolk, Wilton-Hockwold in Norfolk, eight manors and the hundred of Cannington in Somersetshire, and sixteen manors and the hundred of Folkestone in Kent; had also a joint part with Sir Robert Manners of the goods and chattels of Sir Robert Ogle, outlawed; possessed Dagenham and another manor in Essex, fifty-eight manors in Lincolnshire, the manor of Foston in Leicestershire, the castle and manor of Cockermouth, and eight and a half manors, besides parcels of another manor, several advowsons of churches, and a fourth part of the "barony of Egremont," in the county of Cumberland. His son Henry was at the time in his thirty-fourth year, and had already served in several very important capacities. He had married, through the influence of Cardinal Beaufort, the heiress of the three Baronies of Poynings, Fitzpayne, and Bryan, and, with his paternal estates, possessed, therefore, in all probability, a larger territorial dominion than the family have ever since held,—one of the largest ever owned by a British subject. It was all staked again, —the Earl supporting the Lancastrian cause by force throughout the North, and falling sword in hand while leading Margaret's vanguard in the decisive battle of Towton. Three of his brothers also fell fighting in the same cause,—one, Sir Richard, along with him at Towton; another, Sir Thomas, who had been made Baron Egremont, at the battle of Northampton, in 1460; and the third, Sir Ralph, at Hedgeley Moor, near Chillingham Castle, in 1464, exclaiming as he died, "I have saved the bird in my bosom!" i.e., his faith to King Henry.* The next heir was thrown into the Tower; the Yorkist Parliament held in November attainted the family; the earldom and estates were granted to John Neville, Lord Montagu, brother to the King-maker, and once more the house seemed to have been torn up by the roots. This time the eclipse was of short duration. In October 1469, King Edward, jealous of the excessive power of the

* He had previously submitted and taken the oath of fealty to King Edward.

Nevilles, bethought himself of the Percy, and summoned the prisoner to his presence. The Percy, believing further resistance hopeless, or tamed by eight years of confinement, took the oath of allegiance, and regained at once his honours and his estates,—Lord Montagu receiving in exchange the barren title of Marquess.* The battle of Barnet, which crushed the Nevilles so completely that the clergyman who now holds the lands of Abergavenny is the only Peer directly representing that almost regal house, confirmed the Percies in their inheritance. They resumed their old function of ruling the Border, and in 1482 Earl Henry was second in command to Richard of Gloucester on his triumphant march to Berwick and Edinburgh. He acquiesced in the revolution which placed Richard on the throne of his nephew. Disgusted, however, with Richard's tyranny, or annoyed by his obvious determination to break down the baronial power, the Earl, on Henry Tudor's arrival, obeyed the Lancastrian instinct of his house, and at the battle of Bosworth drew off his forces to a neighbouring hill, and there remained only a spectator. The act was treacherous, and it was expiated; for Henry VII. contrived to bring the Percy, for the first and only time in the history of the house, into direct conflict with the people. Parliament, in 1489, granted

* The ease with which these transfers were effected is one of the many difficult social questions presented by the Wars of the Roses. We believe, however, the explanation is this. All the classes benefiting by the feudal system admitted the royal right to transfer estates after attainder; and the people, however deeply irritated, could not resist the armed class. They, however, liked their old lords best; and the moment the King's word replaced them resistance became impossible. A transfer *from* them was accepted like an act of conquest—a re-transfer *to* them like a grace.—(M. T.)

a heavy subsidy to the King for the war in Bre-
tagne; the Earl in vain endeavoured to obtain an
abatement, and the people of the north, still Yorkist
in their leanings and wild with disappointment and
rage, rose in rebellion, and murdered him in his house
at Cocklodge, near Thirsk, in Yorkshire.   Skelton
wrote an elegy on his death.   His successor, the fifth
Earl, was a man in whom the second attribute of the
family—a stately fondness for learning and magnificence—flowered out so fully as to conceal or efface
their first—the passion for military success.   In 1497,
at the age of twenty, he was one who fought and
defeated James Touchet, Lord Audley, in the battle
of Blackheath, and was with Henry VIII. at the battle
of the Spurs, in France; but he disliked active life,
obtained leave to resign the Wardenship of the Marches
to the Earl of Surrey, and devoted himself to study
and stately ceremonies.   The "Household-Book" of
this Earl, which has been preserved, presents a singular picture of the semi-regal state of a great noble of
those days—a state which combined the feudal power
with the social magnificence of later times.   There
was a council of the great officers of the household,
who assisted the Earl in drawing up his code of eco-
nomic laws; the constables and bailiffs of his castles
waited on his person in regular succession; all the
officers of the household were gentlemen, and the
table at which they sat was called the Knights' Board.
He kept eleven resident priests, and a doctor or bache-
lor of divinity as dean of his chapel, with a regular
establishment of choristers.   The number of persons
permanently supported in his household was two hundred and twenty-three, and the annual cost of house-

keeping was, in our money, £8951. This magnificent
Peer died in 1527, and was succeeded by his son,
Henry Algernon, sixth Earl of Northumberland,
who as a lad had been educated in the household
of Cardinal Wolsey, and had fallen in love with
Anne Boleyn. It is still doubtful whether they had
not entered into a contract of marriage when the
Cardinal interfered, and Henry Percy was married
offhand to a daughter of the Talbots. The interference seems to have permanently affected his
character. He plunged into debt till he acquired
the nickname of Henry the Thriftless, and was compelled to sell the Poynings estates, lived unhappily
with his wife, and separated from her without children.
His brother, Sir Thomas Percy, in 1536 joined the
rebellion known as the Pilgrimage of Grace, was executed at Tyburn, and his whole family attainted in
blood. Within a month, June 1537, the Earl died of
heartbreak ; and, as the nephews could not inherit,
the house of Percy-Louvain came momentarily to an
end.

During this temporary interregnum, the title and
the estates were transferred to the Dudleys, the
Northumberland, minister of Edward VI., being of
that and not of the Percy family ; but the catastrophe
of Lady Jane Grey swept them out of the road.
Thomas Percy, nephew of the last Earl, regained Scarborough (seized by a son of Lord Stafford), and Queen
Mary annulled the attainder, and regranted estates and
earldom to him, with a clause in the patent including
his younger brother Henry. Queen Elizabeth confirmed these grants, and reappointed Earl Thomas Warden ; but he fell under suspicion as an ardent Catholic,

D

the Wardenship of the Middle and West Marches was bestowed on Lord Grey de Wilton, and a copper mine, discovered on the Percy estates, and from which the Earl appears to have expected unbounded wealth, was appropriated by the Crown. The Earl, greatly disgusted, already secretly a friend of the Papacy, most probably involved in some of the many plots of that dangerous period, on the arrest of the Duke of Norfolk, took up arms with two other northern Earls, in the movement known as the "Rising in the North," and he is the hero of the ballad which bears that title.* The forces of the insurgents were soon discovered to be inadequate for the enterprise, and after some slight successes, Northumberland fled, taking refuge in Scotland with an old friend, Hector Graham of Harlaw. In January 1570 Graham betrayed him to the Regent Murray, and in July 1572 Morton delivered him up to Lord Hunsdon, and he was beheaded at York, affirming with his last breath the supremacy of the Pope. He left no heir, but the clause in Mary's patent saved the house, and his brother Henry was summoned to Parliament as eighth Earl of Northumberland. Though he had opposed his brother in the field, and at first, at any rate, was hostile to his schemes, Earl Henry had offered to assist in liberating Queen Mary of Scotland, which offer was refused through distrust of him. Elizabeth's ministers, however, seem to have considered him in earnest, for they sentenced him to a fine of 5000 marks. It was never levied, and no opposition was offered to his accession to the earldom; but

---

* " Listen, lively lordings all,
   Lithe and listen unto mee,
   And I will sing of a noble earle,
   The noblest earle in the north countrie."

for ten years he had been forbidden to depart from the
vicinity of the metropolis, when he was accused of
complicity in Throckmorton's conspiracy, and committed to the Tower. Here he remained for more
than a year without being brought to trial; but on
the 20th June 1585, a servant of Sir Christopher
Hatton's was substituted as his keeper, and the next
morning the Earl was found dead, with three bullet-
wounds in his chest, and a discharged pistol on the
floor. A coroner's inquest returned a verdict of sui-
cide; but Raleigh at least believed that the death lay
at Hatton's door. Be this as it may, England was
getting too hot for the Catholics; and the Earl's son,
Henry, ninth Earl, accompanied Leicester to the Low
Countries, joined in the siege of Ostend, and when
England was menaced raised a squadron at his own
charge, and under the Catholic Howard of Effingham
helped to defeat the Armada. Elizabeth granted him
a lease of Sion Park, January 15, 1602; and July
5, 1604, James I. granted him Sion House, a dissolved nunnery which the Dudleys had possessed, together with the manor of Isleworth. He might, strong
in the history of his family, have lived down the
jealousy caused by his creed, more especially as he
was himself a Moderate, but unfortunately he did a
Stuart a service—an offence which that family, like
the Bourbons, could scarcely forgive. The Earl was
looked up to by the Catholics as their natural chief,
and James promised him in return for his support all
manner of favour to the members of the oppressed
creed. The negotiations were conducted through a
relative of the Earl's, Thomas Percy (afterwards the
Gunpowder-Plot conspirator), who was at one time

high in favour and confidence with James. But on
the accession of that King, although he at first affected
favour to Northumberland, and made him one of the
Council of State, and Captain of the Band of Gentlemen Pensioners, the influence of Cecil was para-
mount, and Northumberland soon fell under a cloud.
Together with his friends Cobham and Raleigh, he
made secret overtures (not accepted) to the French
Court. However, he had the prudence to stop here ;
and though he was examined strictly on the discovery
of Raleigh's subsequent plot, no evidence could be
found against him, and he was released, after a short
confinement. On the discovery of the Gunpowder
Plot, however, he fell again under suspicion. He had
admitted Thomas Percy into the Band of Pensioners
without his taking the usual oath, and he was
accused of having neglected to use means for his
apprehension when he fled into the North on the
discovery of the plot. The Earl was first ordered
to confine himself to his house (November 7, 1605),
and then brought before the Star-Chamber, where
the first article against him was that " he had
endeavoured to be the head of the Papists, and to
procure them toleration ; " and the King had actually
the baseness to allow the negotiation with the
Catholics, through Thomas Percy, at the end of the
reign of Elizabeth, in his own favour, to be brought
as evidence in support of this charge, Percy himself
being silenced by death. The Earl defended himself
very ably, but was sentenced to a fine of £30,000,
the loss of all offices, and imprisonment for life in the
Tower. James not only confirmed the sentence, but,
pleading some delay in the payment of the first in-

stalment, seized the estates, and leased them for his own benefit.* The Earl remained in prison till July 18, 1621, fifteen years, which he spent in mental culture. He studied mathematics and astronomy—perhaps also astrology—gathered learned men round him, three of whom were called Northumberland's Magi, and earned for himself by his researches the nickname of Henry the Wizard. He was, perhaps, the most accomplished gentleman of his age, and with his fellow-prisoner Sir W. Raleigh, turned the rooms of the Tower into a school, to which the flower of the rising generation resorted for instruction. He fell again under suspicion in 1611, was re-examined, but again baffled his enemies, who could find no new evidence against him. At last, released, after he had paid £11,000, by the intervention of the Earl of Carlisle, who had married his youngest daughter (Lady Lucy Percy, Waller's goddess), he exhibited his contempt for the court in an outburst of characteristic magnifi-

* " In a petition addressed to the King (14th April 1613), the Earl offers Sion as an equivalent for the oppressive fine imposed on him : ' Sion, and please your Majesty, is the only land I can put away, the rest being entailed. I had it before your Majesty's happy entry 48 years by lease, without paying any rent, but such as was given back again certain in other allowances. It hath cost me since your Majesty bestowed it upon me, partly upon the house, partly upon the gardens, about £9000. The land as it is now rented and rated is worth, to be sold, £8000, within a little more or less. If your Majesty had it in your hands, it would be better by £200 a-year more, by the copyholder's estates, which now payeth but two years' old rent fine ; dealing with them as you do with all your copyholders in England, is worth at the least £3000. The house itself, if it were to be pulled down and sold, by view of workmen, comes to 8000 and odd pounds. If any man, the best husband in building, should raise such another in the same place, £20,000 would not do it ; so as according to the work, it may be reckoned, at these rates, £31,000 ; and as it may be sold and pulled in pieces, £19,000 or thereabouts." This proposal, it appears, was not accepted.—Aungier's ' Hist. of Syon Monastery,' pp. *114, *115.

cence. Buckingham drove six horses, so the Earl traversed London with eight, and retired first to Bath and then to Petworth, where he maintained a court thronged by nobles and men of learning. The Stuarts paid for their baseness. Earl Henry's eldest son, Algernon, who, in 1632, succeeded him as tenth Earl —who was in 1637 Lord High Admiral, and a man of such influence that Charles I. said "he had courted him like a mistress," and of so stately a character that even Clarendon half forgets his party hatred—stood through life the unswerving foe of the royal power. On the breaking out of the Civil War he was one of the Peers who remained at Westminster. He tried to negotiate with the King at Oxford, and leaned to the Peace Party in 1643, retiring for a time in ill-humour to Petworth, but after the insincerity of the King became manifest, took his position as a recognised leader of the Independents, and *after* the King's death took the oath to the Commonwealth. On Monk's advance from Scotland, the Earl strove earnestly to secure guarantees before re-admitting the Stuarts, and resisted the punishment of the members of the High Court of Justice which sentenced King Charles, for the avowed reason that the execution, which he had at the time opposed, would be a wholesome warning to future sovereigns. For the rest of his life the stately old man occupied himself with magnificent gardening at Petworth, and, dying October 13, 1668, was succeeded by his son Josceline, namesake of the first of the house, eleventh and last Earl of the house of Percy-Louvain. He died at Turin, 21st May 1670, and once again the line ended in a daughter. It had lasted five hundred years

all but a few months, and during that entire period
had never been named in Scotland without a sense of
fear, or in England without the feeling that here, at
least, was one family which could be trusted to face
the throne. From the signing of Magna Charta to the
last protest against the unconditional re-admission of
the evil Scotch house as kings, the Percies had done
battle with lives and fortunes against the royal power,
were the only great nobles who tried arms against the
imperial Henry VIII., and the last of the barons who
ventured to trust their followers in the field against
the organised power of the Crown.

A brief interregnum carried the family over the
Revolution. Earl Josceline's only surviving daughter,
the Lady Elizabeth Percy,* conveyed the estates, by
her second marriage, to Charles Seymour, Duke of
Somerset; and, as if the family spirit had passed into
his brain as its revenue did into his purse, he was
among the first to welcome the Prince of Orange in
the Revolution by which the great nobles saved England from tyranny and themselves from slow extinction. His son Algernon was created Baron Percy, but
he again had but one daughter, who, on July 18th,
1740, married Sir Hugh Smithson, Bart., of Stanwick,
Yorkshire. The Smithson baronetcy arose with Hugh
Smithson, the second son of Anthony Smithson, Esq.,

---

* She was first married at the age of thirteen to Henry Cavendish,
Earl of Ogle, son of the Duke of Newcastle, who assumed the name of
Percy, but died a few months after his marriage. The great heiress was
then wooed among others by Thomas Thyme of Longleat Hall, Wilts,
and by the adventurer, Count Konigsmark. She leaned to the latter, but
her friends affianced her to the former. Before the wedding, however,
Thyme was assassinated by agents of the Count, who fled from justice to
the Continent. Three months after the murder, she was married (not
being yet sixteen) to the Duke of Somerset.

of Newsome or Newsham, in the parish of Kerby-on-the-Mount, Yorkshire, who was thus rewarded for his past Royalist services in the year 1660. The grandfather of the bridegroom had been brought up as a Roman Catholic, but conformed to the Church. The Duke of Somerset strove for influence, and on 2d October 1749, he was created Baron Warkworth and Earl of Northumberland, with remainder to his son-in-law, Sir Hugh, and *all* heirs-male of the Lady Elizabeth ; and next day Baron Cockermouth and Earl of Egremont, with remainder to his nephew, Sir Charles Wyndham, son of his sister Katherine. With this latter peerage went the estate of Petworth and the Cumberland property, which thus, on the death of the Duke, passed away from the Percies to the family in which they still remain. The Duke dying in 1750, Sir Hugh Smithson succeeded him under the patent, and sixteen years after, on 22d October 1766, was created Earl Percy and Duke of Northumberland. Petworth was almost made up for by the estates at Stanwick, at Armine, in the West Riding, and at Tottenham, in Middlesex, which Sir Hugh brought into the family, and the new house revived to the full the magnificence of the Percy-Louvains. The first Duke rebuilt Sion House, Northumberland House (purchased by the ninth Earl from the Howards), and Alnwick Castle, and planted a great part of the county of Northumberland—planting annually, for twenty years, from eleven to twelve hundred thousand trees. He also devoted great attention to agriculture, and for these services—supported doubtless by the purchase of Werrington in Cornwall, which commands the borough of Launceston—he obtained

in 1784 the Barony of Alnwick, with remainder to his
second son, Algernon, afterwards Baron Lovaine and
Earl of Beverley, the bearer of which titles stands
now nearest to the family succession. The second
Duke (1786), also Hugh, served in America, especially at Lexington; the third (1817)—again Hugh
—was the popular and convivial Lord-Lieutenant
of Ireland ; and the fourth, Algernon, who was
created Baron Prudhoe of Prudhoe Castle, Northumberland, November 27, 1816, and succeeded to
the dukedom February 11, 1847, was first Lord of
the Admiralty to Lord Derby's Administration, and
has been noted for years for a liberality princely in
its degree. He has built, rebuilt, and endowed more
churches than any peer in Great Britain ; and he established, at his own expense, a complete system of life-
boats along that wild north-east coast, where his name
has so long been a household word. "About two
years ago," says a writer in the ' Times ' newspaper
(1864), " the Duke of Northumberland, with the co-
operation of the Ecclesiastical Commissioners, established five new ecclesiastical districts in the large
seaport town of North Shields, and appointed the
requisite number of clergymen to them. It has not
been definitely settled with the Ecclesiastical Commissioners what is to be the exact proportion of the Duke
of Northumberland's contribution to this magnificent
scheme of church-extension, but we believe his Grace
does not expect that it will fall much short of £100,000.
Exclusive of this large outlay for churches and parson-
age-houses, and the immense expenditure upon Alnwick Castle, the following sums have been expended
by the Duke on his estate since he came into posses-

sion in 1847. The amounts, under their respective heads, are made up to December 31, 1863: For roads, bridges, &c., £39,689, 0s. 1d.; buildings, cottages, &c., £308,336, 12s. 9d.; draining, £176,582, 4s.; total, £524,607, 16s. 10d." The vast possessions of his house have been increased to an extent which probably only the Duke knows, by the development of the underground wealth of his estates; and in 1864, as in 1100, there is in the North no rival in magnificence or social weight to the representative of the Percies. Throughout that great interval, the whole of our English history, there has never been a period of twenty years during which the vote of the Percy has not been of the first importance to the Government, scarcely a century in which the lives and lands of the house have not been staked in defence of the popular cause. There is no other house in England with a history approaching theirs; but their career is enough to indicate why England accepts and Liberals bear the aristocratic influence which foreigners believe to be supported entirely by astute but unprincipled intrigue.

The Greys of Howick.

IT seems scarcely fair to tell the story of the Greys immediately after that of the Percies; it will read beside theirs so short and so insignificant. Our object, however, is to explain the existence of the governing families; and for the last sixty years the great house of Northumberland has had less influence over the course of British policy than its comparatively feeble county rival, and once at least the lesser house has performed an incomparable service to the nation. To write a history of the families in the north of England which bear or bore the name of Grey, would be a work in itself. Our present object is simply to give a brief notice of the one Grey family which is a great political house at the present day, viz., the Greys *of Howick,* and of other Greys, only those who can be proved to have been of the same blood. The Greys are, in a genealogical sense, some five hundred years old, though they claim, or the "Peerages" for them, a much higher antiquity.* Sir

---

* The noble family of Gray in Scotland (summoned as Lords of Parliament in that kingdom in 1437), it may be remarked, bear the same arms as the English Greys, and Douglas in his 'Peerage' conjectures them to have been a younger branch of the latter.

Thomas de Grey was a gallant soldier in the wars of
Edward III., and held, among other manors in Northumberland, that of Howick; but, as we have no links
to connect him with the subsequent Greys of Howick,
the historian who cares about accuracy instead of
heraldic probabilities will prefer to date the existing
family from SIR JOHN GREY of Berwick, who was
alive in 1372. His son, Sir Thomas Grey of Berwick
and Chillingham, had two sons, from the eldest of
whom, Sir John Grey, were derived the Lords Grey of
Powys, Earls of Tankerville in Normandy, who became extinct in 1551. This Sir John was a distinguished soldier under Henry V., pushed his fortunes
in the war which so nearly ended in the conquest of
France and ruin of England, and was at last killed
with Thomas, Duke of Clarence, in the disastrous defeat which that Prince suffered at the hands of the
French King's Scotch auxiliaries. From his brother,
Sir Thomas Grey of Warke, descended, through three
intermediate generations, Sir Ralph Grey of Chillingham, in the reign of Henry VIII., who possessed a
moiety of the manor of Howick. His second son, Sir
Ralph Grey of Chillingham, who ultimately became
his heir, was the father of the first Lord Grey of
Warke, who played an important part in the civil war,
fought on the popular side, and for some time acted
as Speaker of the House of Lords. The great-grandson of this Lord Grey, though a man devoted at heart
to the same cause, is probably the one ancestor of
whom the family is ashamed, being Forde, third Lord
Grey of Warke, one of the very few men of his time
and class ever convicted of a want of nerve sufficient
to overpower alike the pride of class and the sense of

duty. On the explosion of the Rye-House Plot he
fled to Holland in 1683; and, returning with the Duke
of Monmouth in 1685, accepted the command of Monmouth's cavalry, but fled with it from the field of
Sedgemoor. He saved himself by giving evidence
against his friends; and his intrigue with his sister-
in-law, Lady Henrietta Berkeley, which gave rise to a
cause célèbre, seems to have outraged even the ideas
of that wild age. His trial (in 1682) is one of the
strangest records of real overmastering passion ever
written. He committed a great crime, but it is impossible to read the dully picturesque report in the
State Trials without perceiving that the private defence of the accused noble, that he was utterly over-
mastered by his over love, was *true*—an admission
which, in the majority of such cases, would be utterly
false—that by one of those strange accidents, which
are never impossible, yet so seldom occur, he had in
Henrietta Berkeley found his double, and that for
once, in open court, before all England, Paul Ferroll's
dream was realised—the dream of a love which could
survive alike ruin, and sarcasm, and crime. At the
last moment, when all ignominy might have been
avoided, and Lord Grey had worked himself up
to promise that he would never see his paramour
again, he broke down, and refused all terms unless he
were permitted to see her. The case was ultimately
withdrawn—why, was never explained. His party
seem also to have forgiven his cowardice and treachery;
for, on June 11, 1695, he was created Viscount Glen-
dale and Earl of Tankerville. His sole surviving
child, a daughter, carried the estate of Chillingham
into the family of Bennet, Lord Ossulston (Arlington

of the Cabal belonged to these Bennets), who was
therefore created Earl of Tankerville; and her descendants to this day own the great Chillingham Park,
and the breed of white wild bulls, and divide with the
Greys of Howick and the Percies the political influence of Northumberland.

Sir Ralph, the father of the first Lord Grey of
Warke, had a younger brother, Sir Edward Grey of
Howick, whose descendant, Henry, was in 1736 owner
of the whole of the manor of Howick, and was created
a baronet. Two of Sir Henry's sons died unmarried,
the eldest having represented the county in 1754 and
1762; another was killed in a duel with Lord Pom-
fret; and the fourth, Charles, was the founder of the
existing peerage. He was a soldier of some mark,
and distinguished himself, so far as anybody did, in
the American war, fought with Earl St Vincent in
the West Indies, and in 1801, under the Addington
Administration, was raised to the peerage as Baron
Grey de Howick, and in 1806 was created Viscount
Howick and Earl Grey. He died on the 14th November 1807, leaving his dignities to his eldest surviving
son CHARLES, second Earl, and founder of the modern
political greatness of the family. He was elected in
1786, being then only twenty-two, member for Northumberland, and threw himself with ardour into political life. Like all his family he was a determined
Whig, followed Fox, shared in the convivialities of
Carlton House, and perhaps believed that the Prince
who had betrayed every human being who trusted
him would not betray a Grey. He was soon known
as one of the small group of aristocrats who clearly
foresaw the future, who contended for Catholic eman-

cipation, the removal of the disabilities of the Dissenters, the reform of Parliament, the suppression of the
slave-trade, and the purification of the administrative
machine, which had slowly rotted into an engine for
efficient corruption. In 1806 he entered the Grenville Cabinet as First Lord of the Admiralty, and
on the death of Fox, succeeded him as Secretary for
Foreign Affairs. The question of Catholic emancipation formed, however, a bar to his further rise under
George III.,—Whigs in those days having convictions
as well as traditions,—and on the Regent's accession,
he was, like the rest of his party, betrayed, the King
hoping to compound for a hundred perjuries by keeping one oath which he did not comprehend. The
Earl, fortified by a pride such as only an English
Whig Peer, a Cardinal, or a Brahmin ever honestly
feels, neither compromised nor gave way; and even
when Canning made a movement towards Liberal
opinions, and drew around him some of the leading
Whig statesmen, Lord Grey stood haughtily aloof,
proclaiming in no whispered voice his want of confidence. The people admired his consistency, and on
the accession of William IV. he was the recognised
head of the Whigs, and in that capacity succeeded the
Duke of Wellington as Premier. Then came the
Reform struggle, in which the unbending character of
the Earl was the very mainstay of his party, and enabled them for the first time in English history to
effect a complete transfer of power without an appeal
to arms or a change of dynasty. Mr Roebuck will
have it that the Earl quailed at last, and would, had
the King been firm, have declined to swamp the Upper House; but the statement is inconsistent with the

fact, that the vote could have been carried by the elevation of elder sons and other devices, without that
possibly disastrous resort. Be that as it may, in the
first Reform Administration the special character of
the Premier and the special uses of an aristocracy
came out in their strongest colours. No Parliament
ever sat in which "dangerous" tendencies were more
apparent. Brains had grown hot in the contest, and
the people were more than half inclined to plunge
at once into the unknown, and effect farther radical
changes in the constitution which had worn so well.
Fortunately for all the empire, except Ireland—which
under the new middle-class power lost its best chance
of final reorganisation—every mood of the popular
mind had to be strained first through the aristocratic
sieve, which when it included Earl Grey had very
close meshes indeed, and time was allowed for the
trial of an organisation which, after thirty years of
determined and not inglorious effort, now once more
seems feeble, because, throughout an empire whose
power, as Pozzo di Borgo said, "has earth for its
base," there is not out of Ireland a grievance sharp
enough to stir the national blood. Earl Grey retired
in 1834 from official life (dying July 17, 1845) ; but
the political influence of his family, founded on his
reputation, has not been diminished in the hands
of his successor, Henry, second Earl,—a man in
whom all his father's qualities seem intensified. If
he were not the most impracticable of mankind, there
would be in England no statesman with a chance
against Earl Grey ; and his administration of the
colonies, still but partially understood, will one day
be found to have involved as bold, as successful, and

as important a revolution as that which his great father carried through. At this moment there is, perhaps, no family in England more largely employed in the public service than that which looks to Earl Grey as its head, and scarcely one in which there have been so few conspicuous failures.

E

The Lowthers.

HE history of the Lowthers is that of immense and almost unbroken civil success. Though they date from the earlier feudal period, and possess to this day a power more nearly feudal than that of any family in England except the Percies and the Wynns, they would be defined on the Continent as belonging rather to the peerage "of the robe" than the nobility of the sword. A race of proud, sensitive, and singularly efficient men, they have filled high office as lawyers, battled bravely as politicians, and performed once or twice great service as Ministers of the State; but they have not contributed generals, or reared up great admirals, or flung back invasion at their own cost and charge. They have been great servants of the State, not great members of it. Their original ancestry is hard to trace, but it cannot have been a high one, for the family takes its name from the little Westmoreland river. The name of William de Lowther appears at the head of the gentry of Westmoreland as witness to a deed in the reign of Henry II., and Sir Thomas and Sir Gervase de Lowther occur in the register of Wetherel Priory, under Henry III. The great-grand-

son of Sir Gervase, SIR HUGH DE LOWTHER, performed
the functions of Attorney-General in the twentieth
year of Edward I., and may be accepted as the
founder of the great fortunes of the house. This Sir
Hugh possessed lands in the hamlet of Whale and in
Thurmby, as well as the manor of Lowther, and was
also seised of the manor and town of Widchope in
Cumberland. Sir Hugh represented the shire of Westmoreland in Parliament in 1300 and 1305, was " a
justice itinerant and escheater on the north side of the
Trent," and for five hundred years there never again
sat a Parliament which was not attended by a Lowther
or a Lowther's direct nominee. His eldest son, also
Sir Hugh, sided with the Earl of Lancaster in the
struggle with Gaveston, but subsequently made his
peace with the King; and a brother, Thomas de Lowther, became in 1330 a justice, and in the following
year Chief Justice of the King's Bench in Ireland. It
was a habit of this house, as we shall see, to export its
cadets to Ireland. The second Sir Hugh married the
daughter and heiress of Lucie Lord Egremont, Baron
of Cockermouth, and obtained licence to make a park
in his manor of LOWTHER. This feudal privilege
obtained, the family rested for years, though Sir
Hugh's great-grandson was at Agincourt; but the
grandson of the Agincourt hero married the daughter
of Sir Lancelot Threlkeld, a half-sister of Henry Lord
Clifford—the " Shepherd Lord" of ballad and romance
—and his grandson again intermarrying with his
cousin, the daughter of the "Shepherd Lord," the double
alliance greatly increased the consequence of the Lowthers. Sir Richard was made Warden of the West
Marches and High Sheriff of Cumberland—then a

quasi-military dignity—and was sent by Queen Elizabeth to receive Mary of Scotland after her flight from
the field of Langside. He earned the Queen's displeasure in this office; but he had not incurred the
hate of any of the Queen's Ministers, and died peacefully in his bed, having "kept up plentiful hospitality
for fifty-seven years." His fourth son, Sir Gerard, who
possessed the manor, town, and park of Lowther in
Fermanagh, besides other landed property in Ireland,
became Chief Justice in that kingdom, was *ex officio*
one of the Lords Justices who carried on the government, and in 1654 was appointed by Cromwell Lord
Chancellor. Another son, Sir Lancelot, of county Kildare, was also a Baron of the Exchequer in Ireland;
but the main line were Royalists, and only kept their
estates by living in close retirement. Their head in
the earlier part of the reign of Charles I. was Sir John
Lowther, nephew of the Irish Chancellor, who purchased for his second son Christopher the lands of the
dissolved monastery of St Bees, at Whitehaven, in
Cumberland, and it is to this son that the rise of that
port is due. The use of coal had then just become
general in England, and Sir Christopher conceived the
idea of making his possessions productive by opening
some collieries, "but no considerable progress was
made till after the Restoration," when his son, Sir
John Lowther, "formed a plan for working the mines
on a very extensive scale, and in 1666 procured a
grant of all the ungranted lands within the district."
Two years afterwards he obtained a gift of "the whole
sea-coast for two miles northward, between high and
low water-mark." He then turned his attention to
the port, and formed the present haven. Besides this

Whitehaven property, out of which he had carved an
estate for his second son Sir Christopher, the head of
the Lowthers left to his eldest son, John (created
a baronet of Nova Scotia in 1640), in the county of
Westmoreland, the manors of Lowther, Helton-Flecket,
Banpton, Knipe, Crosby, Ravensworth, and the moiety
of the tithes in Shaps Land, Sleagill, and Great Strick-
land ; and in the county of Cumberland, the manors
of Thwaites, Threlkeldwaite, Sliddal, Malmesmeburn,
Drunburgh Castle, and the moiety of Regal Grange.

Sir John's eldest son (Colonel John Lowther) dying
before his father, and leaving a motherless boy also
called John, the latter was brought up entirely by his
grandfather, and at the age of fifteen sent to Queen's
College, Oxford, and thence abroad. On the death of
his father, John Lowther was returned as one of the
Knights of the Shire for Westmoreland, which county
he continued to represent as long as he remained a
commoner. He was in opposition to the Duke of
York during the debates on the Succession Bill, rather
leant to the Crown at the commencement of the reign
of James II., but grew, with most other Protestant
gentlemen, alarmed at the King's favour to Roman
Catholics, and joined in the invitation to William of
Orange. So earnest was he in the cause that he abandoned the somewhat over-pacific tactics of his house,
secured Carlisle, and induced the counties of Westmoreland and Cumberland to declare in the Prince's
favour. He was rewarded with the Lord-Lieutenancy
of Westmoreland and Cumberland ; and in 1690, on
Carmarthen becoming first Minister, Sir John Lowther
assumed the lead of the Lower House. Lowther, says
Macaulay, " was a man of ancient descent, ample

estate, and great Parliamentary interest. Though
not an old man, he was an old senator; for he had
before he was of age succeeded his father as Knight
of the Shire for Westmoreland. In truth, the representation of Westmoreland was almost as much one of
the hereditaments of the Lowther family as Lowther
Hall. Sir John's abilities were respectable; his manners, though sarcastically noticed in contemporary
lampoons as too formal, were eminently courteous;
his personal courage he was but too ready to prove;
his morals were irreproachable; his time was divided
between respectable labours and respectable pleasures;
his chief business was to attend the House of Commons and to preside on the Bench of Justice; his
favourite amusements were reading and gardening.
In opinions he was a very moderate Tory. He was
attached to hereditary monarchy and to the Established Church; but he had concurred in the Revolution; he had no misgivings touching the title of
William and Mary; he had sworn allegiance to them
without any mental reservation, and he appears to
have strictly kept his oath. By Carmarthen's influence Lowther was now raised to one of the most important places in the kingdom. Unfortunately it was
a place requiring qualities very different from those
which suffice to make a valuable county member and
chairman of quarter sessions. The tongue of the new
First Lord of the Treasury was not sufficiently ready,
nor was his temper sufficiently callous for his post.
He had neither adroitness to parry nor fortitude to
endure the gibes and reproaches to which, in his new
character of courtier and placeman, he was exposed.
There was also something to be done which he was

too scrupulous to do, something which had never been
done by Wolsey or Burleigh, something which has
never been done by any English statesman of our
generation, but which, from the time of Charles II. to
the time of George III., was one of the most important
parts of the business of a Minister." We need hardly
say that this was "corruption," and as his agent in
this work in the House of Commons, Carmarthen
passed over Lowther and selected Sir John Trevor.
Lowther underwent the usual fate of a prominent
Minister—unlimited abuse from his political opponents, and for a time alienated the affections of his
friends the country gentlemen also. In one of the
debates on official salaries he was quite overwhelmed
by the storm of objections. "He lost his head, almost
fainted away on the floor of the House, and talked
about righting himself in another place." Such, indeed was his susceptibility on points of honour that
once, while he was First Lord of the Treasury, he actually accepted a challenge from a Custom-house officer
whom he had dismissed, and received a severe wound
in the duel. Such a man was little fitted for the
leadership of the Commons, and in 1692 he accepted
a seat at the Board of Admiralty, and was succeeded
at the Treasury by Sir Edward Seymour. On the
Triennial Bill he differed from Carmarthen, taking
the side of the Tory squires, who strongly opposed it;
and on the 28th May 1696, he was raised to the Peerage as Baron Lowther and Viscount Lonsdale.

He was expected to afford the King's Government
great assistance in the Lords; but his health broke
down, and for the next two years "he employed
himself in beautifying his new house, planting the

neighbourhood, and calling in Verrio to paint gorgeous frescoes representing the gods at the banquet of Ambrosia." In 1698 he, as a trusted personal friend, yielded to the King's importunity, accepted the office of Lord Privy Seal, and resisted the "Resumption Bill," the measure for resuming the Irish grants to the King's favourites. He was named in July 1700 one of the Lords whom Queen Mary was to consult; but his death on the 10th of the same month rendered the appointment a merely nominal honour. He was succeeded by two sons successively, the latter of whom, Henry, Lord of the Bedchamber and Lord Privy Seal, died in 1750, unmarried, the last of the Viscounts Lonsdale. The family succession was not, however, interrupted. The Viscount left his estates to Robert Lowther of Meaburn, Westmoreland, his heir-at-law, the grandson of Richard Lowther, a "Turkey merchant," uncle of the first Lord Lonsdale. James Lowther, son of this Robert Lowther, seems to have caught the commercial instinct. He turned the college building, erected by his predecessor, into a manufactory "for most beautiful stockings, and carpets of strength and look little inferior to those of Persia. A few of these were sold for from £63 to £105; but they were wrought chiefly for his own use, or to be given in presents to his friends." Sir James also erected a steam-engine for the use of the collieries at Whitehaven, in which property he had succeeded his relative, Sir James Lowther of Whitehaven. The new head of the family was for more than thirty years a member of the House of Commons for the counties of Westmoreland or Cumberland, and Lord-Lieutenant of both counties.

On the 24th of May 1784 he was raised to the titles
of Baron Lowther, Kendal, and Burgh (the latter
title derived from a place in Cumberland), Viscount
Lonsdale and Lowther, and Earl of Lonsdale; and
on October 10, 1797, he was created Baron and
Viscount Lowther of Whitehaven, with a collateral
remainder of these titles to the heirs male of the body
of his cousin, the Rev. Sir William Lowther of Swillington, Baronet. In 1761 he married a daughter of
the celebrated Earl of Bute, the favourite of George
III.'s mother, and died May 24, 1802, without issue.
In him the Lowther peculiarities culminated in an
eccentricity which almost approached to madness.
Of a gloomy and morose disposition, full of evil
tempers and great ideas, he was known throughout
Westmoreland and Cumberland as the "Bad Earl."
De Quincey relates how he used to drive through
small towns in which every face was grave from dread
of his oppressive temper; and the people of his estates
felt his arrival as those of a guilty town might feel
that of an executioner. He used to exhibit his contempt for form by driving about in an old neglected
carriage with untrimmed horses, and allowing droves
of wild horses to thunder about his park. He seldom
went to London, but even there his haughty temper
displayed itself; and he actually left an estate to his
successor as a reward for standing as second in a duel
no one else would take up. His carriage had been
stopped by an officer in command of a party appointed
to keep Piccadilly clear for the attendance on a great
levee, and he actually challenged the officer, who
insisted on doing his duty in spite of the remon-
strant's rank. There was, however, a sentimental

side to the character of this gloomy Earl. "He loved with passionate fervour a fine young woman, of humble parentage, in a Cumberland farmhouse. Her he had persuaded to leave her father, and put herself under his protection. Whilst yet young and beautiful she died; Lord Lonsdale's sorrow was profound—he caused her to be embalmed, a glass was placed over her features," and at intervals the Earl paid visits to "this sad memorial of his former happiness." He resisted the payment of all bills on principle—nearly ruining the Wordsworths, among others; and the first task of his successor was to remedy the many acts of injustice of which his cousin's half-lunatic, half-imperial mind—the man offered to give and maintain a seventy-four for a war which he disapproved—had induced him to commit. The memoirs of his day are full of the strange acts of the Bad Earl, and he had the honour of forcing Parliament to pass an Act to restrain his injustice. "The Portland family enjoyed the manor of Penrith by a grant from King William III., and they had likewise, for almost seventy years, possessed the adjoining forest of Inglewood, though not strictly included in the terms of the original grant." Sir James Lowther—it was in the year 1768, before his ennoblement—"the dangerous neighbour of the Bentincks in those parts"—determined to avail himself of the ancient legal maxim that the rights either of Crown or Church are not lost by any lapse of time—*Nullum tempus occurrit Regi vel Ecclesiæ.* He solicited a lease of the King's interest in the forest of Inglewood, and the boon was too readily and too partially yielded by the Ministry, not displeased to mortify a political opponent, as the Duke of Portland

had then become. This act of Sir James provoked a
Bill in Parliament called the *Nullum Tempus* Bill, to
secure the property of a subject at any time after
sixty years' possession from any dormant pretension
of the Crown. The outrage struck half the nobles of
England; and though the Earl had strength enough,
through his influence with Lord North, to get the Bill
postponed for one session, it passed in the next almost
without opposition. The source of that strength is,
perhaps, best indicated in the letters of William Pitt.
Sir James had been induced, through the Duke of
Rutland, to nominate him for Appleby, and "I have
seen Sir James," writes Pitt to his mother, "who has
repeated to me the offer he had before made, and in
the handsomest manner. Judging from my father's
principles, he concludes that mine would be agreeable
to his own, and on that ground, to me of all others the
most agreeable, to bring me in. No kind of condition
was mentioned, but that if ever our lines of conduct
should become opposite I should give him an opportunity of choosing another person. Appleby is the
place I am to represent, and the election will be made
(probably in a week or ten days) without my having
any trouble, or even visiting my constituents." In a
second letter he adds, "I have not yet received the
notification of my election. It will probably not take
place till the end of this week, as Sir James Lowther
was to settle an election at Haslemere before he went
into the north, and meant to be present at Appleby
afterwards." *That* was the system from which the
Reform Bill delivered us, though it has at the same
time prevented the possibility of men like Pitt entering at twenty-one into Parliament. The peerages

bestowed on Sir James Lowther were doubtless tokens of the appreciation by the King and his Minister of the services thus rendered to both. The Earl, however, did not reciprocate this gratitude, for on the occasion of the Regency Bill, in 1788, he yielded to the personal solicitation of the Prince of Wales to oppose Mr Pitt. " The Earl issued his mandate accordingly, and Lord Lonsdale's people," as Mr Grenville terms them—that is, the members whom he nominated—" declared themselves, reluctantly perhaps, against the Government."

All the Lowther estates went (as we have mentioned), on the first Earl's death, to his cousin, Sir William Lowther of Swillington, in Yorkshire, descended from William, a brother of the Sir John Lowther who was grandfather of the first Viscount Lonsdale. One baronetcy had become extinct in this branch, but Sir William's father had obtained a new patent, and Sir William became, by virtue of Earl James's patent of 1797, Baron and Viscount Lowther, and in 1819 was raised to the dignity of Earl of Lonsdale. He seems to have been an amiable man— an amiability not the less appreciated from his contrast to his wild predecessor; but he is chiefly remembered as a munificent patron of the fine arts, and the peer who changed Lowther Hall into the magnificent seat now styled " Lowther Castle." His son, the present Earl, has taken a prominent part in public life from 1810, when he became a Lord of the Admiralty, down to February 1852, when he was Lord Derby's President of the Council. He is the Lord Eskdale of Disraeli's 'Tancred'—a man with every ability except the ability to make his powers useful to mankind.

The race under the present patents is in no danger of dying out; it still rules Westmoreland and Cumberland, and is, perhaps, among English families, *the* best representative of those "lesser barons" of the Plantagenet period who, except in Northumberland, have eaten out their mighty and warlike rivals. In all the qualities which make citizens they are, perhaps, the better class; but the Lowthers are scarcely the men who, in the hour of utter ruin, will say as their single boast, "I have saved the bird in my bosom."

The Vanes or Fanes.

HIS family is now represented by the Earl of Westmoreland in the elder branch, and by the Duke of Cleveland and Frances Marchioness of Londonderry and her son, Earl Vane, in the younger branch. The heralds of the reign of Elizabeth gave it a Welsh pedigree from a supposed "Howel-ap-Vane of Monmouthshire"—time not stated, but who, from a computation of generations, must have lived before the Conquest. No names of residences or any authorities, however, appear in support of this genealogy, until we reach a Henry Vane who is said to have been knighted for his gallantry at the battle of Poictiers. But the pedigree still gives us no *habitat* for the family until we reach the reign of Henry VI., when we find a HENRY VANE of the manor of Hilden, in the parish of Tunbridge, Kent, who would seem to be the undoubted ancestor of the great families above mentioned. This Henry Vane of Hilden, Kent, had three sons — John, Thomas, and Henry, of whom Thomas left a son, Humphrey, who died without issue. By his will, dated 1455, their father devised the manor of Hilden to his eldest son, John, and the par-

sonage to his youngest, Henry. The manor was sold
in the tenth year of Henry VII.; and the parsonage
was also sold in the reign of Edward VI. Henry
Vane had a son, Ralph, who was knighted at the fight
at Boulogne, 1544; and in the thirty-sixth year of
his reign, Henry VIII. granted to him (as Sir Ralph
Fane) and to Anthony Tutsham, Esq., the manor of
Shipborne, Kent, with its appurtenances, lately belonging to the monastery of Dartford, and the manor
of Shipborne *alias* Puttenden, lately belonging to
the monastery of Tunbridge, and the lands in the
tenure of John Hart, and the lands and chapel of
Shipborne with all their appurtenances, to hold of
the King *in capite* by knight's service; soon after
which Anthony Tutsham released all his interest to
Sir Ralph. The latter, for his valour at the battle of
Musselburgh in the first of Edward VI., was made a
Knight Banneret, and became a favourite and leading
counsellor of the Protector Somerset. He shared
his downfall; and, being engaged in the conspiracy
against Dudley, which proved fatal to the Duke, he
was apprehended in October 1551. He had escaped
over the river, but was taken in a stable in Lambeth
hidden under the straw. Palmer, the informer, stated
that Sir Ralph Vane was to have brought 2000 men
to assist the Duke in his enterprise. He was brought
to trial, found guilty, and executed on Tower Hill,
February 26. Burnet says of him : " Sir Ralph Vane
was the most lamented of them all. He had done
great services in the wars, and was esteemed one of
the bravest gentlemen of the nation. He pleaded for
himself that he had done his country considerable
service during the wars, though now, in time of peace,

the coward and the courageous were equally esteemed.
He scorned to make any submissions for life. But
this height of mind in him did certainly set forward
his condemnation ; and, to add more infamy to him
in the manner of his death, he and Partridge were
hanged, whereas the other two were beheaded." On
the scaffold he protested with the rest that he had
never been guilty of any design either against the
King or to kill the Lords ; and he added "that his
blood would make Northumberland's pillow uneasy
to him." He died without issue. John Vane, the
elder brother of Sir Ralph's father, Henry, obtained
either by grant or purchase the mansion and estate
of Hadlow Place, in Tunbridge, and had four sons
and three daughters. He took or used the spelling
"Fane ;" and by his will, bearing date April 16, 1488,
writing himself "John Fane of Tunbridge, Esq.," he
makes certain bequests to the church of Tunbridge,
and also 6s. 8d. to every one of the churches of Hadlow, Leigh, East Peckham, Seale, Morden, Lamber-
hurst, Betburgh, Wittersham, and Snargate, in Kent,
in all of which places he held lands. He bequeathed
to Richard Fane, his second son (ancestor of the Earls
of Westmoreland), the manor of Snargate, and, after
his wife's death, his lands in Morden and Lamber-
hurst ; to his third son, Thomas, the mansion, &c.,
that was his father's ; and to his youngest son, John
(ancestor of the noble families of Vane), when he
came of age, all his lands and tenements called
"Holynden." The rest of the landed property is left
to his eldest son Henry, and his other sons in succession—his lordship called "Albonys" being left to this
Henry in fee. John Fane or Vane's will was proved

on June 8 of the same year. His eldest son, Henry, resided at Hadlow, and was Sheriff of Kent in 23d Henry VII. He died without issue in 1538; and by his will, left to his youngest brother, John, all his lands lying in Great Peckham, Kent; and in default of issue male, to Ralph Fane his cousin and the heirs male of his body; remainder to Richard Fane, his next brother; and after several other remainders, to Ralph Fane and his heirs for ever; and his manor and place wherein he then dwelt, with all his lands in Hadlow and Capel, to Ralph Fane in tail male; remainder to each of the sons of his youngest brother, John Fane, successively in like tail. The heir to the rest of his property was his brother, Richard Fane. The third brother, Thomas (of London), had died before Henry Fane in 1532, and bequeathed to his brother, John Fane, his grey ambling mare which he had of his gift, and his lands lying in Tunbridge, called the "Vault-ney." From this Thomas descended Thomas Fane of Fairlane, Kent, who died in September 1692, and left his estate of £30,000 per annum to Mildmay Vane, seventh son of Vere Fane, Earl of Westmoreland.

We will first pursue the fortunes of the elder branch —the Westmoreland Fanes. Richard Fane, elder brother of the above Thomas Fane and of John Fane, the ancestor of the Vane or younger branch of the Fanes, married Agnes, daughter and heir of Thomas Stidolph, Esq., of Badsele, in Tudeley, Kent, with whom he had that estate, on which he resided. His only son, George Fane, was seated at Badsele, which was settled on him by his father. He was Sheriff of Kent in the 4th and 5th of Philip and Mary, and died February 4, 1571. He married Joan, daughter of William Waller, Esq., of Groombridge, Kent, and was succeeded by his son Thomas, who in his youth was one of the gentlemen of Kent that engaged in Sir Thomas Wyat's insurrection in Mary's reign, was committed prisoner to the Tower, and attainted of high treason, but was pardoned by the Queen. He was knighted at the Castle of Dover August 26, 1573, by Robert, Earl of Leicester, in the presence of Queen Elizabeth. The fortune of the Fanes was made by his second marriage (December 12, 1574, at Birling, in Kent) to Mary Neville, daughter and heiress of Henry, Lord Abergavenny. On the death of her father she inherited the manors of Birling, Ryarshe, Ealding *alias* Yalding, Luddesdon, the rectory of All Saints in Birling, and advowson of the vicarage of Birling; the manor of West Peckham and Maplecomb in West Peckham, and advowson of the church; the manor of Mereworth, and advowson of the church, and farm of Old Haie *alias* Holehaie, all in the county of Kent. Her husband, Sir Thomas Fane, died March 13, 1589. He resided sometimes at Badsele, sometimes at his wife's seat of Mereworth Castle. Mary, Lady Fane, his widow, had on the death of her father in 1587 laid claim to the title of Baroness of Abergavenny or Bergavenny, in opposition to Edward Neville, son of Sir Edward Neville, younger brother of George Lord Abergavenny, Lady Fane's grandfather, on which Sir Edward Neville the Castle of Abergavenny had been settled by will and by Act of Parliament. The claim was not determined till after Sir Thomas Fane's death, May 15, in the 1st of James I., when the barony of Abergavenny was adjudged to the heir male, the ancestor of the present Earl of

Abergavenny, the only existing heir male of the great house of Neville. As some compensation to Lady Fane, the old barony of Le Despencer was called out of abeyance in her favour, with the ancient seat, place, and precedence of her ancestors, to her and the heirs of her body, as being descended from Elizabeth, eldest daughter of Isabel, sister and heir of Richard le Despencer, Earl of Gloucester and Lord le Despencer, son of Edward Lord le Despencer (by Elizabeth, daughter and heir of Bartholomew, Lord Burghersh), descended from Hugh le Despencer, Earl of Winchester, and Baron le Despencer (Edward II.'s favourite), son of Hugh le Despencer, Justice of England in the reign of Henry III. The barony of Despencer continued in the Fane family till 1762, when it fell again into abeyance between the sisters of the Earl of Westmoreland, and was called out again in 1763 in favour of the Dashwood family, from whom in a similar manner it has passed to the Stapletons. Mary Fane, Baroness le Despencer, died June 28, 1626, and the barony then devolved on her eldest son, Francis, who was made a Knight of the Bath, July 15, 1603, and on December 29, 1624, was advanced to the titles of Baron Burghersh and Earl of Westmoreland. He married Mary, daughter and heir of Sir Anthony Mildmay of APETHORP, Northamptonshire, with whom he had a great estate. He died in 1628. His eldest son, Mildmay, succeeded him as second Earl of Westmoreland, adhered to Charles I. in the Civil War; but in 1643, with several other noblemen, abandoned that cause in disgust at the Irish " Cessation," submitted to the Parliament, and on April 22, 1645, with the Earls of Holland, Thanet, and Monmouth, and the Lord Saville, took the oaths required from those who adopted this course. He was author of a volume of poems, ' Otia Sacra,' privately printed in 1648, and died February 12, 1665. He was twice married, his second wife being a daughter and co-heiress of Horace, Lord Vere of Tilbury ; and his two sons by these marriages, Charles and Vere, became successively third and fourth Earls of Westmoreland, the latter dying December 29, 1693, and being succeeded by his sons, Vere, Thomas, and John, successively as fifth, sixth, and seventh Earls of Westmoreland. The sixth Earl held the household appointments of a Lord of the Bedchamber to Prince George of Denmark, and Gentleman of the Bedchamber to George I., was Chief Justice of the Forests south of the Trent, and sworn of the Privy Council in 1717. On May 19, 1719, he was appointed First Lord Commissioner of Trade and the Plantations, which office he resigned in May 1735, and died June 4, 1736. His brother and successor, John, seventh Earl, distinguished himself in the wars under the Duke of Marlborough, and had the command of several regiments. On October 4, 1733, he was created a peer of Ireland as Baron Catherlough, and served in the English House of Commons during several Parliaments. In 1737 he was appointed Warden of the east bailiwick in Rockingham Forest, and joint Chief Ranger with the Earl of Exeter. In 1739 he became Lieutenant-General in the army. He then retired to his seat of Mereworth Castle, which he rebuilt after a plan by Palladio. On January 1, 1754, he was appointed Lord High Steward of the University of Oxford, and in 1759 he was elected Chancellor of that University. He died

August 26, 1762, without issue, when the barony of
Despencer, as we have said, fell into abeyance, and the
earldom of Westmoreland and barony of Burghersh
devolved on his cousin Thomas Fane, of Brympton, in
Somersetshire, merchant in Bristol, great-grandson of
Sir Francis Fane, younger son of Francis the first Earl
of Westmoreland. Sir Francis had obtained some
reputation as a dramatic writer, and as Governor of
Doncaster Castle and Lincoln for the King in the
Civil War. His third son, Henry, was made a Knight
of the Bath in 1661; and, April 18, 1689, was appointed by William III. Commissioner of Excise, and
sat in several Parliaments of that reign. His son
Charles was of the Privy Council to George I., and
was created in 1718 Viscount Fane and Baron of
Loughairne in the Irish Peerage, which titles became
extinct in 1782.

Thomas Fane, who succeeded as eighth Earl of
Westmoreland, died November 12, 1771, and was
succeeded by his son John, ninth Earl, who as well
as his father represented Lyme Regis in Parliament
before their accession to the Peerage. He died April
26, 1774, and was succeeded as tenth Earl by his son
John, who married first Sarah Anne, sole daughter
and heiress of Robert Child, Esq., of Osterley Park,
Middlesex, the celebrated banker; and his eldest
daughter by her, Lady Sarah Sophia, by the will of
her grandfather Child, inherited his large fortune,
which by her marriage to Mr George Villiers, afterwards Earl of Jersey, she carried away to that family.
The Earl of Westmoreland, her father, died December
15, 1841, and was succeeded as eleventh Earl by his
son John, a distinguished officer during the French war,

and well known afterwards as Ambassador at Berlin and Vienna, and still better as an amateur composer and patron of music. He died October 16, 1859, and was succeeded by his son Francis William Henry, twelfth and present Earl of Westmoreland. The Fanes have for some time been supporters of the Tory or Conservative interest, but have not been prominent in domestic politics.

We must now turn to the other branch of the Fanes or Vanes—descended from John Fane, younger brother of the ancestor of the Westmoreland family. John Fane had received, as we have seen, some lands at Holynden, Kent, from his father, and by the will of his elder brother, Henry, lands lying in Great Peckham. He married Joan, daughter and coheiress of Edward Haute, Esq., by whom he had three sons, Henry, Richard, and Thomas (of Winchelsea). Henry succeeded, by virtue of the entail made by his uncle Henry, to the manor of Hadlow, after the execution of Sir Ralph Vane, and he seems to have also obtained the rest of his unfortunate kinsman's property at Shipborne and elsewhere. He engaged, like his relative of the Westmoreland branch, in Wyat's insurrection, like him was sent to the Tower, and also pardoned by the Queen. The whole family, indeed, were among the early and most zealous Protestants. In the two first Parliaments of Elizabeth he was returned for Winchester, and became a leading member of the House of Commons. He died June 11, 1581, leaving his son and heir, Henry, of the age of twenty years. He repaired to the camp at Tilbury on the occasion of the Spanish invasion in 1588, the county of Kent contributing thereto 150 horse and 5000 foot, a larger force than any county except Middlesex. He had afterwards a command in the forces sent to France to the assistance of Henry of Navarre, and died at Rouen, October 14, 1596. His will and that of his father show that they were strongly imbued with the religious tone of the more earnest Protestants of that age. It appears by the inquisition taken after his death that he possessed, besides the manors already enumerated, those of Goodins *alias* Fromonds, Crowberry *alias* Croweberry, and Camiston *alias* Cawstons, all in Kent, which descended to his eldest son and heir, Henry, then of the age of seven. This Henry Fane, born in 1589, resumed the old form of the family name— *Vane.* He was knighted by James I. in 1611, and afterwards travelled for three years and mastered several foreign languages. On his return to England he was elected to the Parliament of 1614 for Carlisle, and from this time for many years was very influential in the counsels of James and Charles. The former King appointed him, soon after his entrance into Parliament, cofferer to the Prince; and the latter retained him on his accession to the throne, and made him one of his Privy Council. He sat for Carlisle in the Parliaments of 1620 and 1625, and in every succeeding Parliament during his life, for Thetford in Norfolk, the county of Kent, and (in the Long Parliament) for Wilton in Wiltshire. He was eminent as a diplomatist, but in other respects a mere self-seeking, laborious man of business, without the slightest elevation of character. But he was an ambitious man, and he seems to have desired to emulate the kindred Westmoreland branch by founding in his own family a peerage. The great estates of the Nevilles Earls of

Westmoreland in the north, which had been forfeited
for their rebellion in the reign of Elizabeth, were at
this time in the hands of the citizens of London, to
whom they had been granted by the Crown as trustees
for the purpose of sale; and probably it was the fact
of the Fanes having obtained by marriage some of the
Kentish estates of the Abergavenny branch of the
Nevilles that led Sir Henry Vane of Hadlow to turn
his attention to the Neville estates in the bishopric of
Durham. Accordingly he purchased, during the reign
of James I., the great lordship and manor of RABY
Castle in that county, and seems to have continued
his purchases over several years, in 1626 becoming the purchaser of the honour of Barnard Castle
in the same county, and acquiring altogether a
large estate in that district, of which he made Raby
Castle the chief seat. He also purchased about the
year 1639 another estate in Kent, viz., the mansion of
Fairlawn, with the lands belonging to it, in Wrotham;
and at a subsequent period he disposed of the family
estate of Hadlow, and Fairlawn became the centre of
the Kentish estate of the Vanes, including the manors
of Shipborne, &c. In 1631 Sir Henry was appointed
Ambassador Extraordinary to Denmark, and in a
similar capacity to confirm a peace and alliance with
Gustavus Adolphus of Sweden, and concluded both
missions successfully. He returned home in 1632,
and the next year gave a princely entertainment at
Raby Castle to King Charles, then on his way to
Scotland to be crowned. He again entertained him
at the same place in 1639, in the expedition against
the Scots, in which Sir Henry also held the command
of a regiment. In this year he was made Comptroller

of the Household, and some months afterwards Principal Secretary of State. He experienced in this last elevation the greatest opposition from Wentworth, who managed to delay the appointment for some months. But the Queen's influence secured it at last for Vane, who received a further affront from Wentworth in the January following when the latter, on being created Earl of Strafford, chose also for an additional barony that of Raby of Raby, Durham, a title which Sir Henry Vane had doubtless anticipated for himself. This led him to grow cooler in those courtier-like feelings by which he had been hitherto actuated, and during the Long Parliament he gradually allowed his eldest son Henry to carry him over to the popular party, to whom his experience and business habits made him a welcome recruit. Charles, at the close of the year 1641, marked his displeasure by dismissing him from the office of Secretary of State, which he still nominally held, and giving it to Viscount Falkland. Vane sat on in the Long Parliament, following in the wake of his son, but being otherwise a nonentity. On December 1, 1645, the Parliament, in its propositions for peace, voted to recommend to the King the creation of Sir Henry Vane to a barony. He was among the members who retained their seats in the House after Pride's Purge and the establishment of the Commonwealth, sitting on Committees, but taking no leading part in public affairs. He died at his seat of Raby Castle in the latter part of the year 1654. He had married Frances, daughter of Thomas Darcy, Esq., of Tolleshunt-Darcy, in Essex, and had by her three sons who grew to maturity, the eldest of them being the famous SIR Henry or HARRY VANE. The

second son, George, was knighted at Whitehall,
November 22, 1640, and had his seat at Long-
Newton, in Durham. He espoused the Royalist side
in the Civil War, and in July 1645 surprised Raby
Castle, which was held in his father's name for the
Parliament. He obtained the estate of Rogerley, in
Durham, with his wife, daughter of Sir Lionel Maddi-
son, and died in 1679. We find his name, as well
as those of his father and brother, still sometimes
spelt "Fane." His great-grandson, the Rev. Henry
Vane, Prebendary of Durham. was created a baronet
in 1782, and married Frances, daughter of John
Tempest, and sister and at length heiress of John
Tempest of WINYARD and Old Durham; and their only
son, Sir Henry Vane, Baronet, on succeeding to his
maternal uncle's estate, assumed the name of Tempest
in addition to that of Vane. In 1807 he was elected
member for the county of Durham in the independent
interest against a powerful coalition, and in 1812
re-elected without opposition. He died in 1813,
having married Anne, Countess of Antrim and
Baroness Dunluce in her own right, by whom he had
an only daughter, Emily Frances Anne, who became
the second wife of Charles William Stewart, afterwards
Marquess of Londonderry. This lady still survives,
and is the present possessor of the great Vane-Tempest
property in Durham. Her eldest son, George Henry
Charles Robert Vane, is the present Earl Vane and
Viscount Seaham, of Seaham, Durham, in which titles
he succeeded his father (who had been created to
them 1823, with limitation to the sons of his second
marriage) in 1854. The collieries on the Vane-
Tempest property have rendered it exceedingly valu-

able, and the political influence of the family in the
county—now exerted, as is that of the Fanes, in the
Conservative interest—is very considerable, and more
active than in the case of the kindred family.

Charles Vane, the third and youngest son of Sir
Henry Vane the elder, was an eminent diplomatist in
the service of the Commonwealth and Cromwell, and
envoy to Lisbon. One of Sir Henry's daughters married Sir Thomas Liddell of Ravensworth, ancestor of
the present Lord Ravensworth, and another married
Sir Thomas Pelham, ancestor of the family now represented by the Duke of Newcastle and the Earls of
Chichester and Yarborough.

But the most famous by far of Sir Henry's children
was his eldest son Henry, without whom indeed the
family would have little claim to a place among the
political houses of England. He was born in 1612,
and educated at Westminster School. " I was born
a gentleman," he himself says, " had the education,
temper, and spirit of a gentlemen, as well as others,
being in my youthful days inclined to the vanities of
this world, and to that which they call *good-fellow-
ship*, judging it to be the only means of accomplishing
a gentleman. But about the fourteenth or fifteenth
year of my age God was pleased to lay the foundation or groundwork of repentance in me, for the
bringing me home to Himself, by His wonderful rich
and free grace, revealing His Son in me, that by the
knowledge of the only true God and Jesus Christ
whom He hath sent I might, even whilst here in the
body, be made partaker of eternal life in the first-
fruits of it." His father, the worldly old courtier,
was much puzzled and disturbed at this religious

manifestation—much as Shelley's father was at *his* philosophical vagaries. He sent the lad as a gentleman commoner to Magdalen Hall, Oxford. But when he was called upon at his matriculation to take the usual oaths, young Vane "quitted his gown, put on a cloak, but studied notwithstanding for some time in the said hall,"—much being forgiven to a Minister of State's son. He then left Oxford for the Continent, passing through France to Geneva, and there imbibed opinions on Church matters little congenial with the doctrines fashionable at the English Court. His father, still more perplexed, on his return got Laud, then Bishop of London, to talk to the young heretic; but the Bishop, who had little command of his temper, only quarrelled with young Vane. The latter had already, in the opinion of the courtiers, suffered "much hurt" from the society of Sir Nathaniel Rich and Mr Pym, and soon announced his intention of quitting England and going to the newly-formed Puritan colonies in New England. He landed at Boston in 1635. Here he was received with all the *éclat* attendant on the accession of the son and heir of one of the King's Ministers, was admitted to the franchise of Massachusetts, and in 1636, before he had completed his twenty-fourth year, elected Governor of that colony. In this position, however, the young English gentleman soon came into collision with some of the religious and republican prejudices of his new subjects, and we find him remonstrating against excessive scruples of conscience and defending the Royal authority against provincial democracy. He found also a formidable rival in Winthrop, the leading and most talented of the New England emigrants, who no doubt viewed with some jealousy the sudden elevation of the young son of an English courtier. They engaged in controversy, both orally and in pamphlets, and ultimately the influence of Winthrop proved the stronger, and the authority of Vane grew less. Matters were precipitated by the part he took in defending Mrs Anne Hutchinson (a female preacher, who by her personal allusions to the clergy and interference in families had caused much heartburning in the colony, but, on the other hand, was persecuted with great and cruel intolerance for her " Antinomian" opinions by the leading Puritan clergy of New England), and Vane quitted the colony for the old country in August 1637, leaving behind him many friends and a general reputation for high character and ability which survived the temporary differences with Winthrop and the clergy, and bringing home with him views matured and sobered, but not substantially altered, by experience. He lived for some time after his return in retirement, marrying Frances, the daughter of Sir Christopher Wray, of Ashby, in Lincolnshire. A Parliament, however, being at last called in April 1640, young Vane entered the House of Commons as member for Hull. His father, to add the *ballast* of office to his new political career, obtained from the Earl of Northumberland, Lord Admiral, the appointment of young Vane to the office of joint Treasurer of the Navy (with Sir W. Russell), a place of great trust and profit, and the King backed the appointment by conferring on him the honour of knighthood. " Young Sir Henry Vane," as he was now called, maintained silence during the Parliament of April, though he courted the society of Pym and Hampden ; but with the meeting

of the Long Parliament a career at last opened before
him on which he was not slow to enter. No longer hampered and embarrassed by the narrowness and petti-
ness of colonial prejudices, his genius rapidly made
itself felt in the House of Commons, and under Pym's
guidance he acquired by degrees a considerable share
in the confidence of the popular party. His discovery
of the celebrated notes of the Privy Council taken by
his father, and his communication of them to Pym,
their production in the House of Commons during
Strafford's trial, and the scene which followed between the cautious old Vane and his son, are to be
found recorded in the 'Journal' of Sir Simmonds
D'Ewes, or less authentically in Clarendon's 'History.'
There was still some of the rash impetuosity of youth
which at times detracted from the political weight of
Henry Vane. He made an enemy, for instance, very
unnecessarily, of the Earl of Essex, by his indiscreet and
inopportune manner of speaking the truth respecting
that dilatory and jealous general. He was more in his
element in religious matters, and we find him busy in
the committees on Church government. Here, as in
all other matters, he displayed great subtlety of mind
and depth of thought, with a considerable power of
reasoning, though he was apt to overlook broader
practical facts in following out his reasonings to their
consequences. Some of the distinctions which he
made in estimating motives were of a curiously subtle
kind, and may well have gained him the character of
a visionary even in that age of speculation. But he
was no mere visionary. When real practical work
had to be done, no one was more practically efficient,
or ready in sagacious practical expedients, than Sir

Henry Vane the younger. There were times, indeed, when the natural tendency to casuistry in his mind seems to have somewhat affected the frankness of his conduct; but the cause of this was so apparent that it never permanently injured his reputation as an honest high-minded Englishman. We cannot pretend to follow his career in detail, for it is henceforth identical with the history of the Great Revolution. His next important service to the Parliament was negotiating in 1643 the National League and Covenant with the Scots. Here, again, he is accused of having juggled with the Presbyterian Covenanters, and persuaded them by an ambiguous form of words to embark in a cause entirely alien to their views of Presbyterian exclusiveness. But there is ample evidence that if there was any ambiguity it was intentional on the part of the leading men of both nations. There was a special explanation published by Parliament at the time, which is decisive against the narrow interpretation set upon the Covenant afterwards by the more intolerant Presbyterians; and a glance at Principal Baillie's 'Journal' and 'Letters' is sufficient to show that the Scotch Presbyterians were as studious, in courting the Independent party in England, to sink for the time their intolerance, as young Vane was in Scotland careful not to put forward prominently his notion of the indifference of forms of Church government. He became one of the most eminent of the Independent party, and at length divided the leadership of that section of the Parliament with Oliver Cromwell. They differed as to the execution of the King, Vane disapproving of the interference of the army and Pride's Purge, and withdrawing from

the House until brought back, after the death of the
King, by Cromwell's own earnest exertions. Vane,
however, had now in his own mind moulded the existing state of things into a theory of government,
and was prepared to abide by this as the basis of any
future settlement. He regarded the existing frag-
ment of a Parliament as the only remaining representative of the national will, and applied to it in this
capacity all the arguments properly applicable to the
nation at large. Thus he regarded it as the only
source of all authority in the nation, while Cromwell,
on the other hand, looked upon it as only a useful but
temporary instrument for working the Government,
and was desirous, as much as possible, to distribute
again among several co-ordinate bodies the powers
which necessity had concentrated in this one body.
Vane was willing and desirous to recruit the House
of Commons by new elections; but he could see no
ultimate authority in the nation but the House of
Commons; and though he framed, or joined in fram-
ing, a new scheme of representation, he hesitated long
to fix a day for the dissolution of the existing House.
There was also no doubt a personal jealousy between
the two leading men of the Commonwealth, of which
neither of them was entirely conscious. Vane was no
soldier, but he had experience at the Navy Board, and
he devoted himself to perfecting the fleet of England
as a counterbalance to the army. He also opposed
the officers of the army in the House in an injudicious
manner. But the real point at issue between the two
men was this: Was the House of Commons to be
supreme and irresponsible, or was it to be checked
and balanced by other co-ordinate authorities? The

real facts of the final struggle in the Long Parliament in 1653 between Cromwell and Vane have yet to be unravelled. There seem to have been some meetings between them to arrange matters, at one of which, as Cromwell considered, there was an understanding arrived at to delay the bill for dissolution until it could pass in a form agreeable to all parties. Vane seems to have carried away, or at any rate acted on, a different impression, and when he was hurrying the Bill through the House during Cromwell's absence, the latter, as is well known, hastened to the place, and the scene ended in the employment of force to put an end to the sitting of the House. Cromwell certainly lost control over his temper on the occasion, and the words he used respecting Vane, " One man might have prevented all this, but he is a juggler, and hath not common honesty," must be held to convey the irritation of the moment rather than his deliberate estimate of his former friend. " Oh, Sir Harry Vane! Sir Harry Vane! the Lord deliver me from Sir Harry Vane!"— his famous retort to Vane's protest that this was not honest conduct—was no doubt an equally impatient outburst against the over-subtle policy of the philosophical statesman. Vane remained in opposition to Cromwell's Government throughout, but on more than one occasion showed a disposition to come to a friendly compromise, recognising " the wise and honest General" if he would consent to hold his authority *under* the House of Commons. This Cromwell never would, believing (independently of any personal ambition) that the only way to bring back a really national government was to prevent all authority from being concentrated again in that one body. After Crom-

well's death Vane pursued the same course towards
his son, not hostile to the person but the Government.
On the restoration of the Long Parliament he resumed his seat in the Council of State ; but on the
second dissolution of the Rump by the army, having
learnt wisdom by experience, he acquiesced in the
change, and consented to take his seat in the new
Committee of Safety which governed till the eve of
the Restoration, thus quarrelling with Hesilrige and
others of the Republicans who had the folly to call in
Monk to subvert the authority of Lambert and Fleetwood.   On the Restoration, Vane was arrested, thrown
into the Tower, and removed from thence at length to
the Scilly Islands, where he remained a prisoner till
his fate was decided in Parliament.   After much debate as to excepting him from the Act of Indemnity,
in which the Lords appeared against him and the
Commons in his favour, as a compromise he was ex-
cepted, but the two Houses joined in a petition to
the King, that if Sir Henry was convicted he should
not be executed.   The King gave a general but favourable answer ; and on 2d June 1662, Vane was
arraigned before the Court of King's Bench for com-
passing King Charles II.'s death and aiding in his
exclusion from the throne, and after considerable argument consented to plead " Not Guilty."   He was
brought to his trial four days subsequently, and after
a spirited defence of himself, convicted.   The King's
promise should now have been fulfilled, but Charles
wrote that Vane was " too dangerous a man to let
live if we can honestly put him out of the way," and
on the 11th of June he was sentenced to be executed,
having vainly offered a paper of exceptions to the

judgment. He was beheaded on Tower Hill on June 14, dying, as a Cavalier present said, " like a prince." Sir James Mackintosh has pronounced a high eulogium on his genius as a profound thinker, and there can be little doubt that, with all his failings of temperament, England lost in him an eminent statesman as well as a high-minded gentleman.

He had four sons, three of whom died without issue. Christopher, the survivor, was more pliant or more fortunate than his father. He was knighted by Charles II., sworn of the Privy Council to James II. (July 25, 1688), and created by William a Peer of the realm July 8, 1699, as Baron Barnard of Barnard Castle, Durham. He married Elizabeth, eldest daughter of Gilbert Holles, Earl of Clare, and sister and coheiress of John Holles, Duke of Newcastle, and died October 28, 1723. He suffered from long-continued ill health, and this perhaps added to his general disinclination to politics ; but he is spoken of as an excellent manager of his estate, and is said to have thrown large sums of money into the Bank of England when there was a run upon it, in order to support public credit. He was a tolerant member of the Established Church, without the genius or the dangerous speculations of his father. His younger son, William, a man of ex-tremely amiable character, and who represented the county of Durham and other places in Parliament, had Fairlawn and the Vane estates in Kent left to him by his father, as well as a large fortune out of the Newcastle estates. On June 12, 1720, he was created Viscount Vane and Baron of Duncannon in the Irish Peerage ; but his son William, the second Viscount, ran through nearly all the property, and died in a state of great embarrassment in 1789 without issue, leaving Fairlawn to the Papillon family, who afterwards sold it.

Gilbert, the eldest son of Lord Barnard, succeeded him as second Lord Barnard, and died April 27, 1753, leaving several sons, of whom the second, Morgan, Comptroller of the Stamp Office, is represented by the present Henry Morgan Vane, Esq., to whom the second Duke of Cleveland is understood to have left a considerable fortune. Henry, the eldest son, who succeeded as third Lord Barnard, represented Durham and other places in Parliament, and was appointed Vice-Treasurer and Paymaster-General of Ireland in 1742, a Lord of the Treasury in 1749, and on April 3, 1754, was raised to the English Peerage as Viscount Barnard and Earl of Darlington, was made joint Paymaster of the Forces, and died March 6, 1758. He married Lady Grace Fitzroy, third daughter of Charles Fitzroy, Duke of Cleveland (eldest son of Charles II. by Barbara Villiers). His eldest son by her, Henry Vane, succeeded as second Earl of Darlington, having previously served in Parliament for the county of Durham and other constituencies. He was Master of the Jewel Office, Governor of Carlisle, Lord-Lieutenant of Durham, &c., and a Colonel in the army, and died September 8, 1792, being succeeded by his only son, William Henry Vane, third Earl of Darlington, who married Catherine, daughter of Henry Pawlet (or Powlett), sixth and last Duke of Bolton. He was created Marquess of Cleveland 5th October 1827, and, supporting the Reform Bill at a great sacrifice of borough interest, was raised on the 29th January 1833 to the Dukedom of Cleveland,

with the additional creation of Baron Raby, of Raby
Castle—the coveted title of his ancestor Sir Henry
Vane the elder. He died January 29, 1842, having
been throughout his life a stanch Whig, and leaving
all his disposable property to his youngest son, Lord
Harry George Vane, of Battle Abbey, also a consistent
Whig. His second son, William John Frederick, succeeded to his grandfather the Duke of Bolton's large
disposable estates, and assumed the name of Powlett.
Henry, the eldest son of the first Duke, succeeded as
second Duke of Cleveland to the entailed Vane
estates, and died without issue, January 18, 1864.
He was at first devoted to field sports, afterwards a
practical agriculturist, and throughout a strong Tory.
The same politics in a modified form were professed
by his brother William, who succeeded him as third
Duke of Cleveland. He has had a very brief tenure
of the dignity, dying September 6, 1864 ; and his
brother, Lord Harry George Vane, is now fourth Duke
of Cleveland, the family thus resuming its place
among the great *Whig* houses. Their wealth is now
very considerable, the Vane property having increased
in value enormously.

The Stanleys of Knowsley.

THEY are a strange race these Stanleys, and not precisely the men that the popular opinion formed during the agitation for the Reform Bill would make them out to be. Strong, brave, and efficient, with marvellous luck in marriage and at Court, they have owed their prosperity in no slight degree to a less winning power, so often and so successfully exerted that we may call it political " divination." They have almost always foreseen before other men the side which was going to win, and on that side at its moment of supreme triumph the Stanley has usually appeared. The house, now, perhaps, the greatest among our Parliamentary families, the only one which in modern days has seated father and son at the same time in the Cabinet, now comprehends one baronetcy—Stanley (now Errington) of Hooton, in Cheshire, representing the eldest branch —and two peerages, the Earldom of Derby of Knowsley, in Lancashire, and the Barony of Stanley of Alderley, in Cheshire ; besides inferior branches at Dalgarth, in Cumberland, in Staffordshire, Sussex, Kent, and Hertfordshire. The history of the Knowsley branch, the only one with which we have now to deal, commences properly with Sir John Stanley, who was born in the twenty-eighth year of Edward III., and died in the very beginning of the reign of Henry V. He represented indirectly or claimed to represent Adam de Audley, who in the reign of Henry I. held Reveney in Cumberland, and whose grandson William, obtaining by a family arrangement the manor of Stoneleigh or Stanleigh, in Staffordshire, adopted the name of Stanley. His son, Sir William, obtaining by marriage the manor of Stourton and bailiwick of Wyrrel Forest in Cheshire—the family were, as we shall see, as lucky in their marriages as the Hapsburgs—assumed the arms still borne by the ennobled house. Of *his* two grandsons, again, the younger, John, is the ancestor of the Cumberland Stanleys, and their offshoots in the south of England; the elder, Sir William, had sons, of whom the eldest, Sir William, was the ancestor of the Stanleys of Hooton, the second, Sir John, of the Knowsley race. SIR JOHN STANLEY, founder of the latter branch, inherited the old seat of Newton in Macclesfield, Cheshire, and marrying Isabella, heiress of Sir Thomas LATHOM, whose ancestress again had been heiress of Thomas de KNOWSLEY, became master of the estates around which his descendants' princely property has accreted. The rise of Sir John Stanley, a cool, shrewd, and efficient man, during the reign of Richard II., was unusually rapid. In 1385 he was Lord Deputy of Ireland, obtaining in that capacity a grant of the manor of Blake Castle, in that kingdom ; in 1399 first Lord-Justice, and then Lord-Lieutenant. Between these last two appointments occurred the revolution which seated the house of Lancaster, and the first of

those political "transactions" which enriched the
house of Stanley. Sir John accompanied King
Richard on his return from Ireland to Wales, and was
in Conway Castle with him when Bolingbroke and
the Percy approached in their successful career, but
foresaw the catastrophe, and at once hastened to join
Henry. As his reward he went back to Ireland as
Lord-Lieutenant under the new king, and on his return, after two years' service, his brother Sir William
remained as his deputy. In the year 1405 the revolt
of the Percies gave him an opportunity of rising still
further. He was commissioned with Roger Leke to
secure the city of York and the Isle of Man, succeeded, and in the following year, 1406, the Isle of
Man, taken from the Percies, was given to him, at
first for life, but afterwards in perpetuity, to be held
of the king by homage, and the presentation of two
falcons on coronation days. By this grant the Stanleys obtained an absolute jurisdiction over the people
and the soil—*a hundred and eighty thousand acres*
—and became, with the exception of a few baronies,
immediate landlords of every estate in the island—a
semi-regal position which they retained till 1765,
when Charlotte Duchess of Atholl sold the royalty to
the Crown for £70,000. The authority exercised
there, and which was very different in degree if not
in kind from that of an ordinary feudal lord, affected
the character of the house, and perhaps justified in
their own eyes their habit of making alliances with
their kings rather than keeping fealty to them. Besides this magnificent grant, Sir John was custodian
of endless royal palaces and parks and castles, and in
the first year of Henry V. was appointed Lord-Lieu-

tenant of Ireland for six years, with almost regal
powers. He landed in Ireland once more in October
1413, but died in the following January, having during his long life raised his family from simple country
gentlemen to the head of the lesser baronage. His
second son, Sir Thomas, founded the Stanleys of Pipe,
in Staffordshire; and the elder, again a Sir John, was
Knight of the Shire for Lancaster, Constable of Caer-
narvon Castle, and Justice of Chester. He died in
1431, and his son, Thomas, after serving as Lord-
Lieutenant of Ireland, and Lord-Chamberlain to
Henry VI., emerged from among the country gentry
(in or before 1456) as Lord Stanley. He also died in
1459, and from his third son, Sir John Stanley, who
married the heiress of Sir Thomas Weever, of Weever,
in Cheshire, the Stanleys of Alderley are descended.*
This first Lord Stanley was supposed to be an adherent of the house of Lancaster, but from first to
last, throughout the Wars of the Roses, the house
fought for its own hand, changed sides at its own
discretion, and usually received an enormous reward for its far-sighted adhesions. The Stanleys
always, however, stanchly protected their own
people, and throughout that frightful period no
battle was ever fought in Lancashire, neither side
caring to make a deadly enemy of a family whom
the people would always follow. Sir William, indeed,
second son of the first Lord, managed to get himself
attainted by the Lancastrian Parliament called after

* Sir John Thomas Stanley, Baronet, was created Baron Stanley of
Alderley, Cheshire, May 9, 1839. His son, Edward John, the present
Lord, was created May 12, 1848, Baron Eddisbury, and has been pro-
minent in the Whig administrations.—See 'Ormerod's History of
Cheshire,' a very valuable work.

the battle of Ludlow; but the elder son, Thomas, ran a career of successful faithlessness almost without a parallel in English history. His sister's husband, Sir Richard Molyneux, of Sefton (ancestor of the Earls of Sefton), fell fighting at Bloreheath on the Lancastrian side; but Lord Stanley himself had married a daughter of the Earl of Salisbury, who commanded the Yorkists in that battle, and sister of Warwick the King-maker, and fell, therefore, under suspicion of the Lancastrians. The Commons framed articles against him in the Parliament of 1459, which record a line of conduct so precisely like that he afterwards pursued that the accusations may be accepted as substantially true. He seems to have declined summoning his tenantry till the last moment, sending excuses of every kind. When at last he took the field, he halted his men, 2000 in number (he increased that by-and-by), six miles short of Bloreheath, where he remained during the engagement and three days afterwards, and then excusing himself to Margaret, marched home again with unbroken array. The night after the battle he wrote to the Earl of Salisbury (commander-in-chief of the enemy), "thanking God for the good speed of the said Earl," which was natural to his father-in-law, "trusting in God he should be with the Earl in another place to stand him in as good stead as he should have done had he been there," *i.e.*, at Bloreheath, which was treason. He appears, moreover, to have given Salisbury private assurance of his friendly feeling, and countenanced his tenants in serving under his brother on the Yorkist side. Still, so powerful was Lord Stanley, or so open did he seem to both parties, that the King was advised to reject the Com-

mons' impeachment with "*Le Roy s'avisera.*" The
battle of Northampton which followed in July restored
the Yorkist fortunes, and we read that Queen Margaret and her son were nearly taken near Chester in
their flight by a retainer of Knowsley.   Lord Stanley
accordingly appeared as a Yorkist when Edward
ascended the throne in 1461, but contrived to keep
neutral between the factions into which the dominant
party split.   He married his son George to the heiress
of Lord Strange, of Knockyn, Salop, whose wife was
a sister of Elizabeth Woodville, but held aloof from
the Woodville party, the new people Edward was
trying to build up.   When Warwick and Clarence
revolted they had strong hope of Stanley's aid, and
when Lord Welles was defeated and Warwick compelled to fall back, the applications became urgent.
The wily chief, however, looked to his own interest,
and never struck a blow either for Warwick or
Edward, took no share in hastening Edward's flight
to the Continent, brought no aid to his gallant return, but on his re-accession in 1471 re-appeared at
Court as the sovereign's right hand.   He then struck
the boldest and most adroit stroke of his whole life.
Still nominally a Yorkist, he married as second wife
the Countess of Richmond, mother of Henry Tudor,
the new Lancastrian chief, and thus guaranteed himself on both sides.   On the fall of the Woodvilles, he
entered on a sort of alliance with Lord Hastings, and
with him the two Archbishops and Bishop Morton
formed a kind of neutral *junto* at Ely House, apart
from Richard of Gloucester's cabal at Crosby Hall.
Nothing, however, ever deceived his scent.   He divined
that Richard would strike Hastings, warned him of

his danger by relating a dream of a boar who had grazed both their shoulders; and in the violent scene when Hastings was arrested and hurried to execution, Lord Stanley also (wounded during the scuffle) was arrested and committed to the Tower. Here he was visited by Richard, who freed him and made him Lord Steward and Constable of England for life—and when the revolt of Buckingham exposed the treason of the Countess of Richmond, remitted the death penalty on her for her husband's sake, and specially ordered that the forfeiture ordered of her property should not be allowed to damage the interests of the Lord Stanley. Even in January 1485, when Richmond's invasion was expected, Richard appointed Lord Stanley with his brother William and his son George to the command of the forces raised in Cheshire to oppose the invaders. Yet at this very moment Lord Stanley was pledged to Richmond's cause, and as Steward of the Household was sending him information of all Richard's plans. As the time drew near, however, he shrank from the charge of the Wild Boar, and retired to Cheshire, leaving his son George, created Lord Strange, as his hostage. When Richmond landed Richard summoned Lord Stanley to his side, but he pleaded sweating sickness, and his son made an unsuccessful effort to escape. He was captured, and confessed his father's treason, and prayed for mercy, pledging himself that the Stanleys should abandon their designs; and Richard, who did not want to make the father an inveterate enemy, contented himself with placing the son under ward. At last the opposing parties arrived at Bosworth, Richard with 23,000 men, Richmond with only 5000. Of the 23,000 no less than 8000 obeyed the Stanleys, 5000 under the noble on the right, and 3000 under Sir William on the left flank of the army. Lord Stanley, as Richmond's men dashed to their first great charge, threw off his disguise and charged boldly against his master on his stepson's side. The royal army recoiled, but a desperate charge, headed by Richard himself, who, hunchback or none, was one of the first generals of that age, restored the day, and Richmond might have been lost, when Sir William Stanley on the left also threw off his disguise, and with a final assault of his fresh troops left Richard dead on the field. The crown was hewn from his helmet, and Sir William, amidst the shouts of the army, placed it upon the victor's head, ending in the act, though he knew it not, the Wars of the Roses, the Plantagenet line, and the power of the feudal barons. Henry was not ungrateful. On the 27th October in the same year Lord Stanley was created Earl of Derby, confirmed Lord Steward and Lord High Constable for life, and died in 1504, almost the only baron who survived the Wars of the Roses with added power and splendour. His originally great possessions had been swollen throughout his life by enormous royal grants. Early in his reign Henry VII. gave him almost all the estates forfeited in the north, and thus he acquired (after the battle of Stoke, in 1487) the estates of Sir Thomas Broughton of Broughton, of Sir James Harrington of Hornby, of Francis Viscount Lovel, of Sir Thomas Pilkington, and what Sir Thomas had in right of his lady, the heiress of Chetham. From this Sir Thomas Pilkington came all the Stanley property in Salford Hundred. The Earl had also the estates of Pooton of Pooton,

Bythom of Bythom, and Newby of Kirkby, in Lancashire, "with at least twenty gentlemen's estates more." A record in the Duchy Office, in enumerating these estates, mentions Holland, Nether Kelleth, Haleswood, Samlesbury, Pilkington, Bury, Chetham, Chetewood, Halliwall, Broughton in Furness, Bolton in Furness, Underworth, Shuttleworth, Shippelbotham, Middleton, Oversfield, Smithells, Selbethwaite, Tottington, Elleslake, Urswick, and many others forfeited by attainder.* He had also a grant from the King, in 1489, of Burford St Martyn in Wiltshire. Before, however, the Earl terminated his prosperous career he had to witness in silence a tragedy in his family which must have shaken even his equanimity. The career of his brother Sir William Stanley, whose chief estates were Holt Castle in Denbighshire and Ridley in Cheshire, had been, except in one point, as prosperous as his own. At the commencement of the reign of Edward IV., as a reward for espousing openly the Yorkist side, he was made Chamberlain of Cheshire, and by Richard III. Justice of North Wales. During the reign of the latter King he received from the royal demesne lands an immense grant in Cheshire and Wales, stretching to Shropshire, chiefly as a royal bounty, but partly in exchange for money and other manors, and in the fourth of Henry VII. this grant was confirmed by Act of Parliament to him and his heirs. He was also made Chancellor of the Exchequer and a Knight of the Garter. Lord Bacon says, he was "the richest subject for value in the kingdom,"

---

* Baines's 'History of Lancashire' contains much interesting local information bearing on the fortunes of the Stanleys ; but it is unfortunately most inaccurately compiled.

having in his castle of Holt "40,000 marks in ready money and plate, besides jewels, household stuff, stocks upon the ground, and other personal estate exceeding great. And for his revenue in land and fee it was £3000 a-year old rent, a great matter in those times."

But he was not, like his elder brother, raised in the peerage, and it was said he had solicited and been refused the great Earldom of Chester. Some said that Henry coveted his great wealth; but be the excuse what it may, during the Perkin-Warbeck affair, Sir Robert Clifford, who had turned informer against the adherents of Warbeck, accused Sir William Stanley of being in league with the Pretender, and instanced his saying to him, "That if he were sure that Perkin Warbeck was King Edward's son he would never bear arms against him." The King appeared astonished at the accusation, and cautioned Sir Robert, who, however, persisted in his charge. The next day Sir William was himself examined before the Lords of the Council, when it is said he neither denied nor attempted to extenuate his guilt. Henry probably seized the opportunity of striking a blow at the Stanleys, which would intimidate the Earl from following his brother's example, without the awkwardness and danger of a direct attack on the husband of his own mother and the powerful head of the county of Lancaster. No intercession availed to save Sir William, and six weeks after the time when the accusation was preferred he was arraigned of high treason, found guilty, and on the 16th of February 1495, was beheaded as a traitor. His granddaughter carried his blood into the family of the Breretons of Malpas in

Cheshire, whose head during the Civil Wars of Charles
I.'s time took the lead in those parts against the Stanleys. It was, perhaps, to ascertain by personal observation how the Earl bore the death of his brother, that
King Henry in the summer of the same year " did
make his progress into Lancashire, there to make
merry with his mother the Countess of Derby, who
then lay at Lathom in the country." And Kennett
tells us " a notable tradition, still believed, how Henry,
after a view of Lathom, was conducted by the Earl to
the top of the leads for a prospect of the country. The
Earl's fool was in company, who, observing the King
draw near to the edge of the leads not guarded with
banisters, he stepped up to the Earl, and pointing
down the precipice, said, 'Tom, remember Will!' The
King understood the meaning, and made all haste
down stairs and out of the house; and the fool long
after seemed mightily concerned that his lord had
not courage to take the opportunity of revenging himself for the death of his brother." This was, then, the
old splendid Lathom House as built by the Lathoms.
The Earl's eldest son, Lord Strange, preceded him to
the grave. His principal act of historical interest after
his narrow escape from Richard's heavy hands, and
before his death in 1497, was his gallantry at the
battle of Stoke, where he was one of the commanders
under Henry VII. against De la Pole, Earl of Lincoln.
This led to the grants of some of the forfeited lands
which we have enumerated to his father the Earl.
Lord Strange himself had also a grant in the fourth
of Henry VII. of the manors of Hasilbeare, West Ludford, and Blackdon in Somersetshire. His younger
brother, Sir Edward Stanley, who lived at Hornby

Castle in *Lancashire*, won great glory for the house of Stanley at Flodden Field (September 9, 1513), harassing the Scots so much, it is said, by his archers, that they abandoned their advantageous position on the hill, and breaking their ranks in descending, exposed themselves to the disastrous defeat which followed. This is the Stanley of "On, Stanley, on!" The story is that it was in reference to this hill exploit and to the crest of the Stanleys that Sir Edward was created by Henry VIII. Baron Monteagle. His grandson, the third Lord Monteagle, left an only child, a daughter, who married Edward Parker Lord Morley, and their son William Lord Morley and Monteagle was the lord to whom the celebrated Gunpowder Plot letter was addressed in the beginning of the reign of James I.

George, first Lord Strange, left three sons, of the youngest of whom, Sir James Stanley of Croxhall, Lancashire, the present Earl of Derby is the lineal descendant, tracing thus an unbroken *male* descent back to a man who was great under Henry I.—a rare pedigree of seven hundred and eighty years, surpassed in England by scarcely any noble of the first class, and in Europe by very few. In three hundred years the family had reached by fortunate alliances, rare policy, and great tact in conciliating all *under* their power, a position which brought them close in blood and in power to the Royal House itself; and but for the great qualities of the new line, one with which no noble contended successfully for a month, they might have gone even higher.

The Stanleys continued under the Tudors what they had been under the Plantagenets—a powerful,

H

efficient race, greatly beloved by their immediate followers and neighbourhood, but with an instinct which
their friends called foresight and their enemies faithlessness. Lord Strange's eldest son, Thomas, who
succeeded his grandfather as second Earl of Derby,
was a man of little historic note. He was, however,
a favourite and constant attendant of Henry VIII.;
and was created by a charter of that King Lord
Mohun, Basset, Burnal, and Lacy, and Lord of Man
and the Isles. He died before May 13, 1522; and
besides the Lancashire and other property already
enumerated, most of which descended to him, died
possessed of an eighth of the manor of Hunden St
Kynar, an eighth of the barony and castle of Lewes,
a fourth of the manor of Brighthelmstone (the present
Brighton), and nine other manors in Sussex, of the
manor of Milton or Middleton in Cambridgeshire, and
the manors of Colham and Hillington in Middlesex. He had also the manors of Barlborough in
Derbyshire, Heveringham and Flintham in Nottinghamshire, Bosley in Cheshire, and Cople in Bedfordshire.

The great religious controversies of the age might
have been expected to give to the ambiguous politics
of the Stanleys a more decided character. Edward,
however, who succeeded his father as third Earl, and
lived through the whole time of the struggle, seeing
the faith proscribed by Henry VIII., as a young man
victorious under Elizabeth, then growing old, pursued
the course which, during the Wars of the Roses, had
saved his house, and with the same results. Though
at heart a Catholic, he belonged politically neither to
the Catholics nor the Protestants. The King's middle

scheme suited him exactly, being the one which did not involve the penalties of treason. When the Pilgrimage of Grace in 1536 threatened to involve the whole North of England in insurrection, Lord Derby showed much activity in obeying the King's orders to raise the militia of Lancashire and Cheshire, and by his attitude kept in check the rising in Cumberland, Westmoreland, and the north of his own county of Lancashire. At the coronation of King Edward VI. he was made a Knight of the Garter, and in 1548 he was appointed one of the Commissioners for advancing the Reformation. But when, in the beginning of 1549, the first Act of Uniformity was passed, he strongly resisted the disuse of the Missal; and three years later, 1552, protested against the Act prohibiting the simoniacal practices of reserving pensions out of benefices and granting advowsons while the incumbents lived, and the next and most necessary Act allowing the marriage of the clergy. His son, Lord Strange, was, nevertheless, bred a strict Protestant with Edward VI., and even advised his master to marry a Seymour instead of a French princess—a highly Protestant step. The Earl remained, however, a Catholic, was one of the few nobles who escaped the snare laid by Dudley, Duke of Northumberland, when he ordered the Peers to sign the King's patent appointing Lady Jane Grey his successor, and when Mary appealed to the nobles, rose in arms at the head of 20,000 men. At her coronation he was appointed Lord Steward, the ancient office of his house, and came to Westminster attended by fourscore gentlemen in velvet and 218 yeomen in livery. So completely did he throw off the mask that he, a Commis-

sioner for the advancing of the Reformation, became
a persecutor, and received a pointed rebuke from a
poor Lancashire yeoman. Marsh had become a Protestant curate and schoolmaster, and was brought
before the Earl, whose eldest son was as guilty, to
answer for those high crimes. "It is strange," said
poor Marsh, "that your lordship, being of the Honourable Council of the late King Edward, consenting and
agreeing to acts concerning faith towards God and
religion, should so soon after consent to put poor men
to a shameful death for embracing the same religion."
The remark did not help Marsh, who was committed
by the Earl to Lancaster Castle, confined with common
felons, and then handed over to the Bishop of Chester,
who, being a priest, and unable, therefore, to shed
blood, had him publicly burned alive. Notwithstanding this complicity in Mary's policy, the Earl was so
powerful and so adroit that on Elizabeth's accession
he was sworn of *her* Privy Council, and actually
appointed in the first year of her reign, with others,
to take care that no man in the North held office who
had not taken the oath of supremacy, and named a
commissioner to inquire into the persecutions and to
enjoin the new book of service. The Earl did not
like his task in his heart : the Reformation retro-
graded in Lancashire, hunted Papists found there an
easy refuge ; and Elizabeth, roused in all her Tudor
susceptibilities, wrote one of *her* letters to the Earl.
He was well informed, and before the letter could
reach him, the peer who had surrendered Marsh to
the flames was actively hunting Catholics. In 1569
the Northern Earls were preparing the rising of the
North ; and having gained over two of the Earl's

sons, tried to tempt over himself. The Earl, however, had the family instinct; and, Catholic all the while, he sent their letter to the Queen. Next year, however, he was again under suspicion, as we learn from a private letter of Lord Huntingdon's to Burghley, in which he describes Lathom House as full of Papist counsellors, and accuses Lord Derby of keeping a conjuror. (This charge of witchcraft, as we shall see, stuck to the family for generations.) His son Thomas was, moreover, committed to the Tower for complicity in the Duke of Norfolk's plot to liberate Mary of Scotland; and the Earl lived, therefore, an anxious life. He made amends to himself for political agitations by a princely life in Lathom House; and Camden says that at his death the glory of hospitality seemed to fall asleep. Holinshed and Stow tell us of "his godly disposition to his tenants,—never forcing any service at their hands, but due payment of their rent; his liberality to strangers, his 'famous housekeeping,' and 'eleven score' menial attendants without discontinuance for twelve years; his feeding threescore and odd aged persons twice a-day, besides all comers thrice a-week; and 'every Good Friday, these thirty-five years, one with another, 2700 with meat, drink, money, and money's worth.'" He spent, they tell us, annually, £4000 on his housekeeping. He was also celebrated for his skill in setting bones and in surgery—the explanation, perhaps, of his dealings with the forbidden art.

Earl Edward died 24th October 1574; and his son Henry, fourth Earl, whose mother was a daughter of the Duke of Norfolk, was one of the few members of the family ever constant to one opinion. Favourite

with Edward VI., he was under Elizabeth known as
a bitter opponent of the "recusants"—even presiding
at the trial of his own cousin, Philip, Lord Arundel.
His wife, however, Margaret, granddaughter of Mary
Brandon, Duchess of Suffolk, and younger sister of
Henry VIII., lost the favour of Elizabeth, nominally
for consulting wizards, like her father-in-law, but
really, perhaps, for being one of the Suffolk line. Earl
Henry died September 25, 1592; and Ferdinand,
his son, the fifth Earl, though seemingly a man of
spirit and sense, is noted only for dying "of witchcraft" on April 16th, 1594. He left only three
daughters (among whose descendants the baronies of
Strange of Knockyn, Mohun, and Stanley are in abeyance); and their uncle, William, the sixth Earl, purchased from them the Isle of Man; and procuring a
new grant from the Crown, obtained also an Act of
Parliament to ratify it. He was appointed Chamberlain of Chester for life, and afterwards conjointly
with his son for their joint lives, and died September 29, 1642. His son James, who was summoned
to the Upper House, February 17, 1628, as Lord
Strange, is the well-known (seventh) Earl of Derby
of the Great Rebellion. The romance which has
attached itself to his death, to the character of his
heroic wife Charlotte de la Tremouille, and to his
double position — then beginning to seem questionable—as demi-sovereign in Man, has blinded men's
eyes to the fact that he was a man of haughty temper, little talent, and half-decided views. Before
the King raised the standard he was considered an
adherent of the popular party; and his watchfulness
over Papists in Lancashire and Cheshire was specially

acknowledged by the House of Commons. D'Ewes, a fervent Presbyterian, speaks of him as a great countenancer of religion, and a constant practiser of it in his own family for many years; but in 1641 he was suspected of swaying towards the King; and in 1642, though he was included in the list of Lord-Lieutenants trusted by the Parliament, and presented to the King as their nominee for Cheshire, his Puritan neighbours, headed by Mr Rigby, a lawyer and member of Parliament, prevented the addition of Lancashire to his jurisdiction. Whether this influenced Lord Strange or not, he, on the 20th June 1642, appeared at Preston at a county meeting as chief of the King's party, seized the magazines of Lancashire, joined the King at York, and was invested at once with both Lord-Lieutenancies. From York he proceeded to Lancashire, and was busily engaged in raising troops for the King, when he was stopped by an intimation from the King's Council that the noisy musters which he had made were for his own ambitious designs, and it was not safe for the King to intrust him with so much power. He was also deprived of his Lieutenancy of Chester and North Wales, and it was proposed to invest Lord Rivers with that of Lancashire in his stead. The latent cause of this strange proceeding it is now impossible to discover, unless the King suspected him of pretensions to the throne—and Clarendon accuses him of the opposite vice, inactivity, and attributes it to panic at the excessive hostility of the people around. It is certain that for the rest of his life he entirely lost his power over his people on the mainland—the islanders remained for a time faithful—and that when, his father being dead, he finally declared for the King, he only raised three regiments of foot and three troops of horse—less than a fifth of his house's following. With them he battled bravely against his Puritan neighbours, but was at last compelled to retire to the island, where he was secure, leaving his wife to defend Lathom House. The Countess defended it against the Parliamentary leaders in a style which made her the heroine of local romance, and tempted Scott to give her immortality, until in May 1644 she was relieved by Prince Rupert. The Prince summoned the Earl, and together they attacked Bolton. It was taken by storm, the Earl leading the assault; and either he, or the Prince, or both, put twelve hundred of the people to death after the town was taken—a crime which won for the Earl the deathless hate of the Puritans and their future chief. The Earl soon after retired to Man, Lathom House surrendered, and the estates of the Stanleys were placed under sequestration, a fifth part of the income and the manor of Knowsley being allowed for the children's maintenance. Lord Derby continued to hold his island, at first in defiance, but afterwards with the tacit consent of Parliament, till the attempt of the King of Scots in 1651, when the Prince summoned him to his standard. The Earl obeyed, and endeavoured to raise Lancashire; but alone among that long line he was personally disliked and distrusted, and while gathering feeble forces he was surprised by Colonel Robert Lilburne and completely routed. He fled almost alone to the Prince, to share in the disaster of Worcester, and then fled on again to Cheshire, to be intercepted and surrender on promise of quarter. The court-martial held that "quarter" only exempted him from death on the spot,

and sentenced him to death; but he appealed in a
manly letter to the Lord General Cromwell. Cromwell loved not executions; but the memory of Bolton
stood between the Earl and the Puritans, and on the
15th October 1651 he was executed. His Countess, the
lady who executed Mr Christian of her own sovereign
power, had surrendered Man on the Earl's recommendation, and lived till the Restoration in very
straitened circumstances. Her son Charles, the eighth
Earl, had indeed received a grant of £500 a-year; but
he joined the Cheshire revolt of 1659, and was, after
the battle of Nantwich, taken prisoner. Parliament
spared him, however, and on the Restoration he was
by Act of Parliament restored in blood, and this
chapter in the family history ended.

The remainder we may tell more briefly. The
restored Earl died in 1672, and his son William
George Richard, ninth Earl (1672), and his brother
James, the tenth Earl (1702), adhered with the accustomed fortune to William and Mary and the house of
Hanover, but were not conspicuous beyond their own
great estates. The latter Earl dying (February 1,
1736) without male issue, the barony of Strange (the
creation of 1628), with the sovereignty of Man,
descended to the heir-general, James Murray, second
Duke of Atholl, and grandson of the third daughter
of James, the seventh Earl, who was executed at
Bolton.* The Earldom of Derby reverted, as before
mentioned, to the descendant of James Stanley, the

* The ninth Earl of Derby leaving two daughters, the barony fell
into abeyance between them from 1702 to 1714; then devolved on the
elder, Henrietta, wife of John, Lord Ashburnham. Their daughter,
Anne, succeeded to it in 1718, but dying unmarried in 1732, the barony
reverted to the Earldom of Derby in the person of her uncle, the tenth

third son of the first Lord Strange of Knockyn, of
this house, viz., Sir Edward Stanley of Bickerstaff,
Lancashire, Baronet, who thus became eleventh Earl
of Derby.   His son James (improperly called Lord
Strange) marrying the heiress of Hugh Smith, of
Weald Hill, Essex, took the name of Smith in addi-
tion to his own (whence the curious fallacy that the
Stanleys are not ancient), and *his* son Edward Smith-
Stanley succeeded his grandfather as twelfth Earl in
1776, and died October 21, 1834.   The thirteenth
Earl, Edward Smith-Stanley, called to the Upper
House in 1822 as Lord Stanley, was chiefly remarkable for the stanchness of his adherence to the
Whigs, his great knowledge of ornithology, and his
enormous expenditure; but his son Edward Geoffry
Smith-Stanley, the present Earl, has the hereditary
failing, and more than the hereditary strength,
having, after jumping on a table to protest against
taxes till the Reform Bill was passed, gone over to
the Conservative side and risen to its lead.   He and
his son Lord Stanley—Whig in opinion, Tory Cabinet
Minister in fact—have rebuilt the political influence lost with the execution of the seventh Earl,
and maintain to the full that respect and affection
from their tenantry which, save to that one man, have
never failed.   Lathom House was transferred by
marriage in 1714, and now belongs to the Bootle-
Wilbrahams Lords Skelmersdale; but the Stanleys
have of late been able managers, the growth of Liver-

Earl.   On his death without issue it passed to his heir-general, the Duke
of Atholl, whose daughter and heiress Charlotte (who married her
cousin, the third Duke of Atholl) sold the sovereignty of Man to the
Crown, as already mentioned.   The Dukes of Atholl still enjoy the
barony of Strange.

pool and of the cotton trade has poured wealth into their coffers, and though their island sovereignty has passed away, they may vie in social dignity with the proudest who ever bore their name. They conquered at Flodden for England, supported the Dutchman who gave her the freedom she has used so magnificently, and strove hard and successfully to carry the blood-less revolution of 1831; but it is by an irony of fate that their motto is now, as at Flodden, "*Sans changer.*"

The Grosvenors.

NGLISH respectability culminates in the Grosvenors. As a family, they have in their long career done few striking acts, have furnished no great statesmen, yielded no orators, or generals, or admirals, or men of the highest rank in any one department of life. But they have been steady, sensible men, who have done what they found to do efficiently, have never skulked from difficulties, and though given to accumulation have shown that they could, on adequate occasion, risk their properties for political principle. Consequently they have prospered, and having been lucky beyond measure in marriage and in the acquisition of a great Middlesex tract, are now the wealthiest family in Europe —perhaps, due regard being had to security, the wealthiest uncrowned house on earth. The Lichtensteins have a throne, the Rothschilds are still exposed to the chances of the market, and there is no other family extant which certainly possesses a larger income. The family, though from its want of great men it is never remembered as a feudal house, is still of considerable antiquity. The present branch dates, it is true, only from Henry VI., in whose reign Sir

RAUFE LE GROSVENOR married JOAN or JANE, the heiress of JOHN ETON of Eton (now spelt EATON), in Cheshire, and acquired the manor round which the monstrous wealth of the house has gradually accreted. But he was the second son of Sir Thomas le Grosvenor, whose ancestry stretches away into the Scandinavian mist. Sir Thomas's *eldest* son, Robert, had only daughters, and the patrimony was muddled away amongst coheiresses; but the second, whose marriage rebuilt the house, then became the heir-male of an old stock. He claimed to descend from an uncle of Rollo, a fighting pagan of some mark, and peerage-makers are at liberty to admit his claim.* As it involves, however, some particularly large assumptions, students of history will, in spite of Icelandic sagas, prefer the certainty that in the reign of Richard II. Sir Robert le Grosvenor, grandfather of the Eton bridegroom, fought a celebrated lawsuit with Sir Richard le Scrope, in which most of the English nobles gave their evidence. The Grosvenors said they were lineally descended from Gilbert le Grosvenor, nephew of Hugh Lupus, the great Earl of Chester (the man who gave the Percies Whitby), who, according to the family tradition, gave the manor of Over-Lostock, in Cheshire, to Gilbert's son Robert, in whose family it remained till the year 1465; and affirmed that one Grosvenor (a Robert) was a crusader with Cœur de Lion, another (still a Robert) served with Edward I. in Scotland, a third, Sir Robert le Grosvenor, was with Edward III.

* The story is that the name "Le Grosvenor" is derived from "Le Gros Veneur," "the Grand Huntsman," an hereditary office alleged to have been held by the family in Normandy. Of course it may equally well be translated "the big hunter," but this would spoil the genealogy. All is pure conjecture.

at Crecy and the siege of Calais—all people respectably performing their duty. These claims seem to have been generally admitted, and the house recognised as one of the "early Norman;" but as the estates were chopped up for the coheiresses, the race, but for Sir Raufe's marriage, would have disappeared from the surface. There he was, however, after his wife's death, *circa* 1465, Lord of Eaton, worth ten marks a-year, and lands in Burwardsley, Stockton, Haugton, and Wigland, a burly country squire. His grandson Richard enriched this estate by marrying CATHERINE, one of the four coheiresses of Richard Coton, or COTTON, of Rudware-Hampstall, in Staffordshire, a wealthy landowner in that county, and in Leicestershire, Derbyshire, and Cheshire; and by the inquisition after the death of this Richard Grosvenor (34th of Henry VIII.) he held the manor of Eaton, the toll of the ferry, the fishery, a free boat, and forty messuages therein, as the twentieth part of a Knight's fee—value £26, 13s. 4d.; also lands in Burwardsley, Hargreave, Huxley, Doddleston, Tushingham, Brindley, Stockton, Hampton, Wigland, and Oldcastle—total value, £46, 11s. This fishery and ferry on the Dee are described more particularly in an early legal document, relating to one of the Eaton family, as "the serjeancy of Dee, from Eton Weir to Arnoldsheyre (a rock opposite Chester Castle, now called Arnold's Eye), by the service of clearing the river from all nets improperly placed there, and a moiety of all fish forfeited, and of the fish therein, as far as stall nets are placed, viz., from Dee Bridge to Blakene, and from there to Arnoldsheyre to have one out of all the nets taken, and all the fish therein, and to have a ferry-boat at Eton over the water, for which he shall be paid by the neighbours according to their pleasure, but shall receive from every stranger, if he has a horse and is a merchant, one halfpenny; and if not a merchant, the payment to be at his option." Also toll from every "flote" at Eton, passing through his weir, "de prima knycke unum denarium, qui vocatur hachepeny, et de quaibet knycke sequente, unam quadrantem," as well as waifs and wrecks on his manor of Eton, and two stall nets and two free boats on the Dee. This serjeantcy of the Dee, which must have produced much revenue, has been laid claim to by the Grosvenors as lately as the end of the last century, and is one of the *very* few sources of profit the Grosvenors ever lost. His wife made this Richard father of five sons and eleven daughters, and their great-grandson, also Richard, had by one wife three sons and fourteen daughters; and as most of the ladies married well, the Grosvenors became a very powerful connection. It may have been this tendency to multiply which made them so thrifty, for they grew as no other family ever did, and this Richard, whose fore-fathers since Crecy had done nothing of note, possessed in the 21st year of Elizabeth's reign the manor of Eaton, with certain messuages, a free ferry, and the serjeantcy of the Dee, "by services unknown," from the Queen, as of her Earldom of Chester; and also the manors of Tushingham, *Belgrave*, and Thurcaston, half the manor of Doddleston, and lands in Stockton, Droybayche, Wigland, Stocklach, Hampton, Edge, Horton, Kiddington, Oldcastle, Hargreave, Burwards-ley, Greenwall, Pulton, Pulford, Gorstilow, Rowton, *Oscrofte* (this came from Catherine Cotton), Kynaston, Bromfield, Gresford, and Barton; right of common in Burton, County Denbigh, and *coal mines* in Wrexham.

The house woke out of its torpor with Richard, the son of this wealthy squire. James I., in 1622, made him a baronet, and he sat as Knight of the Shire for Cheshire in the Parliaments of 18th James I. and 2d and 3d Charles I. In the latter he took a high position, and it would appear from a speech of his still extant that he was an able man and a zealous member of the Puritan party. The speech was delivered on 13th February 1629, in a debate in which Oliver Cromwell took part, on the pardons and preferments granted to divines condemned for Arminian doctrines, and preaching the divine right of kings.

Sir Richard seems to have acted up to his professions to his own hurt, for he became security for a brother-in-law, Peter Daniel, of Tabley, and involved himself so deeply that he was thrown into the Fleet, at the suit of one Bennet, and despite the "protection" of the King's Council he disappeared from the political stage—a sad termination for such promise. He did not die till 1645; but his son, Richard, the second baronet, long before his father's death, took the lead of the family, and being of opposite politics raised the *posse comitatus* of Cheshire against Lord Fairfax. He lived and died a consistent upright Royalist, his estate was sequestrated, and he was turned out of Eaton to live in a little house on the border of his own property. Even then Oliver Cromwell found so much reason for suspicion in his conduct that he flung him into Chester Castle. His

eldest son Roger, who died during his father's lifetime, was also an ardent Royalist, and the family
might have perished, had not Charles II., for once,
befriended those who had served him well. They
regained all their property, and Roger was to have
been one of the Knights of the Royal Oak, when that
project was abandoned for fear of reviving animosities.
Roger was killed in a duel in 1661, but he had previously married Christian, daughter of Sir Thomas Myd-
delton, of Chirk Castle, Denbigh, an active Presbyterian,
who became, in 1648, a Royalist. The family fortunes
seem to have been little affected by Sir Richard's
bonds, for Roger, during his father's life, had an income of £3000 a-year; a sum which, though the rise
of prices which distinguished the Tudor period had
reached its maximum, was still very large. His son
Sir Thomas, who succeeded his grandfather as third
baronet, represented Chester in Parliament during the
reigns of Charles II., James II., and William III., and
seems to have been a thoroughly honest, high-prin-
cipled man.

" Sir Thomas was certainly at first supposed to be
a warm supporter of the measures of the Crown, having been singled out by Jeffreys as the foreman of a
jury, who *presented* the necessity of requiring sureties
of the peace from the principal Cheshire noblemen
and gentlemen who paid attention to the Duke of
Monmouth in his progress through Cheshire ; and for
that presentment Sir Thomas Grosvenor had afterwards an action of libel brought against him by the
Earl of Macclesfield. On the bill for the repeal of
the penal laws and test acts being brought into the
House, he was closeted with the King on the subject,

and his support of the measure was solicited, the royal
request being accompanied with the offer of a peerage,
and of the Earl of Shrewsbury's regiment of horse, in
which he then commanded a troop in the camp of
Hounslow. On this occasion the constitutional principles of Sir Thomas Grosvenor were honourably de-
veloped : the offers were rejected ; he resigned the
commission which he already held, and, proceeding to
the House, gave his negative to the measure." He
was Sheriff of Chester during the Revolution, and
died in 1700, having first married in 1676 the third
heiress who had enriched the Grosvenors. She was
MARY, only child of ALEXANDER DAVIES, of Ebury, a
Middlesex proprietor, and brought to him an inheritance then valuable, now princely—viz., the huge slice
of London on which the wealth of the house is now
mainly based, and which includes among other property the whole of the now fashionable region of Bel-
gravia, Tyburnia, and Pimlico. The story is, that
during the general panic and social disorganisation
consequent on the Great Plague of London, a large
amount of valuable property, money, and title-deeds
was left by neighbouring families in Mr Davies's
charge, most of which the owners never lived or returned to reclaim. Alexander Davies made such
excellent use of the capital thus placed at his disposal
—there is no imputation against his honesty—that
he was enabled to bring together, by fresh purchases,
the large landed property in the metropolis with
which his daughter eventually enriched the Grosvenors. His son, Sir Richard Grosvenor, fourth
baronet, sat for the city of Chester in the Parliaments
of the 1st and 8th of George I., and the 1st of George

II., in the latter of which he was associated with his younger brother, Thomas Grosvenor. He was Mayor of Chester in 1715, and at the coronation of George II. officiated as grand cup-bearer of England, in right of his manor of Wymondley, in Hertfordshire. Though twice married, he left no children, and was succeeded in the baronetcy by his next brother, Sir Thomas Grosvenor, who died unmarried at Naples in a consumption in 1733, and was succeeded by a third brother, Sir Robert Grosvenor, sixth baronet, who had sat along with him for Chester, being elected in the room of the fourth baronet. He sat for the same city in four other Parliaments of the reign of George II., and was mayor of the city in 1737. He married Jane, the heiress of Thomas Warre, of Swell or Swill Court, and Shepton-Beauchamp in Somersetshire and of Sandhall in Hampshire, and carved an estate out of this property for his younger son, Thomas Grosvenor, who succeeded him as member for Chester. On his death, in 1755, Sir Robert was succeeded in the baronetcy by his eldest son, Sir Richard Grosvenor (seventh baronet), who officiated as grand cup-bearer at the coronation of George III., and was M.P. for Chester in 1754 and mayor of the city in 1759. In 1758 he purchased the manor of Eccleston, of which Belgrave was a hamlet, and was, on the 8th of April 1761, raised to the peerage as Baron Grosvenor, Lord Bute having been gazetted Secretary of State a fortnight before. His domestic relations were, however, most unfortunate. He married, in 1764, Henrietta, daughter of Henry Vernon of Hilton, Staffordshire; and, while still young and beautiful, Henry, the licentious Duke of Cumberland, seduced her. Lady Grosvenor's husband, Lord

Stanhope observes, "it must be owned, offered her no
small grounds of alienation. The Duke followed her
secretly into Cheshire, meeting her in disguise, yet not
unobserved, at various times and places. On the discovery which ensued, Lord Grosvenor, though from
his own conduct hopeless of divorce, brought an action
for criminal conversation, at which, for the first time,
a Prince of the Blood appeared in the situation of de-
fendant. The verdict was against him, and damages
were awarded to the amount of £10,000." The unhappy lady was, of course, immediately deserted by her
royal admirer. In July 1784, Pitt thought Lord Grosvenor useful enough and powerful enough to be promoted, and he made him Viscount Belgrave and Earl
Grosvenor. The family completely controlled Chester,
sitting for it in Parliament as if the seat had been
an estate; but in return they were magnificent benefactors to the ancient city, whose gates they rebuilt,
one in 1769 and the other a few years after. Robert,
the second Earl, was as a member sufficiently conspicuous for a notice from Lord Stanhope, who, after
observing that, on the 12th of April 1802, Sir Francis Burdett, in moving for a committee of the whole
House to inquire into the conduct of the late administration, " inveighed especially against Pitt, and arraigned with much bitterness the entire course of the
war," continues :—"It may well be supposed that this
attack was very offensive to the large majority of
members who had supported Mr Pitt in all his measures. Lord Belgrave became the mouthpiece of their
indignation. He moved an amendment that, on the
contrary, the thanks of the House should be given to
the late ministers for their wise and salutary conduct

throughout the war.   The Opposition cried out that
such a motion was contrary to the forms of Parliament; but the Speaker decided that it was regular,
though very unusual, and that it might be put.   But
here Pitt rose.   In his loftiest tone he said that he
would not offer one word on the original motion, but
he hoped he might be allowed to suggest that the
amendment was certainly, for want of notice, against
the general course of proceeding in the House, and
that it ought to be withdrawn.   Lord Belgrave did
accordingly withdraw it, and after some further debate
the House divided, and the motion of Sir F. Burdett
was rejected by an immense majority.   Upon this
Lord Belgrave gave notice that he would, after the re-
cess, bring forward a vote of thanks to the late administration.   But a second attack on Pitt being made
on the 7th of May, by a Mr Nicholls, who concluded
by moving an address of thanks to the King for having been pleased to remove the Right Hon. W. Pitt
from his councils," Lord Belgrave rose, "and pointed
out that the foundation of the proposed address was
entirely false.   The King had not dismissed Mr Pitt.
That minister had of himself resigned."   He then re-
stated the arguments he had urged in the former
debate, and concluded by moving the amendment of
which he had given notice.   The amendment was
vehemently opposed by Grey, Erskine, Fox, and Tier-
ney; and supported by Wilberforce, Sir Robert Peel,
Lord Hawkesbury, and Addington.   On a division,
Lord Belgrave's resolution was carried by a majority
of 222 to 52.   The Grosvenor family was therefore
still, nominally at least, Tory.

This Lord Belgrave (second Earl Grosvenor) was a

Lord of the Admiralty in 1789, Mayor of Chester in 1807, and Lord-Lieutenant of Flint, in which county the Grosvenors had now a seat called Halkin Hall. Their old luck with heiresses had not deserted them. The second Earl married Eleanor, heiress of Thomas, Earl of Wilton, the representative of one of the co-heirs of the old Lords Grey de Wilton, of Border renown; and the earldom of Wilton was, therefore, entailed on his second son, Thomas, who has since succeeded to that title, and keeps up the old Tory politics of the Grosvenors.

Earl Grosvenor himself seems to have moved forward gradually to the Canning party, then took his side definitely with the Liberals, and, on 13th of September 1831, was raised to the rank of Marquess of Westminster. He was one of the few great peers who strenuously supported the Reform Bill, and, on 7th October 1831, he made in his place a speech containing the remarkable statement, that he knew of his own knowledge that Mr Pitt had never abandoned his desire for parliamentary reform; that he saw in it the only chance of "salvation" for Great Britain, but that he had thought it useless to contend with the "borough-oligarchy." He never changed his views during the reaction which swept away so many great peers, but, till his death in 1844, remained a consistent and strenuous Whig and supporter of the Grey and Melbourne administrations. An admirable man of business, an honest politician, his character was deformed only by a thrift, always more or less apparent in the family, which in him rose to a mania. The very rich in England are often very economical, for they are bred up with the idea that they are ob-

jects of incessant plunder ; and tradesmen know well
that it is the *nouveaux riches* and not the aristocracy
who pay exorbitant bills without inquiry. Still the
thrift which gives rise to stories such as those told of
the Marquess is unusual, and has done much to lower
the great popularity of the house. On his death his
eldest son, Richard, became Marquess ; his second son,
Thomas, was already Earl of Wilton ; and on the elevation of his third son, Robert, to the barony of Ebury,
three brothers sat side by side as peers of the realm.
Chester, moreover, returns the future heir to the House
of Commons, Flint sends up a cadet, and the family
have a sort of prescriptive claim to one seat for Middlesex. All are liked by the people, as men who,
though ennobled, have a sort of *bourgeois* respectability
and aptitude for business ; and, as the family wealth
develops with every succeeding year, they may yet
carve out more peerages without impoverishing the
main stem. By every law of succession they ought
now to develop some mad spendthrift ; but if they
avert that danger, and can avoid internal disputes,
they may by 1900 be better represented in the Peers
than any family in the land. Their connection is
enormous ; for besides all other links with the great
aristocracy, Earl Grosvenor has married a daughter of
the Gowers, and thus become one of that group of
brothers-in-law who form a clan without a rival in
Great Britain. So high have consistent respectability,
luck, and steady thrift, brought up a Norman squire.

The Fitzwilliams.

HERE is an atmosphere of health about the Fitzwilliams such as does not often surround these great families. Strong, efficient, but thoughtful men, with an eye to their own interest and a hearty sympathy for the people around them, they have come down through history as a family addicted at once to governing and accumulation, forcing all manner of chaotic men and things to assume some semblance of order, redressing all visible grievances, standing always in the fore-front of the popular battle, and withal very dangerous to attack, as their county rivals know. Their character would justify the family legend that they are the children of a bastard of William the Norman, but it is not supported by any ascertained facts. In the misty domain of the pedigree-makers, we hear of William Fitzwilliam, who gave, in 1117, land in Elmley and Sprotborough, in Yorkshire, to the monks of Biland, who may have been the son of another Fitzwilliam, and of Eleanor Elmley of Elmley, and the grandson of this bastard of the Conqueror's, or of William Fitzgodric, cousin of Edward the Confessor, and marshal of the army which conquered at Hastings and changed all

English history. But all this is conjectural. The first
distinct figure who steps out of the mist is an Alderman, Sir WILLIAM FITZWILLIAM, a man, it would seem,
of pure Norman blood ; but who, as son of a younger
son of a Northamptonshire squire, had taken to trade,
prospered exceedingly, and under Henry VII. and VIII.
became a great City magnate, Alderman, and Sheriff
of London, and in 18th Henry VII. purchased the
lordship and manor of MILTON, in Northamptonshire,
which he and his never let go again. That he was of
gentle blood is clear ; for his ancestry, though it cannot be carried to the Conqueror, is distinct to a Fitzwilliam of Elmley and Sprotborough, to whom Edward
I. granted the right to turn the highway which ran
through the middle of his park—a pretty sure proof of
his grade and consideration. These ancestors must
have been, too, somewhat popular persons ; for one of
the family set up a cross, which was standing down
to 1520, and on which these words were engraven in
brass :—

> " Whoso is hungry, and lists to eate,
> Let him come to Sprodburgh to his meate ;
> And for a night, and for a day,
> His horse shall have both corn and hay,
> And no man shall ask him where he goeth away ! "

The family, we may remark *en passant*, threw off,
in the reign of Richard II., a branch from which sprang
William Fitzwilliam, Vice-Admiral of the Fleet, Treasurer of the King's Household, Chancellor of the Duchy
of Lancaster, Admiral of England, Wales, Ireland, &c.,
and Lord Privy Seal in the reign of Henry VIII., by
whom he was created a Knight of the Garter in 1537
and Earl of Southampton. This statesman and soldier
died in 1543, leaving only nieces as his heiresses.

The Alderman—he was Alderman of Bread Street Ward—rebuilt the gates of the Church of St Andrew Undershaft at his own expense, and in 1506 was appointed, on the express command of Henry VII., Sheriff of London. He was again elected in the 2d of Henry VIII., but refused to serve, and was fined a thousand marks, say *ten* thousand pounds, and disfranchised; but four years after he was Sheriff of Essex, in which county he owned the manor of Gainspark Hall, and in nine years more was Sheriff of Northamptonshire. He was a great personal favourite of King Henry, who knew a man when he saw him, and one day came to blows with the stout Alderman. Fitzwilliam had been in early life in the service of Cardinal Wolsey, and in his disgrace entertaining him at Milton, he was asked by the King himself how " he dared " to receive " so great an enemy of the State." Such a question from a Tudor meant death, but the Alderman replied sturdily that he had acted from no contempt of his Majesty, but that the Cardinal had been his benefactor, and had helped to advance his fortunes, and he was bound to receive him. The King declared that *he* had few such servants, knighted Fitzwilliam, and made him one of his Privy Council, being a Tudor who understood other things than etiquette. Sir William had in his prosperity a kindly feeling for the poor, gave a charity of £12, 13s. 4d. a-year to the poor of Marham, in whose church his family lie, payable through his guild—that of Merchant Taylors—and another, secured in the same way, to maintain for ever six poor women in an almshouse at Gainspark Hall ; and in his will, dated May 1534, he gives £100 for the marriage portion of poor maidens among his tenantry, and remits all debts due from poor creditors who " could not content the same," under whose names he had written in his seventh book of debts " *Amore Dei remitto.*" He bequeaths to the poor scholars within the Universities of Oxford and Cambridge £40, to be distributed by the advice of two Doctors of Divinity ; and £30 amongst poor people ; also £50 for the making the highway between Gainspark Hall and Chigwell in Essex ; and the same sum towards mending the highways between Thornborough and Sawtrey Chapel in Huntingdonshire, and to the fellowship of Merchant Taylors his best standing gilt cups with covers, with a perpetual remembrance of him, to be kept in their hall, and they to pray for his soul. For the safety of the same soul he makes plentiful provision in several other quarters. He was three times married—first, to the daughter of a City knight ; next, to Mildred, second daughter of Richard Sackville, of Buckhurst, in Sussex, ancestor to the Dorset family ; and lastly to Jane Ormond. To his eldest son by his first wife, William Fitzwilliam, he bequeathed 300 marks sterling, " with all his harness and coats of fence in his gallery chamber, his rich briganders, his cross of gold with a ruby, set with three diamonds, on condition that he keepeth it as long as he liveth ; likewise his several pieces of plate, and all his household stuff, &c., at Gainspark Hall and his manor-place of Milton." He settles on him, besides (after her death) his wife's portion (the manors of Hennials, Maydells, Marshalls, and Armeways, with other lands and tenements in the county of Essex), his manors of Milton, Marholme *alias* Marham, Etton-cum-Woodcroft, Butlers, Thoroldes, Minskip, and Gainspark Hall, and all his other manors, &c., within the counties of Northampton, Essex, and Lincoln, to him and his heirs male, with remainders in case of default. He also makes very liberal provision in lands or money for his other four sons. He bequeaths to his wife his mansion-house in the parish of St Thomas the Apostle during her life, whilst she remained his widow, on condition of paying £4 per annum to his executors, to be by them bestowed yearly for the relieving of poor prisoners within the city of London that shall be acquitted and remain for their fees. He also bequeathed " to his singular good lord" the Earl of Wiltshire, father of Queen Anne Boleyn, his rich rose of diamond and rubies, "beseeching him to be aiding to his executors in the performance of his will." And he directs that the residue of his plate, jewels, ready money, &c., and what he has not specifically bequeathed, be divided into two parts, the one half among his children indifferently, and the other among his poor kinsfolk and for the benefit of his soul, according to the discretion of his executors. Altogether he was a substantial citizen who meant gain, but meant also justice and mercy, and to go heavenwards as far as he knew how. One of his daughters by his first marriage became the wife of Sir Thomas Brudenell, of Deane, Northamptonshire (ancestor to the Earl of Cardigan) ; and the other, marrying Sir Anthony Coke, of Giddy or Gedney Hall, in Essex, had by him a daughter, Mildred, celebrated for her knowledge of Greek by Roger Ascham in his 'Epistles,' and who became the second wife of Elizabeth's William Cecil Lord Burghley, and the mother of Robert Cecil, the Secretary of State to Elizabeth and James I., and first Earl of Salisbury.

The good Alderman's eldest son and successor at
Milton, also a Sir William, was brought up in the
household of John Lord Russell, first Earl of Bedford
—a kinsman of his mother—and he procured him the
Marshalship of the King's Bench under Edward VI.
On the death of Edward he joined his relative Francis
Earl of Bedford, Sir Maurice Berkeley, and Sir Henry
Neville in proclaiming Queen Mary, was by her employed in Ireland under the Earl of Sussex, then, in
1554, made Commissioner for the Crown, and in the
following year Keeper of the Great Seal. This is the
commencement of the Fitzwilliam connection with
Ireland, where to this day they hold a vast estate,
and where they, almost alone among Norman settlers,
have once at least had the honour of national mourning at their departure. From this date he was, in
various offices, as Lord Justice, Lord-Deputy, Treasurer
at War, and what not, for thirty-nine years virtual or
ostensible ruler of Ireland, retiring only when worn
out with toil and honour to die, in 1599, in his native
hall. He was a real Governor of Ireland in times
when government there did not mean the careful
proportioning of official pay between two rival creeds.

Fuller, in his 'Worthies of England,' speaking of
the repeated renewal of his Irish trust to Fitzwilliam,
says, "A sufficient evidence of his honesty and ability,
Queen Elizabeth never trusting twice where she was
once deceived in a Minister of State. And she so
preserved him in the power of his place that, sending
over Walter Earl of Essex, in 1573, to be Governor of
Ulster, the Earl was ordered to take his commission
from the Lord Deputy." Sir John Davis, in his
'Discourse of Ireland,' bears testimony also that

Fitzwilliam " was very serviceable in the reduction of Ireland ; first in raising a composition in Munster, afterwards in settling the possessions of the lords and tenants in Monaghan, one of the last acts of State (tending to the reformation of the civil government) performed in the reign of Queen Elizabeth. His vigilance was very conspicuous in the memorable year of the Spanish invasion, anno 1588, when the noted Armada, on its return, dared not to land in Ireland, except against their wills, driven by tempest, when they found the shore worse than the sea to them." During one of Sir William's absences in England, Elizabeth displayed her trust in him by constituting him governor of Fotheringay Castle (in Northamptonshire), which was the prison of Mary of Scotland. " He behaved himself with so much civility," says one of his family, to his illustrious prisoner, " that the morning before she was beheaded she presented him with the picture of her son, which picture is still in the family." Fitzwilliam married an aunt of Sir Philip Sidney, a sister of Sir Henry Sidney (who was also one of the Governors of Ireland); and the latter, writing to Burghley by Sir William, on his return to England, in June 1566, says, " I beseech you, sir, be good to this bringer, my brother, Fitzwilliam. In my conscience he is a true man in all his service and charges to the Queen's Majesty. Doubtless I durst be bound, upon forfeit of all my lands, that he hath not willingly deceived the Queen in nothing, and for his cheques I do not think that the Queen shall gain much above that which he hath ever confessed. In debt sure I think he is, and yet far from that sum which hath been reported. He hath deserved well,

which is not to be forgotten, if it were but one day's
service, in which he saved the honour of our nation
in this land, and the lives of as many Englishmen as
were on foot that day in the field. I pray you, sir,
second him, for in truth he is honest." In May 1590,
he suppressed a mutiny among the soldiers; and in
July 1591, Tyrone by his means was made a county,
and divided into eight baronies. In the same year
he made the settlement of the county Monaghan,
already alluded to, on occasion of the forfeiture by
treason of Hugh (Roe) M'Mahon, the Irish chief;
dividing the greatest part of it among the natives,
except the Church lands, which he gave to English
servitors, reserving £400 a-year and upwards to the
Crown. For this service the Queen returned him her
thanks; but the M'Mahons objected in such a practical form that "the good effects of his regulation
were to a great degree frustrated." "Up to this
time," says a biographer, "he was a most disinterested
governor, and it was reported that, thinking his great
services merited some further recompense than the
established entertainment, he sought it from the
Queen; but being answered by a lord in great favour at Court that the Government of Ireland was a
preferment, and not a service, he ever after endeavoured to make his profit of the post." The result
was the gradual aggregation of a large landed estate
in that kingdom, particularly in counties Donegal,
Westmeath, Tyrone, and Wicklow. As already
stated, Sir William was prompt and active against
the M'Mahons, Macguires, O'Neills, and O'Hanlons,
and his other dangerous Irish neighbours; but his
government of Ireland will be chiefly remembered

by the construction of Trinity College, Dublin, the
first stone of which building was laid on the 13th
March 1592 by the Mayor of Dublin; Sir William
having two days before issued a circular letter " to
encourage forwarding and perfecting so good a work,
and, to set an example, gave for his own contribution
£200, and was so zealous in having it finished that
it was made fit for the reception of students on the
9th of January in the following year, his coat-armour
being then placed over the gate to perpetuate the
memory of so great a benefactor."

One of Sir William's daughters married into the
Byron family, and was grandmother of the first Lord
Byron. The Sir William Fitzwilliam, who succeeded
the Lord-Deputy of Ireland, did nothing worthy of
especial notice. His son and successor, William
Fitzwilliam of Milton and Gainspark Hall, was, in
December 1620, created Baron Fitzwilliam of Lifford,
in the county of Donegal—an Irish peerage only—
and died "at his house in the Strand," January 6,
1644, leaving the title and estates to his son William,
second Lord Fitzwilliam. This nobleman had during
his father's lifetime represented Peterborough in the
Parliaments of April and November 1640, and in the
latter (the Long Parliament) attached himself to the
cause of the Parliament, to which he adhered steadily
during all the vicissitudes of the first Civil War.
Joining the party of the Presbyterians, and voting, at
the end of the year 1648, that the King's Newport
proposals were a sufficient basis for an accommodation,
he was one of those excluded on that account by
Colonel Pride. He took no active part against the
Commonwealth, however, and died peacefully at his

house in the Savoy in the beginning of 1658. His second daughter married Sir Christopher Wren, the architect of St Paul's. His successor, the third Lord Fitzwilliam, also a William, was a Whig in politics, and at the accession of the house of Hanover was appointed *Custos Rotulorum* of the city and liberty of Peterborough, and in 1716 raised to the titles of Viscount Milltown of Milltown, in the county of Westmeath, and Earl Fitzwilliam of Tyrone. He also sat for Peterborough in some Parliaments. He married the heiress of Edmund Cremor, of West Winch, in Norfolk, and (his two eldest sons dying before him) the head of the family at length ceased to be a William, and he was succeeded by his son John, second Earl Fitzwilliam (of Ireland), who was also member of Parliament and *Custos Rotulorum* for Peterborough. Earl John married the heiress of John Stringer, Esq., of Sutton-upon-Lound, Nottingham-shire. Their only son, William Fitzwilliam, third Earl Fitzwilliam, of Ireland, who was left a minor, was created by George II. in 1742 a peer of Great Britain, as Lord Fitzwilliam, Baron of Milton in Northamptonshire ; and in September 1746 was further raised to the dignity of Viscount Milton and Earl Fitzwilliam of Norborough in Northampton, and in 1744 he consolidated his fortunes by a marriage with Lady Ann Wentworth, eldest daughter of Thomas Marquess of Rockingham. This family pos-sessed the wide Yorkshire estates of the Wentworths, Earls of Strafford, William Wentworth, second Earl, son of "Thorough," having devised his possessions to his nephew, Thomas Watson-Wentworth, grandfather of Lady Anne. Her brother Charles, second Marquess, the Whig statesman, dying in 1782 without heirs, bequeathed his estates, with WENTWORTH-WOOD-HOUSE, to his nephew William, the second Earl (of Great Britain), who thus became master of the estates possessed by the man for whose execution his ancestor had voted. The Earl remained a Whig till the French Revolution, when, like most of the magnates, he quitted Fox, and in 1794 he, like other friends of the Duke of Portland—the Bentincks are Whigs by right of birth—took office with William Pitt. He was immediately afterwards appointed to his ancestral office in Ireland, and some secret understanding arrived at as to his future policy. The Earl was at heart a strong friend of Catholic emancipation, but he seems to have agreed not to bring any bill on the subject into the Irish Parliament, while Pitt, for his part, promised if Grattan introduced it that it should have full "consideration." This arrangement, however, was not made public, and the Earl and the Premier were alike in a false position. On the landing of the new Lord-Lieutenant, Catholics and Dissenters hurried to him with addresses full of anticipated sympathy on his part with their views. He *did* sympathise with them heartily, and was not the man to disguise his sympathy. The rumour of his friendly feelings soon spread, the agitation for emancipation gained fresh strength, petitions poured into the Irish Parliament, and Mr Grattan was compelled—whatever he may have wished to do out of deference to Pitt—to introduce his bill at once. Then the ultra-Protestants of Ireland burst forth into violent expressions of indignation and alarm. Pitt wrote to Lord Fitzwilliam, stating plainly, though courteously, that the Government could not approve of the bill. Lord Fitzwilliam, with the proud honour of a true Whig, at once summoned the Chancellor to his presence, and announced his intention to lay down his government and return to England within a very few days. On the 25th of March 1795, he quitted Dublin, having only held the office since the preceding January. " The day of his departure was one of general gloom ; the shops were shut, no business of any kind was transacted, and the greater part of the citizens put on mourning, while some of the most respectable among them drew his coach down to the wharf-side ;" and his departure and the arrival of his successor were followed by riots, particularly directed, as the mob said, "to extinguish" Mr Beresford. A challenge was exchanged between the latter gentleman and Lord Fitzwilliam after his return to England. This was occasioned by some words applying to Mr Beresford which occurred in one of two long letters addressed to Lord Carlisle, and published by the Earl in his own vindication. The parties actually met, but the arm of the law arrested the duel, and then Lord Fitzwilliam apologised " in generous terms." The subject of the resignation was renewed in the English Parliament, the Duke of Norfolk and Fox taking up the case of Fitzwilliam ; but Portland and Windham, with the other Whig seceders, adhered firmly to Pitt. The truth seems to have been that the Earl, in his clear-sightedness and sympathy with the people, forgot his official subordination. He lived, however, to see all his dreams realised, and died at the commencement of the first reformed Parliament, having in a long public life steadily postponed his own comfort, position, and reputation to the development of civil and religious liberty throughout the three kingdoms. His son, the late Earl, pursued the same course, strenuously supporting free trade, and so governing his estates and contesting elections as to elicit the warm affection of the people of the West Riding, who, new as the house is in the county, still prefer the Fitzwilliams to any more sleepy race. The great election contest for the county is still talked of, in which the house of Fitzwilliam is said to have expended £100,000, and their competitor all his West India estates. The last Earl at his death divided his vast inheritance into three unequal parts, but the earldom is still supported by revenues which, till the character of their owners change, will not be grudged. A manlier or more competent race does not distinguish the English peerage.

The Cavendishes.

E are among a new order of magnates. The house of Cavendish does not belong to the roll of Norman nobles, conquered no acre of soil, sent no leader to the Crusades, lost no member during the Wars of the Roses, and, though of high historic importance, is as a great house not old. It rose above the surface during that redistribution of England popularly known as the dissolution of the monasteries, the greatest social event between the Conquest and the Reform Bill; but its real founder was a woman, ELIZABETH HARDWICK, who devoted a long life, enduring beauty, matchless wit, and a heart above or below most scruples, to the aggrandisement of the Cavendishes. The first man of the race who can be admitted to have risen above the mass was WILLIAM CAVENDISH, who, in the reign of Henry VIII., obtained an appointment in the Royal Exchequer. He was the second son of Thomas Cavendish, of Cavendish-Overhall, in Suffolk, a well-to-do though undistinguished squire. Genealogists will have it that Thomas was the lineal descendant of Sir John Cavendish, Chief-Justice of the King's Bench in the reign of Edward III., who obtained the lordship of Caven-

dish-Overhall by his marriage with the heiress of John
de Odyngseles ; and that the Cavendishes of Grimston
Hall, in Suffolk, who produced the greatest man of the
name, Elizabeth's illustrious navigator, were of the
same stock ; but the latter pedigree at any rate must
be pronounced untenable.　So must the pleasing story
that it was the first of the house who was gentleman-
usher to Wolsey, who wrote his life, devoted himself
to the Cardinal in his misfortunes, and was, *therefore*,
the honoured friend of Henry VIII.　Great houses
absorb the achievements of all who bear their name,
but this man was George, of Glemsford, Suffolk, elder
brother of the founder,* and the repute of mention by
Shakespeare and aid in the defeat of the Armada must
be struck from the family claims.　All that is *certain*
is, that William Cavendish, a gentleman owning some
small lands in Suffolk, was, in the year of the Cardinal's death, one of the commissioners for taking the
" surrenders" of several religious houses, and in 1539
was appointed one of the auditors of the Court of
Augmentation—a tribunal established to perform a
task which at that time puzzled all English statesmen,
viz., so to "augment" the King's revenue that he
might be able to put England in a condition of decent
defence.　In those days the ox who trod out the corn
was not muzzled, and on the 26th of February 1540,
little more than three hundred years ago, William
Cavendish received a royal grant of the lordships and
manors of Northawe, Cuffeley, and Childewicke, in
Hertfordshire, all abbey property.　Six years after he
was knighted and appointed Treasurer of the Chamber

* See 'Who wrote Cavendish's Life of Wolsey ?' 1814.　A tract, by
the late Rev. Joseph Hunter.

to the King, "a place of great trust and honour," and
no contemptible pickings in the way of small abbeys,
out-of-the-way rectories, and other trifles then going
pretty freely, sometimes in grants, more often in sales
forced on with ruinous speed. The exchequer was
always selling, and the officials naturally knew well
where the fat morsels lay. So well did William
Cavendish employ his opportunities that, in the last
year of Edward VI., he received a royal grant of
"divers lands belonging to several dissolved priories
and abbeys in Derbyshire, Nottinghamshire, Staffordshire, Dorsetshire, Cornwall, Kent, and Essex," in *exchange* for his manors at Northawe in Hertfordshire,
Northawberry in Lincolnshire, the site of the priory
of Cardigan, and other lands in Cornwall and other
counties, and so blossomed from a minor official into
a very considerable landholder. This was pretty well
for one generation, but fortune had fallen in love with
the Cavendish, who seems to have had very indistinct
ideas of any other worship, for he continued to hold
under Mary the office which he had held under Henry
and Edward VI. Two wives had died leaving no
male issue, when he wooed Mistress Barley, widow of
Alexander Barley, of Barley, Derbyshire, the Elizabeth
Hardwick of whom we have already made mention.
She was the daughter and (after her brother's death)
the heiress of John Hardwick, of Hardwick, Derbyshire, and had been married at fourteen—her husband,
who died soon after, bequeathing her his whole estate.
It is probable that she warmly loved her second choice,
for during her long career the single object which lay
close to the heart of this extraordinary woman was
to exalt the name and wealth of the Cavendishes.

Her first command—which, like every other she ever
issued in life, was at once obeyed—was to sell all the
southern estates, and aggregate the Cavendish property round her ancestral farms. Among the consequent
purchases was the manor of CHATSWORTH, then in the
possession of the Agard family, but formerly the seat
of the Leeches, of Leech, who had built there a decent
mansion and laid out a park. Lady Cavendish, however, foresaw her destinies, and persuaded her husband
to pull down the hall, and build what Camden calls a
"spacious elegant house," a quadrangular affair with
turrets, bearing little resemblance to the existing
palace. Sir William did not live to finish it, dying
in 1557; but his widow did, as she did everything
else which might tend to Cavendish advantage.
There were three sons of the marriage, and three
daughters; but Sir William Cavendish, like Alexander Barley, left everything to his widow, who, with
three inheritances, was naturally courted by many
suitors. After a curious list of proposals she found
the connection she wanted, Sir William St Loe, of
Tormarton, in Gloucestershire, owner of several fair
lordships. She insisted, however, on her price, and in
the marriage articles a clause was inserted by which,
in default of more children, all the lordships and
manors of St Loe passed from his race to the children
of William Cavendish, to the exclusion of St Loe's
brothers and his own daughters by a previous marriage,—perhaps the coolest stipulation ever made even
by a widow. This husband, too, died; and the widow,
still beautiful and with a tongue which must have
been of almost magical power, captivated the greatest subject then in the realm, George Talbot, Earl of

Shrewsbury. She made excellent terms with him, too; for besides a great jointure—heaped up always for Cavendishes—he consented to a triple union of the families. His son and heir, Gilbert, was bidden to marry Mary Cavendish, youngest daughter of Sir William; while Henry Cavendish, eldest son,* married Lady Grace Talbot, the Earl's youngest daughter. The Countess married her other two daughters equally well—the eldest, Frances Cavendish, to Sir Henry Pierrepont, of Holme-Pierrepont, Notts, by whom she bore the ancestors of the Earls and Dukes of Kingston, and (through a female) of the Earls Manvers, who at present possess the Pierrepont property; her second daughter, Elizabeth, she contrived to marry into the royal family—viz., to Charles Stuart, Earl of Lennox, younger brother of the unfortunate Henry Lord Darnley, King of Scotland—and Elizabeth Cavendish became by him the mother of the equally unfortunate Lady Arabella Stuart. This relationship, as we shall see, gained the Chatsworth Cavendishes their step to the peerage. The Countess of Shrewsbury led a very unhappy life with her new husband, who complained bitterly of her overbearing conduct. But both Queen Elizabeth, and a bishop, who was called in to mediate, took the lady's side, and the Earl had to bear his lot as he best might. The Countess resided occasionally at Chatsworth during her union with her fourth husband, and the Earl having been intrusted with the custody of Mary Queen of Scots, the hall

---

* Henry Cavendish, a natural son of this Henry Cavendish, had an estate at Deveridge, in Derbyshire, from his father, and is the ancestor of the present Henry Anson Cavendish, Lord Waterpark (an Irish peerage).

" acquired a more than common interest," as having been one of the prisons of that princess.

The Countess survived her fourth husband also,* and lived in great splendour for many years on her rich jointures.   Besides Chatsworth, she built two other houses in Derbyshire, Oldcotes and Hardwick, leaving at the latter place her old family mansion standing near the new edifice, and transmitting them all three to her second and favourite son, William Cavendish, who, we may mention, inherited nearly all his elder brother's fortune (on *his* early death), and stood lord of the greater portion of the vast accumulations carved by his father from abbey lands, and by his mother from the estates of every family with which four wealthy marriages had brought her in contact. Among the exceptions was WELBECK ABBEY, Nottinghamshire, bequeathed with other estates by the mother to her third son, Charles.   He married, as his second wife, Catherine, daughter and heiress of Cuthbert, Lord Ogle, of Ogle Castle, Northumberland, and henceforward the Cavendish stem splits into two mighty branches,—the Chatsworth, or elder Cavendishes, masters of endless abbey and other property ; and the Welbeck, or younger Cavendishes, possessors of the lordships accumulated by the extinct house of Ogle. Such a rise from a petty estate in Suffolk effected in one lifetime is almost without a precedent even in a country where, from the Conquest to the death of William III., the personal favour of the sovereign could in a day make a gentleman an immensely wealthy peer.

We follow the Welbeck branch first.   The Ogle heiress was, on the death of her father and husband,

* See under the history of the Talbots, *postea.*

declared by letters patent Baroness of Ogle, and, dying in 1629, her eldest surviving son, William Cavendish, inherited her title, the vast Ogle and part of the Cavendish estates, and was created successively Baron Ogle of Bothal, Northumberland, and Viscount Mansfield, Nottinghamshire (Nov. 3, 1620); Baron Cavendish of Bolsover, Derbyshire, and Earl of Newcastle-upon-Tyne (March 7, 1628); Marquess of Newcastle (October 27, 1643), and Earl of Ogle and Duke of Newcastle (March 16, 1664); the three last of these dignities being bestowed upon him in reward for magnificent services to the Stuarts. Like all the Cavendishes for generations, he was a man of a large but self-indulgent nature, indolent and voluptuous, with a certain greatness of soul which nothing but severe political pressure—"stormy times," in other words—could bring out of him. By his great power and influence in the North—his property there affording him a gallant regiment of tenants, the renowned Whitecoats—and his steady principles, he managed to overbalance the Parliamentary interest there; and, on the whole (though with great changes of fortune), he kept the advantage over the Fairfaxes till the advance of the Scotch army in 1644 drove him to the shelter of York walls, whence he emerged (against his will) with Prince Rupert to encounter the defeat at Marston which the latter had brought on by his obstinate rashness. After the battle the Marquess took shipping at Hull and returned to the Continent, being unable, as he himself said, to encounter the laughter of the courtiers at his discomfiture. Soon after his arrival at Paris he fell in love with, and married as his second wife, Margaret Lucas, one of Queen Henrietta's maids of honour, daughter of Thomas Lucas, of St John's, near Colchester, and sister of the Sir Charles Lucas shot by Fairfax after the capture of that town in 1648. This is the well-known blue-stocking, and most eccentric and learned Duchess of Newcastle, who was so much admired in her own day and has been so much ridiculed since. Whether she were a wise person or not, she was certainly a devoted and admiring wife, as her writings testify. His estate being under sequestration, he was put to great straits in living, till the death of his younger brother Sir Charles, a mathematician of the highest class, described by Clarendon as a magnificent soul in a frail body, brought him an income of £4200 a-year, on which he lived till the Restoration. Sir Charles had fortunately been induced to compound with the Parliamentarians, and he had bought in as much of his brother's confiscated estates as he could lay his hands on, preserving, for example, Welbeck and Bolsover. On the return of the Marquess to England, however, he found his means sadly crippled, and the statement of his losses will illustrate better than entire histories the position to which the younger Cavendishes had risen, and the sacrifices entailed by the Civil War on a great English landed proprietor.

Of eight parks that he possessed before the Civil War all but Welbeck were destroyed. Clipston Park, Nottinghamshire, seven miles in compass, and filled with magnificent trees, estimated at £20,000, in which he had chiefly delighted, was utterly defaced, not a tree being left standing. He had still, however, remaining in Notts £6229 per annum : in Lincolnshire, £100 per annum ; in Derbyshire, £6128 per annum ; in Staffordshire, £2349 per annum ; in Gloucestershire,

£1581 per annum; in Somersetshire, £1303 per annum; in Yorkshire, £1700 per annum; in Northumberland, the baronies of Bothal, Ogle, and Hepple, £3000 per annum; total, £22,390 per annum.* His losses his wife computes at £941,300, of which she attributes £403,000, without interest, to the Civil War; lands lost, £2000 per annum; and lost in reversion, £3200; and he sold lands to pay his debts to the value of £56,000. His woods cut down she estimates at £45,000. As a compensation for his losses he asked and obtained a step in the peerage, and was, accordingly, in 1664, made Duke of Newcastle. He died in December 1676, and was succeeded by his son Henry (his eldest son Charles, Lord Mansfield, having died before him), who adhered firmly to the Stuart family—was greatly trusted and admired by James II., opposed the Revolution, and, refusing to take the oath of allegiance to William and Mary, retired from public business, and died at Welbeck in 1691. Henry's four sons preceded him to the tomb, and he left five coheiresses; but the bulk of the Newcastle property passed eventually through one of them to the Holles family, thence by a second heiress to Harley, Earl of Oxford, and thence by a third heiress to the Bentincks, Dukes of Portland, who now enjoy it. The younger branch was extinct. It had lasted but two generations; the almost regal Duke, whose opposition to a new dynasty was a great question of State, being only the great-grandson of William Cavendish, clerk in the Exchequer, and manager of the Tudor confiscations. The family had done their work in the world, and their eagerness to accumulate was only equalled

* We have omitted the odd shillings and pence in our statement of the items.

by the splendid decision with which they staked their much-desired wealth on behalf of the cause which, like most of the new *noblesse*, they held to be that of duty.

The elder, or Chatsworth branch, however, remained still in prosperous existence. William Cavendish, son of the Sequestrator, after the ordinary career of a great country gentleman during the latter part of Elizabeth's reign, serving as sheriff and sitting in Parliament, was, on the 4th of May 1604, created by James (through Arabella Stuart's influence), Baron Cavendish of Hardwick. He had caught the passion of the day for geographical adventure, was one of the first "adventurers" who settled a colony and plantation in Virginia, and on the discovery of Bermuda was one of the knot of nobles to whom the King granted the island. They settled and provisioned it in 1612, and in memory of the fact one of the eight counties of Bermuda still bears the name of Cavendish. On the 7th of August 1618, he was created Earl of Devonshire, and died at Hardwick, 1625, at the age of seventy-five. His son William (second Earl) survived him only three years. He was a man notorious for his accomplishments, his dissoluteness, and his half insane expenditure. The King married him to Christian, the daughter of his Scotch favourite, Edward Lord Bruce of Kinloss—*his* younger brother is ancestor of the Earl of Elgin, the late Governor-General of India—taking that means of rewarding Lord Bruce by marrying him into an already great family. He gave the bride himself £10,000 on the wedding, and on the father of the bridegroom making a second marriage, enjoined him not on that account to diminish the inheritance which he would leave to his eldest son. Before his father's death, however, Lord

Cavendish had already contracted a large debt, and when his fortunes were by that event reinstated he launched out into still larger expenses, making his house more like a palace than the dwelling of a subject. He was, however, more than a spendthrift and a *roué*. Hobbes had been his tutor, he had travelled, he knew European languages so well that he was used as courtly interpreter to foreign ambassadors, and he was a magnificent patron of literature and the fine arts. His vices have been obscured by the praises heaped upon him in return, but he nearly undid all the efforts of the Sequestrator and Elizabeth Hardwick. At his death (June 20, 1628, at his house near Bishopsgate, on the site of the present Devonshire Square), his affairs seemed in hopeless confusion—a vast and increasing debt, and upwards of thirty lawsuits, constituting the inheritance. For the second time, however, a woman built up the house. His widow Christian was guardian of the minor, and she calmly devoted her life to the unravelling of the skein. She had a jointure of £5000 a-year, a clear head, a fascinating tongue, and that incapacity of blundering in matters pecuniary which is included in Scotch descent. With this, and still more with her own woman's wit, perseverance, and fascination of manner, she fought successfully all the lawsuits against powerful adversaries, and brought them to an end in moderate time, so that King Charles said to her in astonishment, "Madam, you have all my judges at your disposal." Some of the debts she liquidated by the sale of some estates disentailed by her husband by Act of Parliament (a rare act of grace in those days), the rest she fairly paid off by more prudent management of the property, and she handed over to her son his inheritance scarcely impaired by his father's mad extravagance. When her son came of age she retired to her seat, Leicester Abbey, and resided there till the Civil War broke out, remaining, we may add, the Providence of the family. The Earl, under her advice, flung in his lot, like his great cousin of Newcastle, with the King, voted for the King at Westminster to the last minute, obeyed his summons to York and to the Anti-Parliament at Oxford, and then ran away to the Continent. The motive for this act will never now be explained; but it seems possible that Christian had made the blunder of all women of her kind, and governed her son till his manliness was somewhat questionable. She saved him again, however. Parliament admitted him to composition, and on her advice he got over his obstinacy, came to terms, returned to England, and lived in strict retirement till the Restoration, dying a highly respectable nonentity in 1684. His younger brother, Charles, had more of his mother's spirit. The Templars chose him captain of the body-guard they raised for the King. He distinguished himself at Edge-hill, took Grantham and Burton-on-Trent by storm, became his cousin Newcastle's lieutenant-general of horse, and seems to have had in him the qualities of a great and successful commander. His destiny, however, crossed Cromwell's, and instantly snapped. Cromwell met him near Gainsborough, broke his force, and drove him into a quagmire, where he was slain by the famous Captain Berry (Baxter's friend), with "a thrust under the short ribs." Thirty years after his mother ordered his body to be exhumed, that it might lie next hers, and all Royalist England mourned loudly for the perfect Cavalier.

By 1664, then, the Cavendishes, who but began to grow in 1530, had advanced thus far. They had earned a dukedom and earldom, had contributed three great captains to the royal cause, and were collectively, without exception, the richest landed proprietors in Great Britain. In 1691 only one branch remained ; but that still held the earldom, nearly all the Sequestrator had seized, and most of all his wife had gathered so patiently, and had commenced with William, fourth Earl, a new and far brighter career.

The second history of the Cavendishes, their career as a great Whig house, devoted to the cause which in those days represented freedom—the cause, that is, of aristocratic as opposed to regal government—commences before the death of the third Earl. He lived for years, as we have said, as a respectable nonentity ; but his son, after receiving the usual education, and making the grand tour, married a daughter of the house of Ormond, served in a naval action, went in the suite of Mr (afterwards the Duke of) Montagu to France, where he was nearly killed in an encounter with three of the French King's guards at the Opera House, on his return was elected for Derbyshire, and threw himself warmly into the "country party," of which Lord Russell was the acknowledged head. By his determined conduct he greatly incensed the Court party, distinguishing himself particularly by his zeal for the Protestant religion and against Popery. In 1679 he was appointed with his friend Lord Russell one of the Privy Council, exerted himself strenuously in support of the Exclusion Bill, and suffered from the reaction produced by that violent measure. Accordingly, we find in the 'Gazette' published at Whitehall, January

L

31, 1680, this curt notice :—"This evening the Lord Russell, the Lord Cavendish, Sir Henry Capel, and Mr Powle prayed the King to give them leave to retire from his Council Board. To which his Majesty was pleased to answer, 'With all my heart!'" Lord Cavendish continued to attend all the consultations of Russell and his friends, till at length he objected to something brought forward as too dangerous, and absented himself thenceforth, though he kept up his political connection with the party. This probably saved his head when Russell and Sidney suffered, but he never flinched from their side, appearing at the trial as a witness in Lord Russell's favour, offering to change clothes with him and remain in prison in his stead, and attending him to the last with unswerving devotion and affection. In 1684 his father's death made him Earl of Devonshire, and from this time he assumed the leadership of the Opposition in the Upper House. "He was well qualified to do so," says Macaulay. "In wealth and influence he was second to none of the English nobles; and the general voice designated him as the finest gentleman of his time. His magnificence, his taste, his talents, his classical learning, his high spirit, the grace and urbanity of his manners, were admitted by his enemies. His eulogists, unhappily, could not pretend that his morals had escaped untainted from the widespread contagion of that age. Though an enemy of Popery and of arbitrary power, he had been averse to extreme courses, had been willing, when the Exclusion Bill was lost, to agree to a compromise, and had never been concerned in the illegal and imprudent schemes which had brought discredit on the Whig party." In the

following year the Prince, whom he had endeavoured
to exclude, succeeded as James II., and a mischance
befell the Earl which is differently related by different writers. We will confine ourselves to Kennet's
account, who affirms that a Colonel Culpeper was
instigated to insult the Earl in the precincts of the
Court. Devonshire, though a man of quick temper
and proved courage, at first scornfully pardoned his
antagonist; but after the defeat of Monmouth, Culpeper
was prevailed on to encounter the Earl again in the
presence-chamber, and give him an insulting look.
The proud Peer lost all patience, seized the bravo by
the nose, led him out of the chamber, and then struck
him with his cane. For this offence, a great one
against etiquette, but against etiquette only, he was
summoned to the King's Bench, vainly pleaded his
privilege as a Peer, was fined £30,000, and was committed to the King's Bench until the sum should be
paid. The amount was probably more than one year's
income, or equivalent to a fine at the present day of
£150,000; and the Earl, boiling with indignation,
broke prison, and betook himself to Chatsworth. The
Sheriff of Derbyshire was ordered to arrest him; but
by this time the Cavendishes had a hold on their
tenantry other than that of money, and the Earl
turned the tables by arresting the official, and keeping
him in Chatsworth in honourable custody till he had
made terms with the King. His mother offered James
bonds for £60,000, signed by Charles I. and II., for
monies received during their necessities from the third
Earl; but the faithless tyrant cared as little for the
honour of his house as for justice, repudiated the debts,
and demanded a bond for the whole amount. It was

given, and was found among James's papers after his flight, and cancelled by William III., while the House of Lords reversed the sentence as contrary to Magna Charta. The Earl, during his seclusion from business, which lasted nearly four years, occupied himself with rebuilding Chatsworth, laying out the grounds afresh, and furnishing the house in a style which excited the envy of foreign magnates. As the tendency of the King's Government, however, became more evident, he secretly plunged into politics once more, and opened a correspondence with the Hague, strenuously urging the Prince of Orange to interpose. On the first alarm of the preparations in Holland, James summoned the Earl to Court, but he excused himself; and when his cousin, the Duke of Newcastle, visited him and talked much of the danger of revolution, he answered only in general terms. The instant the Duke had disappeared he held a meeting with his old enemy the Earl of Danby, for whose impeachment he had voted; and after a full reconciliation and avowals of past indiscretion, they concerted measures with Lord Delamere, Sir Scroop Howe, and others of the greatest influence, to raise Derbyshire on behalf of the Prince. The smaller gentry, however, were terribly afraid of another "Bloody Assize," and when the Deliverer's fleet was driven back by the storm, there was danger lest the Earl himself should be seized and retained in arrest. He, however, never lost heart, and the moment the Prince arrived, placed himself at the head of his tenantry—an act which, had James succeeded, would have cost him his life and lands—and read to the corporation of Derby the Prince's first declaration. The town refused to move, and the Earl, with his force swelling at every step, marched to Nottingham, where he issued a declaration of the views and desires of his party, and where he was joined by the Princess Anne. He escorted her with his whole force to Oxford, and thence repaired to Sion House, where he was welcomed by William as one of his steadiest friends. In the Convention Parliament he was the most conspicuous supporter of extreme Whig ideas, and it was at his house that the Lords assembled to devise some compromise between the claims of William and Mary. It is to him, too, that the sentence which, for the first time in our history, assigned the supreme power in the State to the House of Commons, is ascribed. The Tory Lords wished to proceed to business on the 25th January, but Devonshire proposed and carried a delay till the 29th, "by which time," he said, "we may have some lights from below which may be useful for our guidance," a pregnant remark for which he was severely censured. On the accession of the new sovereign he was made Lord-Lieutenant of Derbyshire, and sworn of the Privy Council, in which capacity he is recorded to have refused an enormous bribe. In January 1691, he attended William to the Hague, distinguishing himself as usual by the magnificence of his life ; but he resented keenly William's leaning towards the Tories. He could not comprehend that the Prince had become King of England, not of the Whigs, and expressed himself so bitterly that Macaulay thinks his language gave rise to what Lord Preston stated on his trial—that William Penn had told him that Devonshire was in communication with the Court of St Germain's. No one, however, credited the assertion ; and when Preston was proceeding to repeat this part of his

accusation in the King's presence, William stopped
him, saying to Carmarthen, "My lord, we have had
enough of this." In 1694 William showed his sense
of the Earl's services by creating him, on the 12th of
May, Marquess of Hartington (Derbyshire) and Duke
of Devonshire, on the same day that the Earl of Bedford was raised to a similar dignity. In 1695, the
Queen being dead, Devonshire was appointed one of
the Lord - Justices during the absence of William,
and in that capacity received the confessions of Sir
John Fenwick, implicating Shrewsbury, Godolphin,
and Marlborough, and transmitted them direct to the
King, without showing them to his colleagues—a proceeding which the accused ministers much resented,
but William, probably, much appreciated. On the bill
of attainder against Sir John, however, Devonshire, at
the head of a small section of the Whigs, while supporting the earlier stages of the bill, to intimidate, as
he said, the prisoner into further revelations, refused
to support the third reading unless the prisoner's life
were guaranteed, and his sentence commuted to perpetual banishment, declaring his dislike of bills of
attainder. He strongly opposed, however, the "Resumption Bill" for royal grants in Ireland, and continued in the King's favour to the last, being one of
those present at his death. Queen Anne continued
him in the office of Lord Steward, and he consistently
supported the measures of the Whig party, the war
with France, &c., and was appointed one of the English commissioners to settle the union with Scotland.
He died on the 18th of August 1707, at Devonshire
House, Piccadilly, in the sixty-seventh year of his age,
leaving one of the few unblemished memories of that

period of political demoralisation. He was the flower
of his race, the one member of the house to whom it
had been given to stake lands and life on a side which,
though that of an order, was also that of the people.

His eldest son, William, the second Duke, was not
a man of any great political weight beyond the influence attaching to his position as the head of a great
Whig house. This secured him on three several occasions the office of Lord President of the Council, and
he was more than once appointed a Lord - Justice
during King George's absence in Germany. He attached himself in politics more especially to Townshend and Walpole, in opposition to Stanhope and
Sunderland, and died in June 1729, having married
Lady Rachael Russell, daughter of his father's friend,
Lord William Russell. His third son, Lord Charles
Cavendish, was the father of Henry Cavendish, one
of the founders of the present science of chemistry.
Henry Cavendish had been alienated from most of his
family by his refusal to enter on a political or public
life; but an uncle, approving of his conduct, left him
a large fortune. He lived in strict retirement, being
eccentric in his habits,—he would not see a female,
and if any of his maid-servants came near him, she
was at once dismissed; accumulated a splendid
library, and died in 1810 at an advanced age, leaving
funded property to the amount of £1,200,000, of which
he bequeathed £700,000 to his cousin, Lord George
Cavendish; £200,000 to the Earl of Bessborough;
and the remainder in legacies to other members of the
Devonshire family. The Duke's eldest son, William,
third Duke, like his father and grandfather, acted as
Lord Steward of the Household. He was four times

one of the Lord-Justices during the King's absence from England, and in 1737 was appointed Lord-Lieutenant of Ireland, in which office he continued for seven years. His talents, though not brilliant, were respectable and solid. Sir Robert Walpole, to whom he was consistently attached throughout life, even said of him that on a subject that required mature deliberation he would prefer his opinion to that of any other person ; and Horace Walpole, calling on him one day at Devonshire House, and finding him from home, left the following epigram on his table :—

> " Ut dominus domus est ; non extra fulta columnis
> Marmoreis splendet ; quod tenet intus habet ;"

which may be translated :—

> " Like host like house ; *without*, no pillared show
> Of marble shines ; *within*, their wealth they stow."

In his administration of Ireland he only followed the instructions of Walpole, without leaving any mark of personal character on the Government; but he has the merit of at least once intimidating into submission Dean Swift, who had had the cathedral bells muffled lest they should ring a peal in honour of his arrival. After the fall of Walpole, disgusted with the character of the Duke of Newcastle, and the timidity of his brother, Mr Pelham, the Duke, in 1749, resigned his post of Lord Steward (to which he had been re-appointed on his return from Ireland, with a seat in the Cabinet), and retired to Chatsworth, where he died, December 5, 1755. His eldest son and successor, William, fourth Duke of Devonshire, had filled several public offices during his father's lifetime. He had sat for Derbyshire in the Commons, and had been called up to the House of Peers in the barony of 1605. He was Master of the Horse in 1751; one of the Privy Council and a Lord of Regency in 1752. In January 1754 he was made Governor of the county of Cork; in the February of the following year, Lord High Treasurer of that kingdom, in room of the last Earl of Burlington. These two offices he retained all his life. In March 1755 he was made Lord-Lieutenant of Ireland, in which post he continued till November 1756, when he was made First Lord of the Treasury. This last appointment ensued on the resignation of the Duke of Newcastle, the elder Pitt becoming Secretary of State. Up to that time Devonshire's connection had been with Fox—of course the elder Fox. Lord Stanhope says of him, "This nobleman was, like his father, naturally averse to public business, but, like his father also, was highly esteemed by all parties for probity and truth. Dr Johnson, for example, though opposed to the Duke in politics, bears a strong testimony to his character: 'He was not a man of superior abilities; but strictly faithful to his word. If, for instance, he had promised you an acorn, and none had grown in that year in his woods, he would not have been contented with that excuse,—he would have sent to Denmark for it.'" Devonshire continued to hold this office after Pitt's resignation down to June 1757, when Newcastle and Pitt forced their way into power again. With the new reign, new influences, and, indeed, a new policy, came into play; and the Duke, whom the Princess-Dowager sarcastically called the "Prince of the Whigs," was naturally an object of intense dislike to the Earl of Bute and the King, who was striving to break the power of the great Whig connection. In October 1762, a crisis occurred. The Duke of Newcastle, driven from power, intrigued with the great Whigs, and persuaded two of them—Devonshire and Rockingham—to resign their places in the Household. A few days afterwards, the King in Council called for the Council-book, and ordered the Duke of Devonshire's name to be struck from the list. Soon after, Newcastle, Grafton, and Rockingham having been dismissed from the Lord-Lieutenancies of their counties for censuring the terms of the peace, Devonshire, whose dismissal also had been designed, but averted by Fox, threw up his commission voluntarily. After this, though in the prime of life, his health gave way; he sought relief at Spa, in Germany; but on October 2, 1764, a renewed attack of palsy carried him off at the latter place, at the age of forty-four. Lord Stanhope, observing on the great loss sustained by the Whig party in his death, says that "it is not easy to discriminate between his character and his father's, whom he seemed to have succeeded in principles and disposition as much as in title and estates." Had he survived a little longer he might have assumed again high place on the return of Pitt to power, and have proved an ally in Pitt's real policy—that of pursuing liberal measures by the aid of the great aristocratic faction.

His eldest son and successor, William, fifth Duke, was then only sixteen years of age, and "at no time did he study State affairs. But the importance of the house of Cavendish was, in great measure, upheld by the late Duke's brothers. Lord John especially, the youngest of all, was well read, held in just esteem for his truth and honour, and resolute in his views, though shy and bashful in his manner 'Under the appearance of virgin modesty,' says Horace Walpole, 'he had a confidence in himself that nothing could equal.'" "In reality, however," continues Lord Stanhope, "his abilities were only moderate, nor yet did he bring to public life any very steady application." Burke, notwithstanding his eulogies of him after his death, during his lifetime writes in a much more subdued tone respecting him, and in a letter expresses a wish that Lord John could be induced to show "a degree of regular attendance on business." "Lord John ought to be allowed a certain decent and reasonable portion of fox-hunting; but anything more is intolerable." Lord John was Chancellor of the Exchequer in 1782 and again in 1783, and died unmarried in December 1796. His elder brother, Lord George Cavendish, who died two years before him, also unmarried, brought to the Cavendish property an accession—the Holker estate, in North Lancashire, left him by Sir James Lowther, of Whitehaven, in 1753. We may also mention here that the Cavendishes have added to their influence in this part of the kingdom by purchasing the estates of the old family of Curwen, in the western part of the adjacent county of Cumberland—estates the Curwens had received, we believe, during the great distribution of the abbey lands, and which, had they been retained, would have made them by this time peers, and enabled them, perhaps, to win their brave but hopeless fight of two centuries with the Lowthers.

We are approaching the present day. The fifth Duke was chiefly remarkable as the husband of Georgiana, daughter of John Earl Spencer, the beau-

tiful Duchess who won the vote of a Westminster
butcher for her friend Fox with a kiss. This Duke
had inherited Chiswick House, Middlesex, Lismore
Castle, County Waterford, and other large Irish estates,
with the title of Lord Clifford of Lanesborough, from
his mother, Charlotte, daughter and heiress of Richard
Boyle, Earl of Burlington and Cork; and on September 10, 1831, his younger brother, George Augustus
Henry Cavendish, was raised to his maternal grandfather's title of Burlington, and also created Baron
Cavendish of Keighley, Yorkshire. This first Earl of
Burlington of the Cavendish family married Lady
Elizabeth Compton, daughter and heiress of Charles,
seventh Earl of Northampton, who brought him
Compton Place, Eastbourne, Pevensey Castle, and other
property in Sussex. *His* eldest grandson is Duke of
Devonshire, the sixth Duke, son of the fifth (whom he
succeeded in 1811), dying unmarried. Another peerage
was created, January 15, 1858, in the person of Charles
Compton Cavendish, youngest brother of the present
Duke of Devonshire; and his son, William George,
is now the second Baron Chesham, both father and
son having represented the county of Buckingham
in Parliament. The sixth Duke, William Spencer,
was remarkable for his marvellous taste in horticul-
ture, which he gratified with the assistance of Sir
Joseph Paxton, whom he picked up as an under-
gardener at Kew, till Chatsworth and Chiswick became the noted centres of all that was novel and
magnificent in his favourite pursuit. A true Cavendish in every instinct, magnificent, accomplished, and
dissolute, he was pursued through life by a story
which asserted that he was a changeling, bound by a

family compact not to marry. He did not marry, and he did dip the estates; but in those two facts lay the only evidence in support of a charge probably based on the tale of some discarded waiting-maid. There is scarcely a noble in England whose title is not assailed by some such rumour, though it more generally takes the form of a secret or Scotch marriage, made by some half-forgotten ancestor. The sixth Duke died January 17, 1858. The present and seventh Duke— also a William—has taken little part in public life, though the conjoined wealth of the Devonshire and Burlington titles gives him enormous influence; but his heir, the Marquess of Hartington, has devoted himself to politics, and bids fair, with the assistance of a brother who is just coming forward, and from whom the advanced Whigs hope much, to revive the political influence of the house of Cavendish. Their further rise will be watched without annoyance; for though founded by a sequestrator, made by marrying a widow, and distinguished throughout their history by a personal character which is that rather of Continental than of English *noblesse*, they have deserved well of their country. There was no English royalist like the chief of the younger branch, no Whig who dared or suffered more than the head of the elder race, who made of a family of courtiers a steadily liberal house. Their use in politics has been that of men ready to lead forlorn hopes; and as magnates they, at least, teach the middle class that there are modes of life more brilliant and many-coloured, if less virtuous, than the steady pursuit of *bourgeois* respectability. For three hundred years the Cavendishes have been gentlemen.

The Bentincks.

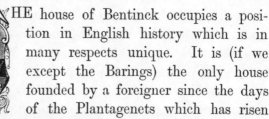THE house of Bentinck occupies a position in English history which is in many respects unique. It is (if we except the Barings) the only house founded by a foreigner since the days of the Plantagenets which has risen to the first rank—the only one built by a favourite which can look back to its origin with a glow of honest pride. Other men whose pedigree is not English are found in the Peerage, but the highest among them is only of secondary rank; other houses have been founded by favourites, but their representatives anxiously veil the personal career of the founder. The Bentincks are proud of theirs, and with reason. In the long and splendid roll of English statesmen there is probably not a man who has accomplished more for English greatness than the bad-mannered Dutchman who loved money so much and Englishmen so little.

HANS WILLIAM BENTINCK, founder of the house which now rivals the Howards, the Percies, or the Seymours, was the third and youngest son of Hendrick Bentinck, Lord of Diepenham, in the Dutch province of Over-Yssel, where his family had flourished for ages as

men of knightly, if not of noble rank. He was born in
the year 1645, and appointed, while still a lad, page
of honour to the young Prince of Orange, then first
among Dutch nobles, and with admitted though somewhat indefinite claims to a civil primacy in Holland.
He was then appointed gentleman of the bedchamber,
and, with the growing confidence of his Prince, acquired
a hold over his affections which continued through
life, and placed the two men, who were in many
respects strangely alike, on a footing, so to speak, of
schoolboy intimacy exceedingly rare in courts. An
incident which occurred in 1675 deepened this intimacy into unbounded trust. The Prince had taken
the smallpox in its most malignant form, and all his
attendants fled. Bentinck alone remained by his
side, doing what thousands of women have often
done, but what seemed to our hard ancestors so wonderful that Sir William Temple recorded it on the
Stadtholder's own authority :—" I cannot forbear to
give Monsieur Bentinck the character due to him of
the best servant I have known in princes' or private
families. He tended his master during the whole
course of his disease, both night and day ; and the
Prince told me that whether he slept or no he could
not tell, but in sixteen days and nights he never
called once that he was not answered by Monsieur
Bentinck, as if he had been awake. The first time
the Prince was well enough to have his head opened
and combed, Monsieur Bentinck, as soon as it was
done, begged of his master to give him leave to go
home, for he was able to hold up no longer. He did
so, and fell immediately sick of the same disease, and
in great extremity ; but recovered just soon enough

to attend the Prince into the field, where he was ever next his person." William never forgot this service, and through life Bentinck was the single human being whom he publicly acknowledged as a man favoured by his own heart. From this time forth, through life, he gave him but one employment. He never made him premier either in England or Holland, never used him as, what he was, a very competent soldier, never gave him defined or permanent high office. Only, whenever it seemed necessary that the Prince himself should do some work which it was impossible for him to do, he rayed out Bentinck from his side as *alter ego*. If there was a nearly hopeless mission to be performed, Bentinck was sent to do it; and though personally, like his master, a stern, cold man, with a gloomy manner, made endurable only by its grave dignity, and the sense of repressed force which it inspired, he was in such missions uniformly successful. He had a knack, it would seem, like William, of persuading people that they had not a great many alternatives. Thus, in 1677, he was sent by the Prince to England to negotiate a marriage between himself and the Princess Mary, eldest daughter of the Duke of York, and heiress presumptive to the throne—a work of singular difficulty, and, as matters turned out, of singular importance. William was a great man, but in 1688, had not the Tory squires been able to conceal the fact of an election to the throne under the fiction of James's abdication and Mary's consequent title, England would have run with blood. In 1677, however, the Duke of York was strongly opposed to the match, liking neither the Dutch Protestantism nor William's hostility to France; but

Charles wanted to please his people, and Bentinck managed his task so adroitly that he brought over the Duke to a favourable answer. The marriage was completed, but in 1683 all its good effect for England, as well as Europe, seemed to have passed away. The Rye-House Plot had just exploded, and all Whigs were looked upon with acute disfavour. William was counted among them, and at this moment Austria was so menaced by Turkey that Holland might have been left alone to encounter the sleepless wrath of Louis XIV. Bentinck was, therefore, hurried over to assure Charles of his master's detestation of the proceedings of the Whigs, and so to conciliate him as to preserve intact the English alliance with Holland. He succeeded, but after the accession of James II. the new monarch made a demand for a proof of all this concern in the shape of the surrender of the Duke of Monmouth, Lucy Walters's all-popular bastard. The States agreed to surrender the Duke, when William despatched his confidant to warn him of the danger and offer him high command in the Hungarian war. Monmouth evaded the offer, reached the Texel and England, and endeavoured to lead the Whigs in arms. William, who, though a Whig, did not want to see Lucy Walters's boy mount a throne, to the prejudice of his wife and his own collateral claim— people always forget that William, on the mother's side, was a Stuart—and who did want very much to command an English army, seized his opportunity, and through Bentinck offered his personal services to his father-in-law, though without success. The offer, indeed, was scarcely sincere, for William was even then preparing for a descent on England, and Ben-

M

tinck, soon after his return, was sent to acquaint the
Elector of Brandenburg (afterwards first King of
Prussia, a person of little ability but much magnificence) with the design, and obtain from him, who
dreaded France nearly as much as his descendant,
promises of assistance. He received them, and then
returning, took charge of the hardest detail in the
design,—the secret gathering of the transports, and
finally, when all was complete, stepped on board by
William's side.

The Revolution triumphed, and Bentinck, who had
incidentally contended for William as against Mary,
was one of the first to experience the Royal Stadtholder's gratitude. He was appointed Groom of the
Stole and First Lord of the Bedchamber, an office
which then resembled more nearly that of *Ministre
de la Maison de l'Empereur*, with £5000 a-year, and
was created Baron Cirencester, Viscount Woodstock,
and Earl of Portland, with some considerable English
grants of land. In 1690 he sailed with William for
Ireland, shared in the battle of the Boyne, and routed
the Irish before Limerick. He received the general
direction of the military operations in Scotland, where
he steadily supported General Mackay against the
Scotch councillors, who were anxious to supersede
him. Mere defeat never struck either Bentinck or his
master as any proof of want of generalship. In 1693
he was despatched on an errand of singular delicacy—
to consult Sir William Temple, then residing at Moor
Park, Farnham, on the wisdom of the opinion which
the King had conceived, that he ought to veto the
Triennial Bill. Temple gave his opinion decidedly
against the King's opinion, and despatched his humble

secretary, Jonathan Swift, to explain to William more fully the grounds of the view which he took of the matter. It is said that he did this because he was afraid of trusting the matter to the report of Bentinck alone, as that statesman was so imperfectly acquainted with the history and nature of the English Constitution. Here, indeed, lay the great drawback to Bentinck's public career in England. He could not converse in the English language—he knew little of, and cared still less for, English feelings, habits, and prejudices; he regarded England only as an instrument in the advancement of his master's greatness in Europe, and was interested in her prosperity simply in so far as it was directly involved with the fortunes of William himself. He never could understand or appreciate the English,—he never was understood or appreciated by them. All the dislike to foreign favourites which was instinctive in the English nation was exaggerated tenfold in his case by his unconcealed want of sympathy with the people from whose resources he was building up a gigantic fortune. For Bentinck was, as his advocates admit, fond of accumulating wealth, avaricious, indeed, and grasping in the pursuit of personal aggrandisement, so far as the limits of honour permitted. Wherever pickings could be obtained from the public purse or the private bounty of the Sovereign without violating the rules of justice and honour, there Bentinck was always on the look-out, and generally a successful candidate. Large slices from the royal domain in many counties of England were carved out for the King's confidential friend; many more estates he purchased with the large sums of money which came to his hands either from the direct gift of the King, or as the salary or perquisites of his various offices and commissions. The English people, cognisant of this unseemly craving for the loaves and fishes on the part of one who refused to be an Englishman in anything but name —he had been naturalised—suspected Bentinck of a hankering after dishonourable gain. They confounded that passion for acquisition, often found in men who are aware that they use acquisitions well, with ordinary greed, and accused him privately of taking bribes. Fortunately for his career they were splendidly undeceived. A Parliamentary inquiry, in 1695, into the distribution of secret-service money by the East India Company, for the purpose of unduly influencing persons in official or Parliamentary positions, disclosed the fact that not less than £50,000 had been offered to Portland, and rejected; and that the money had been held at his service for a whole year, in the hope that he might change his mind, until at length Portland told the Company that if they persisted in thus "insulting" him by this offer, he would become their irreconcilable foe. It is still more characteristic of Bentinck that he resented as an affront the compliments which were paid him on all hands when these facts became known. Still the proud, reserved, money-loving, but honourable Dutchman never made himself tolerable to the English. High and low alike called him morose and boorish, and it became a fashion among the English nobility to speak of him as a mere heavy blockhead—"a Hogan Mogan"—only just fit to carry royal messages. The facts of history return a very different verdict, and show that his cool, clear, sagacious intellect was of inestimable service to the interests of his adopted as well as his native country. Nor do the French writers and statesmen of that time confirm the English estimate of his morose and unmannerly demeanour; on the contrary, they are loud in their praises of the chivalric courtesy and polished manners of M. Bentinck, as well as distinct and unanimous in their appreciation of his diplomatic ability. But Bentinck spoke French as fluently as if it were his native tongue, and (notwithstanding the political chasm between him and the countrymen of the Grand Monarque) evidently was much more *en rapport* with French manners than with English. It is curious that, at the same time that Bentinck was the object of a popular outcry in England as a Dutch favourite, the Burgomaster and Senate of Amsterdam were moving heaven and earth, appealing to the Constitution of the United Provinces, petitioning and protesting both to Holland and England, against the same individual taking his seat in the States Assembly of Holland and West Friesland. Bentinck had been enrolled as Baron of Rhoon in the body of the nobility of Holland as far back as 1676, but the deputies of Amsterdam declared that his right of sitting was forfeited because he had become a naturalised English subject and a member of the English Parliament, and might be supposed, therefore, to be entirely devoted to the interests of England. This was in the year 1690, and the King was greatly incensed at the proceeding, declaring that it arose out of the animosity of the city of Amsterdam to himself personally. The Dutch nobles also resented the interference of the burghers in a matter affecting their own order, and

Amsterdam, not being supported by the other towns, had to give way. The same question, however, was, at a later period, raised with respect to Keppel, who was finally allowed to sit as one of the nobility of Holland, but with the *special* permission of the States; and was obliged to solicit their permission whenever he desired to go to England. Thus some in both countries seemed disposed to repudiate a man to whom both were so eminently indebted, and of whom, with all his faults, either of them might have been proud. In the campaign of 1693 Portland shared the danger of his master in the disastrous rout of Landen (29th July). One musket-shot passed through his peruke, a second through the sleeve of his coat, and a third inflicted a small contusion in his side. He seems, also, from a letter of Archbishop Tillotson's, to have received some injury in his hand. William, who had lost sight of him in the flight, and knew that Portland was in bad health, was full of anxiety for his safety, and on learning his escape wrote off a hasty note of joy and congratulation.

On his return from this campaign, William resolved to reward his unequalled services once for all, and ordered the Treasury to make out a warrant granting to Portland a magnificent estate in Wales—viz., the lordships of Denbigh, Bronfield, and Yale, said to be worth more than £100,000, and the annual rent reserved to the Crown was only 6s. 8d. "With the property were inseparably connected extensive royalties, which the people of North Wales could not patiently see in the hands of any subject." A century before, when Elizabeth made the same grant to *her* favourite, Leicester, the people of Denbighshire had risen in arms, and Leicester thought it expedient to relinquish the grant. The principal gentlemen of the district on the present occasion had recourse to the Lower House, who voted *unanimously* an address to the King begging him to stop the grant. Portland had the discretion, like Leicester, to beg his Majesty that he might not be the cause of a dispute between him and his Parliament. The King gave way, though with a bitter feeling of mortification, saying, " Gentlemen, I have a kindness for my Lord Portland, which he has deserved of me by long and faithful services, but I should not have given him these lands if I had imagined the House could have been concerned. I will, therefore, recall the grant, and find some other way of showing my favour to him." Accordingly, soon afterwards, William conferred on him a grant of the royal house of Theobalds, with the demesnes belonging to it in Hertfordshire and Middlesex, and also the office of ranger of the great and little forests at Windsor. It should be added that the remonstrance of the Commons took place *before* the disclosure of Bentinck's integrity in the East Indian affair, and was argued as a constitutional question. In the February of the following year (1696), Portland had the opportunity of repaying William's indiscreet generosity on his behalf by saving his life. Hearing from two quarters that the assassination of the King was planned for a particular hunting day, he hastened to the palace and implored William not to leave the house on that day. The King positively refused to credit the story, or to alter his plans. Portland persisted, and at length threatened he would make the intelligence at once public if the King did

not give way. William then gave way, and the disappointed conspirators exclaimed, " The fox keeps his
earth." On the 9th of February 1697, William made
him a Knight of the Garter, and in June of the same
year, finding that there was little but a solemn farce
going on between the negotiators at Ryswick, he
resolved to avail himself of Portland's friendship with
Boufflers, and endeavour to cut matters short by a private interview between these two honourable straight-
forward men. Portland accordingly requested half-
an-hour's conversation with the French Marshal, and
the latter, having sent off an express to Louis and
obtained his sanction, complied with the suggestion.
In the conferences which thereupon ensued between
these two men, the leading points were settled which
were afterwards embodied in the peace of Ryswick.
In this private negotiation Bentinck displayed talent
of the highest order, and it is probable that it was
this service which induced William to perform the
most indefensible action of his great career. He gave
his able but greedy servant a second colossal grant.
Nearly a third of Ireland had fallen to him by seques-
trations, and he had promised Parliament to bestow
these lands only with their consent. Bills were
accordingly introduced into the House, but defeated,
and William was persuaded to believe himself absolved
from his promise. He gave the whole to his personal
following, one enormous estate going to Elizabeth
Villiers, the only woman whom William ever trusted
with State secrets, and who rivalled Mary in his somewhat cold affection. The jealousy of the Commons
took fire. They would not remember that most of
these men had, in saving England, forfeited European

careers, and saw only new men and foreigners raised
above the old nobility. They appointed a Commission,
and the Commissioners reported that the number of
acres was 1,060,692, of the annual value of £211,623,
or present value of £2,685,138. These estimates were
said afterwards to have been greatly exaggerated for
party purposes. Among the grants figured one to
William Bentinck, Esq., Lord Woodstock (Bentinck's
eldest son, who died before him), of 135,820 acres.
In the ensuing session (1700) the Tory party brought
in the famous Resumption Bill, founded on this report,
by which the grants were all *resumed* and placed in
the hands of Commissioners for the public service,
one-third being reserved to the King to grant out for
eminent public services. To insure its passing, the
bill was tacked on by the Commons to the Army and
Navy Supply Bills. The Lords angrily resented this
as an infringement of their rights, a money bill not
being subject to *amendment* by them, and, treating
the Resumption Bill separately, sent it down amended.
The Commons refused to recognise it in this form,
and many angry discussions ensued between the two
Houses. At first, William thought of fighting the
battle in the Lords, and on the 5th of April he told
Portland that if the bill was not stopped in the Upper
House he should count all as lost, and the same day
he declared that he was resolved not to assent to the
bill. But his Dutch prudence and good sense got the
better of the Stuart blood he derived from his mother,
and he intimated privately to the Lords that he wished
them to give way. The bill was accordingly voted
by them, Bentinck and Keppel both making a point
of voting in the *majority,* and on the 11th of April

William went down to the House and gave it the royal assent without another word. He then immediately prorogued Parliament without a speech from the throne.

This, however, is anticipating a little. A more serious danger awaited Bentinck than the loss of a grant, vast as it would have made his possessions. Bentinck loved his master dearly, but he regarded him with all the exacting affection of a lover, and could not endure the slightest approach to a rivalry in the place which he held in his confidence. "He had tolerated Zulestein and Anverquerque, for they were contented to be the honoured servants and respectful friends of the King, and left to Bentinck the position of bosom friend. But a younger man was now creeping into the affections of William." This was Arnoud Joost Van Keppel, a young Dutch gentleman who had accompanied William in his expedition to England. " Keppel had a sweet and obliging temper, winning manners, and a quick, though not a profound understanding. Courage, loyalty, and secrecy were common between him and Portland. In other points they differed widely. Portland was naturally the very opposite of a flatterer, and having been the intimate friend of the Prince of Orange at a time when the interval between the house of Orange and the house of Bentinck was not so wide as it afterwards became, had acquired a habit of plain-speaking which he could not unlearn when the comrade of his youth had become the Sovereign of three kingdoms. He was a most trusty, but not a very respectful subject. There was nothing which he was not ready to do or suffer for William ; but in his intercourse with William he

was blunt and sometimes surly. Keppel, on the other
hand, had a great desire to please, and looked up
with unfeigned admiration to a master whom he had
been accustomed, ever since he could remember, to
consider as the first of living men. Arts, therefore,
which were neglected by the elder courtier were assi-
duously practised by the younger. So early as the
spring of 1691, shrewd observers were struck by the
care with which Keppel observed every turn of his
master's countenance. Gradually the younger courtier
rose in favour; he was made Earl of Albemarle and
Master of the Robes," and Earls of Albemarle the
Keppels still continue. This elevation, however, gave
little offence, for the suave courtier was popular, liberal,
and almost affectedly English, while his rival, as Keppel advanced, became at once more unbearably reserved and more avowedly Dutch. At last William,
partly for peace, partly because Bentinck alone could
carry out his designs, made him Ambassador to France.
The "grudging Dutchman" accepted the post, and
in five months spent in his master's honour eighty
thousand pounds, say a quarter of a million of to-
day. A day or two after his departure William
wrote a most affectionate letter to Bentinck :—"The
loss of your society," he says, "has affected me more
than you can imagine. I should be very glad if I
could believe that you felt as much pain at quitting
me as I feel at seeing you depart; for then I might
hope that you had ceased to doubt the truth of what
I solemnly declared to you on my oath. Assure yourself that I never was more sincere. My feeling towards you is one which nothing but death can alter."
Bentinck took the historian Rapin with him as tutor

of his son, Lord Woodstock, and Prior as the Secretary of Legation; and never was embassy conducted in more stately, dignified, and able manner. The French people worshipped the magnificence of his equipages and household. The French courtiers were astonished at the grave but courtly dignity of his bearing in the presence of the great King. The French statesmen were deeply impressed with the calm, shrewd sagacity which characterised his diplomacy. In this atmosphere of respect Bentinck was himself again; but on his return he found Keppel still higher in favour, and though he shared in the negotiations of Loo in 1699, he flung up all his posts, and retired to the noble seat—Bulstrode Park, in Buckinghamshire—which he had lately purchased of Lord Jeffreys's son-in-law, and which had once belonged to Bulstrode Whitelocke. Here, as in his other seats, he adorned the interiors, laid out the grounds, erected aviaries, and spent on all other matters as little as he possibly could. He was still consulted on State affairs, and in 1700 he and Lord Jersey were employed to sign the Partition Treaty which settled the respective claims of the Bourbon and Hapsburg houses. It was a fair treaty for Europe, but the Spaniards, who were signed away without their own consent, resented the indignity: their imbecile King was made to sign a will in favour of the Bourbon claimant, which was endorsed by Louis, notwithstanding the treaty; and the Commons, in wrath at the aggrandisement of France, impeached Bentinck, who had negotiated the treaty, his colleague escaping without a reprimand. They also impeached Lords Somers, Halifax, and Orford, and, anticipating the result of the trial, prayed

William to dismiss them all from his councils. This burst of party spite was, however, too much for the Lords, who first presented a counter-address, and then, quarrelling over points of form, threw out the articles. This was the Earl's last public appearance. He attended his master's deathbed on the 8th of March 1702. With his last articulate words the King asked for Bentinck, who "instantly came to his bedside, knelt down, and placed his ear close to the King's mouth. The lips of the dying man moved, but nothing could be heard. The King took the hand of his earliest friend, and pressed it tenderly to his heart. In that moment," adds Macaulay, "no doubt, all that had cast a slight passing cloud over their long and pure friendship was forgotten." Bentinck, after that event, for six years devoted himself to Holland. In 1708 he found his intellect failing, and he returned to England, to die on the 23d November 1709, and be buried in Henry VIII.'s Chapel, in Westminster, by the side of the Prince whom he had so dearly loved and so faithfully served. Though a foreigner in feeling, both his wives were Englishwomen—the first a Villiers, sister of Earl Jersey ; the second a Temple, sister of Henry Viscount Palmerston. His only surviving son by his first marriage, Henry, succeeded him as the head of the English house of Bentinck ; his two sons by his second marriage, William and Charles John, succeeded him as nobles of the United Provinces. The Earl also left nine daughters, of whom seven married into high English families, and one died unmarried. The remaining daughter married one of the chief noblemen of Holland.

The character of Hans Bentinck, like that of every

hero of a revolutionary period, has been variously represented; but to those who understand 1688—and
who that can read English does not?—it is not hard
to decipher. He was William III. in homespun—and
that was the impression which he stamped upon the
family he had built. Whenever a Bentinck comes to
the front it is as a great Dutchman that he succeeds;
whether, like Lord George, he risks a fortune upon a
horse without a quiver of the lip; or, as Lord William, he earns the hate of every contemporary Anglo-
Indian by his ungenial manners, and the reverence of
every subsequent proconsul by his administration—so
wise, benevolent, and far-sighted. When Hans died
he had accumulated lands worth half a million, and
had surrendered as much more, and contemporaries
murmured at the greed which stood so horribly in
their way. Since his death, however, no historian
has ever adjudged him overpaid.

Henry, the second Earl, was a widely different person from his father. A man of so sweet a disposition
that it is said all were at ease around him, he had
neither his father's bad manners nor his unerring
judgment. His first step was fortunate, for he married, during his father's lifetime, the Lady Elizabeth
Noel, eldest daughter and coheir of Wriothesley Baptist, Earl of Gainsborough, with whom he received,
besides other estates, the moiety of the lordship of
Tichfield, Hampshire, and the manor-house of the
Wriothesleys, Earls of Southampton. There he resided up to his father's death, effacing by a profuse
hospitality the grudge felt in England against the
close-fisted Dutchman. So successful was he in society that King George, in July 1716, created him

Marquess of Tichfield and Duke of Portland. Unfortunately, his judgment was weak, the family love of acquisition was still latent and strong, and he engaged deeply in the great South Sea bubble, to the serious injury of his fortune. On the explosion he accepted the governorship of Jamaica—a post no duke would now look at—and died at St Jago de la Vega in July 1726, in the forty-fifth year of his age. The family, it may be remarked, still kept up their connection with Holland, one of the first Duke's three daughters marrying a Dutch noble.

William, the second Duke, elder of Henry's two sons, was seventeen at his father's death, and was sent to travel in France and Italy, where he acquired the passion for antiquities by which he was afterwards distinguished. He neglected politics for science and cognate pursuits, was Fellow of the Royal Society, and Trustee of the British Museum, and seems to have been considered in that day a man of singular learning for a peer. His pursuits did not, however, prevent him from aggrandising his house, for he married the Lady Margaret Cavendish Harley, only child of Edward, second Earl of Oxford—the title somewhat impudently taken by Harley, the statesman, after the extinction of the mighty house of De Vere—by his wife Henrietta, only daughter and heiress of John Holles, Duke of Newcastle, by the daughter and heiress of Henry Cavendish, Duke of Newcastle. This lady brought to the dukedom nearly all the vast estates of the younger Cavendishes, *i.e.*, WELBECK ABBEY and other lands, and the property of the Lords of Ogle. Bulstrode had been sold by the first Duke to the Duke of Somerset, and Welbeck Abbey was permanently selected as the family seat. The Duchess of Portland survived her husband, who died May 1, 1762, more than twenty years, and seems to have partaken largely of some of his favourite tastes and pursuits, for she added greatly to the celebrated Portland Museum, which had been the legacy of her own ancestors, and which she enriched by a rare and extensive collection in *vertu* and natural history —especially in conchology.

The fortunes of the family as English aristocrats— *i.e.*, as owners of vast masses of land—may now be said to have culminated, for William Henry, the third Duke, succeeded in 1762 to the united properties of the Bentinck, Harley, Holles, and younger Cavendish families—whence the names of the streets around the present Duke's house—and was on his accession to the title one of the wealthiest and best educated men in Britain. He threw himself ardently into politics, associated with Burke and Fox, and became under their influence a very vehement Whig, and very especially obnoxious to George III., whose single leading idea was to emancipate himself from the control of the great houses who had governed the country from the death of William III. When Lord Rockingham returned to power in 1782, the Duke was appointed Lord-Lieutenant of Ireland, an appointment for which the singular coolness of judgment, characteristic up to the present generation, of all the Bentincks especially fitted him, and from his despatches to Fox it would seem that the Irish were warranted in their favourable impression. He was earnestly desirous that some arrangement should be come to by which the *spirit* of what the Irish hoped from an independent legislature would be conceded, without impairing more than was absolutely necessary the central authority of the English Government, or lowering the *prestige* of England. "There is still an *appearance* of government," he writes confidentially to his friend at the close of April 1782 ; " but if you delay or refuse to be liberal, Government cannot exist here in its present form, and the sooner you recall your Lieutenant and renounce all claim to the country the better ; but, on the contrary, if you can bring your minds to concede largely and handsomely, I am persuaded that you may make any use of this people, and of everything they are worth, that you can wish ; and in such a movement it will be happy for them that the Government of England shall be in hands that will not take undue advantage of their intoxication." It is usual to speak of Portland as a man of high honour and excellent intentions, but a mere political nonentity. But there is a shrewd sense in his despatches, which, though far removed from *genius,* is equally removed from insignificance. He had, at any rate, the sagacity to see where talent lay, and to follow its guidance without jealousy, though not blindly. At this time he looked chiefly to Fox, and in the despatch from which we have quoted are unreserved intimations that he had not the slightest confidence in Lord Shelburne and his section of the Cabinet. These were the old following of Chatham whose Whig ties had always been secondary and unessential to their personal attachment to that great man. Hence Fox and the "Whigs proper" on the death of Rockingham refused to accept the leadership of Shelburne, and made it their ultimatum that the Duke of Portland should be the head of the new Ministry. This was refused by the King. So Fox,

Cavendish, and Portland resigned (followed out of office by Burke and Sheridan), and Shelburne, with his own party, a section of the Whigs, and a fraction of the former friends of Lord North, led by Dundas (afterwards Lord Melville), formed a new administration. To these was now added young William Pitt, at the age of twenty-three, in the important post of Chancellor of the Exchequer. The history of the short Shelburne Ministry is one of incessant intrigue and counter-intrigue, ending, as is well known, in the coalition between Fox and North, and the entrance of the two latter in conjunction into a new Cabinet, under the headship of Portland. In all these negotiations Portland stood as steadily by Fox as Fox had by him. After a ministerial *interregnum* of seventeen days the King sent for Lord North, and proposed a *broad* administration. Lord North suggested the King should *see* the Duke of Portland himself; but the King refused, and told Lord North to desire the Duke to send him his arrangement *in writing*. This was as positively refused by the Duke, who sent word that, if his Majesty condescended to employ him it would be necessary for him to see his Majesty. The negotiations went on. At last Lord North declared he was tired of carrying messages, and the King consented to see Portland, but demanded from him a complete list of the intended administration *in writing*, which the Duke refused. After another interval and an appeal to Pitt, the King saw Portland again, and he brought a written list of the Cabinet; but the King would not look at it, and said he would have one of the whole administration. This the Duke refused. He implored the King to look at *his* paper, and held it out; but the

King held his hands behind him and would not take
it. The King sent again for Pitt, and again failed.
He sent for North again, who merely said, " The Duke
of Portland is ready to be Minister." " Then," said
the King, " I wish your Lordship good night." But on
the 1st of April the King sent again for North, and
said, " Well, so the Duke of Portland is firm?" " Yes,
Sir." " Well then, if you will not do the business, I
will take him." So, on the 2d of April 1783, the new
Cabinet Ministers kissed hands—Portland as First
Lord of the Treasury, Fox and North as joint Secretaries of State ; and when Mr Fox kissed hands, the
old Marquess Townshend observed King George " turn
back his ears and eyes, just like the horse at Astley's,"
said he, " when the tailor he was determined to throw
was getting on him !" And thrown, accordingly, the
Cabinet was, on the East India Bill—the King, whose
hereditary want of courtesy was always in his way,
sending for the seals at midnight, and declining an interview. The Whigs deserved their fall, for they had
excluded Burke from the Cabinet, and filled it entirely
from the great governing families. Then, in 1783,
ensued Pitt's daring attempt to carry on the Government without a majority in the Lower House—an attempt maintained with wonderful courage and dex-
terity, but which must have failed had it not been for
the outburst of the Democratic spirit in France. This
alarmed a section of the great houses, who, with Portland at their head, first supported the King's proclamation against " divers seditious writings," directed at
Tom Paine,—and so successful, that to this day country people who never read a line of Paine's writings
hold the poor needleman to have been a demon,—and

then went over to Pitt. Portland had a bitter struggle with his personal affection for Fox ; but political conviction conquered, and (July 11, 1794) he accepted the Home Office. The game was won. The immense, though indefinite influence of the King, Pitt's strange hold over the middle class, and the great Lords' control of votes in the Lower House, were at last united, and a Ministry arose almost as powerful as Parliament itself. In July 1801 Portland became President of the Council under the Addington Ministry, which office he resigned in June 1805, remaining, however, in the Cabinet till Pitt's death, and the accession of Fox to power. On Fox's death the Duke was again summoned (March 1807), this time, as First Lord of the Treasury—to form a kind of stately drapery for Perceval, the real Minister—which office he retained till the autumn of 1809, when he retired from active life, to die within a few weeks, on October the 30th. He is a man whose character has been variously described, but he was in reality a cool, sagacious, determined oligarch, very anxious for England, but more anxious for his order, and so immersed in politics that he suffered his vast estates to be half ruined by mere neglect, and sudden loans raised to fight the Lowthers in the North, or carry some great political end.

This Duke had four sons, the second of whom, Lord William Cavendish Bentinck, was by many degrees the ablest man who has appeared in the family since the founder. Born in 1774, he entered the army, rose to be major-general, and in 1803, when only twenty-nine, was appointed Governor of Madras. The sepoys of the Presidency, long manipulated for a rising in favour of the Princes of Mysore, took advantage of a departmental order about uniform to put forward their invariable cry of " caste in danger," and broke into the petty revolt known as the Vellore Mutiny. The Court of Directors, a body which always disliked and distrusted the Queen's officers, and, acting usually with the cold delay of an ancient mercantile firm, behaved at intervals with the unreasoning hurry of a mob, lost their senses with fright. Before they had received a single despatch from Lord William—whose only share in the orders was to obviate their effects— they censured and recalled him, a proceeding which he compelled them formally to condemn, in a letter in which they admitted that he had no share in the orders, but refused reparation, " because the misfortune which happened in his administration placed his fate under the government of public events and opinion, which, as the Court could not control, so it was not in their power to alter the effects of them." In 1810, he was sent as Plenipotentiary to the assistance of Ferdinand of Sicily. Here he soon divined the real character of the King, and of the unscrupulous though accomplished Queen Caroline, and so irritated her by his advocacy of reforms in the Government, and his support of the Liberal party in Sicily against the treacherous conduct of the Court, that in 1811 the Queen left Sicily and repaired to Vienna, where she intrigued with Napoleon against England. During her absence, the English Plenipotentiary wrung from the Court a Constitution for Sicily, drawn up by him on the most liberal basis of constitutional government. This was in 1812, and the Constitution was guaranteed by Lord William as representative of the English

Government. It was afterwards, as it is well known, shamefully violated, or rather altogether disregarded, by the restored Bourbons, who have at length reaped the fruits of their treacherous folly, and by oppressing Sicily have lost both Sicily and Naples. In 1813, Lord William conducted an expedition from Sicily to Catalonia as a diversion in the rear of the French armies; but was beaten, and forced to retire to Italy. In 1814 he was more fortunate in Italy, where he compelled the French garrison in Genoa to surrender. In the convention concluded by Lord William on this occasion, it was agreed that the old republic of Genoa should be reconstituted under the protectorate of England. Lord Castlereagh, however, disowned Lord William's agreement, and gave Genoa up to Piedmont—a proceeding still resentfully recollected by the inhabitants, though it has proved, by the unexpected change in the political course of Piedmont, so great an advantage both to Genoa and Italy. Lord William, incensed at this disavowal, threw up his appointment. and returned to England, where he entered Parliament as member for Nottingham. He was next sent on a mission to Rome, and on the formation of the Canning Ministry, in 1827—in which his brother held high office—he was appointed Governor-General of India. No man so qualified ever held that great position. Cold, sarcastic, and sagacious, he saw that India needed peace and retrenchment, and he secured both. In his long reign he made but one expedition—to dethrone the atrocious Rajah of Coorg, the horrible being who was recently so well received by British society, and who was, so to say, to General Mouravieff what Mouravieff is to Howard,—defied and re-organised the Civil

Service, and, in defiance of all Anglo - India, threw open the judicial service to the people of the country. He was contemplating much wider reforms, for which his admirable thrift gave scope, when his health failed, and he returned to England, to find, like every other Indian, that the successful government of a sixth of the human race had thrown him back in the struggle for influence in England. He was Hans Bentinck over again, with a larger love for humanity and a higher education.

His elder brother, the fourth Duke of Portland, pursued his father's life, living and dying a great English peer, loved by his tenantry, consulted by political allies, and used every now and then as key-stone in some political arch. Always a foe to injustice rather than a party Liberal, he moved, in 1822, the second reading of the Bill for admitting Roman Catholic peers into the House of Lords, in 1827 accepted the office of Privy Seal under Canning, was President of the Council under Lord Goderich—whose son is a Minister, as Earl de Grey and Ripon—voted for the Reform Bill, and died March 27, 1854, a moderate Conservative. He had repaired by strict attention to business the family fortunes, and acquired a great Scotch property by his marriage with the heiress of General John Scott of Balconie, Fifeshire. His second son, George, preceded him to the grave, having been at the age of twenty-five successively King of the Turf and leader of the Conservative party; and he was succeeded by his son, William John Scott-Bentinck, fifth and present Duke of Portland. This Peer has taken no part in politics, living a life of somewhat remarkable seclusion ; but it is understood that, unlike most of his family, he remains a firm and consistent Whig.

The house of Bentinck has not yet been two hundred years among us; but it has produced three great men, besides two Premiers, and it retains its full vitality. No house has benefited more by the vast rise in the value of land and of London property, and few who have courted popularity so little have ever acquired a stronger hold on the regard and respect of Englishmen. Had Lord George Bentinck lived, the House might even now be ruling us; but as it is, its cadets are deeply engaged in politics, and it still ranks among the most active as well as potent of the great governing families.

The Clintons.

LWAYS in front but never in command, is the sentence which best describes the fortunes of the house of Clinton. They have always been important, have furnished Admirals, and Generals, and possible Ministers without end, yet have never risen absolutely to the top; and at this moment, though Dukes, would, but for their pedigree, scarcely stand in the front rank of English nobles. Even their pedigree has somehow escaped the popular notoriety which attaches, say, to that of the Talbots; and one-half of our readers outside the Peerage will be surprised when we remind them that his Grace of Newcastle is the single Duke out of the Royal Family whose house was certainly ennobled by the early Plantagenets, or who can prove his male line to have been great before the Crusades. There is not a clearer pedigree in Europe, or one about which there has been more determined and scientific lying. Peerage-makers carry the Clintons up to who knows what Scandinavian hero, trusting to English reverence for Dukes and English ignorance of ancient English history. All the while their rise is fixed within a few years by the precise and express testimony of a trustworthy

and contemporary historian—Ordericus Vitalis, who
thus describes their position when their founder first
emerged into sunshine :—" Henry I. reduced all his
enemies to subjection, either by policy or force, and
rewarded those who served him with riches and
honours. Many there were of high condition whom
he hurled from the summit of power for their pre-
sumption, and sentenced to the perpetual forfeiture
of their patrimonial estates. On the contrary, there
were others of *low origin* (*de ignobili stirpe*) whom
for their obsequious services he raised to the rank of
nobles, *lifting them, so to speak, from the dust,* surrounding them with wealth, and exalting them above
earls and distinguished lords of castles. Such men as
GEOFFREY DE CLINTON (Goisfredus de Clintona), Ralph
Basset, Hugh de Bochêland, Guillegrip, and Raimer de
Bath (*Bada*), William Troissebot, Haimon de Falaise,
Guigan Algazo, Robert de Bostare, and many others,
are examples of what I have stated, who acquired
wealth and built themselves mansions far beyond
anything that their fathers possessed. These and
many others of humble birth, whom it would be
tedious to mention individually, were ennobled by
the King, his royal authority raising them from a low
estate to the summit of power, so that they became
formidable even to the greatest nobles." Ordericus
Vitalis, one perceives, did not foresee that to be mentioned by him at all would one day be a certificate of
pedigree of which kings might be proud. This *novus
homo*—man from the gutter—whose original name is
hopelessly lost, is supposed by Dugdale to have taken
his name from Clinton, a village in Oxfordshire, now
called Glympton ; but that is avowedly only a clever

guess. It is, at all events, certain that he rose to be Chamberlain and Treasurer to the King, and possibly Justice of England, and that he received immense grants from Henry, who, wearied to death with the conquerors — who had a perverse notion that they had conquered England for others besides the sons of the Bastard—tried successfully to elevate new men as a counterpoise to their power—a policy which ceased only with the death of William III. Geoffrey de Clinton had grants in Warwickshire, Oxford, Nottingham, Buckingham, and, probably, in other counties; and the largest being in Warwickshire, the family fortunes clustered around that centre, Kenilworth being chosen as his seat from his delight in its woods, and the large pleasant lake nestling among them. It is also probable that he thought his career would not bear the scrutiny of Heaven, for he founded near Kenilworth a monastery for Black Canons. This was the priory, afterwards abbey, of Kenilworth, and the date of its foundation is about the year 1122. By the first charter, Geoffrey de Clinton gives to the Black Canons, for the redemption of his sins, as also for the good estate of King Henry, whose consent he had thereto, and of his own wife and children and all his relatives and friends, all the lands and woods of Kenilworth (excepting what he had reserved for the making of his castle and park), and several manors and churches in the counties we have referred to and in Staffordshire, granting further unto them right of pasturage—viz., that wheresoever his own cattle and hogs should be, whether within his park or without, there also might theirs have liberty to feed, and their tenants' hogs to have the same freedom in all other

except his enclosed woods and park as his own tenants
had. By another charter he makes them a grant of
a full tenth of whatsoever should be brought to his
castle—viz., either to his cellar, kitchen, larder, granary,
or "hallgarth;" as well as of all bought or given,
either in hay, corn, hogs, muttons, bacon, venison,
cheese, fish, wine, honey, wax, tallow, pepper, and
cumin, though they had been tithed elsewhere before,
as of his own proper revenue, together with all his
lambkins throughout all his manors, as well those as
should be killed to eat as of others that might die
casually. He also gave to the said canons liberty to
fish with boats and nets, one day in every week, namely,
Thursday, in his pool in Kenilworth. His son and
grandson (Geoffrey and Henry de Clinton), and his
daughter Leoscelina, were also donors and benefactors
to this monastery, their gifts including the greater
part of Leamington and the mill of Guy's Cliff. Geoffrey de Clinton continued high in favour with Henry
I. till 1130,—so high that his nephew, Roger, was able
to buy the Bishopric of Coventry for 3000 marks, and
was ordained priest and consecrated bishop at Canterbury on two successive days, 21st and 22d December
1129 ; but in that year Geoffrey fell under a cloud.
What he did no man will probably ever know ; but Ordericus Vitalis says he was arraigned for treason, and
the fact is confirmed, though the date is altered by a
few months, by Roger de Hoveden. The latter says he
was "disgraced," but the eclipse was probably only
temporary, for it never affected the territorial position
of the house, the eldest son of the founder—also a
Geoffrey—being Chamberlain to Henry II. in 1165.
With the grandson of this second Geoffrey, however,

the elder branch came to an end, the stock terminating, in 1232, in heiresses.

Another branch of the same stock had, however, in the interim, attained baronial rank. Besides Roger, the simoniacal Bishop of Coventry, the founder had a nephew named OSBERT, said to have been an elder brother of that very prompt prelate. This person is the lineal ancestor of the gentleman who was so recently governing the Colonies, and he received from his cousin Geoffrey a grant of the lordship of Coleshill in Warwickshire, being, therefore, styled " of Coleshill " in the Rolls of Henry II., just seven hundred and three years ago. The new baron enriched himself still farther by marrying Margaret, the daughter of William de Hatton, who brought as her marriage portion the manor of Amington, in Warwickshire. Their son, Osbert de Clinton, Lord of Coleshill and Amington, was a keen supporter of the Barons who tore Magna Charta from John Lackland, had his estates seized by the King, and remained in overt rebellion until that monarch's death, when he made his peace with Henry III. and had his lands restored to him. He died in 1222, and his son Thomas, third Baron Clinton (by tenure), was one of the Justices of Assize for the county of Warwick,* and in the thirty-eighth year of Henry III. had a charter of free warren in the lordship of Coleshill. He married Mazera, heiress of James de Bisege, of Badsley in the same county.

---

* There is no fact in feudal history so strange as the loss of the power of "high and low" justice by the English Barons. Their compeers had it in France to 1660, and in Scotland to 1745; but the English Peers never used it on questions of life and death after the death of Stephen. The Plantagenets could not abide it, and as it was not the interest either of Church or Commune, the Kings won.—(M. T.)

This manor was left by Thomas de Clinton to his
fifth son, James, on payment of one penny annually
to his father's heirs, and from him it passed eventually through an heiress into other families. Besides
this James, Thomas de Clinton's other sons were Thomas, his heir, who succeeded him at Amington; Sir
John (whose male line expired in 1353), who succeeded
him at Coleshill, and was one of the barons who
fought with Simon de Montfort against the Crown,
but was afterwards restored to favour; Osbert, lord of
the manor of Austrey, in Warwickshire (who dying
without issue, the lordship went to his eldest brother,
Thomas); and William, rector of the church of Austrey.

Thomas de Clinton (fourth Baron Clinton by tenure)
married a Bracebridge of Kingsbury, and was succeeded by his son by her, John de Clinton, fifth Baron
Clinton by tenure. He resided at Amington, as his
father had done. He was a distinguished soldier and
attendant of King Edward I. in his wars, particularly
in Scotland. On February 6, 1299, he was first *summoned* to Parliament as Baron Clinton of Maxstoke,
he having married Ida, eldest of the sisters and coheirs
of Sir William de Odangseles, Lord of Maxstoke
Castle and other possessions in Warwickshire. John
de Clinton was high in power with King Edward, who
called him, as a special honour, "his beloved Esquire,"
and by his letters patent at Glasgow, April 2, 1301,
granted to him lands in Scotland of the value of £40
per annum, part of the possessions of Malcolm Drum-
mond (ancestor of the Perth family), then in arms
against Edward. Edward II. continued his favour to
Clinton, for in 1308 he had the custody of the castle
and honour of Wallingford. He died in or before the

sixth year of this reign, leaving two sons, minors, of whom the younger, William de Clinton, rose to high distinction. In the third year of Edward III. William made a great match, marrying Julian, the heiress of Sir Thomas de Leybourne, a great Kentish heiress, and widow of John, Lord Hastings, of Bergavenny. This, says Sir William Dugdale, was a great step in his advancement. He appears, however, to have risen to a considerable position, at least as regards wealth, previously, since after his accession, Edward III., in a deed, recites that the said William de Clinton had performed great services to him and his mother, Queen Isabel, when beyond the seas, for which they had promised him lands of the value of £200 per annum, in confidence of which he had enlarged his family *et se posuit ad Vexillum*. So he now grants to the said William the castle, manor, and hundred of Halerton, in the counties of Chester and Lancaster. He accompanied the King the same year in an expedition to Scotland, and in the fourth year of the reign—the year after his Kentish marriage—he was constituted Governor of Dover Castle and Warden of the Cinque Ports. In 1333 he was appointed Admiral of the Seas, and attending the King again into Scotland, fought in the battle of Halidon. He still continued to rise in the King's favour, and on March 16, 1337, he was created by a royal charter Earl of Huntingdon. Among other martial exploits the Earl was at the sea battle with the Spaniards off Winchelsea; but he died August 25, 1354, without issue, and upon an inquisition, his nephew, Sir John de Clinton, Knight, was found to be his heir, and to be then of the age of twenty-eight years.

The younger brother who thus enriched his brother's son had far outstripped in his fortunes that brother, Sir John de Clinton, second Lord Clinton (by writ), who, however, was summoned to Parliament as a peer, served creditably in Guienne, spent funds of his own on his King's service, married the daughter of Sir W. Corbett, of Chadsley-Corbett, in Worcestershire, and left by her the lad Sir John de Clinton (third Lord Clinton), who inherited the uncle's possessions in addition to his own. He was a soldier of mark, fought at Poictiers with the Black Prince, went to France in the great expedition organised by Edward III., in the thirty-third year of his reign—an expedition which killed off nobles like privates—and ten years afterwards, the French King breaking the treaty, he and Thomas Beauchamp, Earl of Warwick, earned the priceless honour of mention by Froissart, who says, " They took many strong towns and gained great honour by their conduct and valour." On 30th May 1371, he was directed by the King to repair to his manor of Folkestone, in Kent, to repel an expected invasion of the French. The same order was repeated six years afterwards ; and in 1380 England, tired of expecting invasions, began one. Landing in France with Thomas of Woodstock, the King's uncle, Lord Clinton, devastated the country from Calais to Brittany ; and, says Froissart, " the Lord Clinton rode with his banner displayed, and performed certain feats of arms at Nantes with Sir Galoys Daunoy." In the sixth year of Richard II. he was again campaigning in France and the Low Countries, and was at the taking of Gravelines, Bruges, Nieuport, and Dunkirk. Two years afterwards he was at Newcastle-on-Tyne, on his road against the Scots, who had taken

Berwick, but abandoned it on the approach of the English troops. The man altogether was one of the efficient sort whom able kings love, never *quite* at the top, but always ready for severe work, and unapt to make blunders. He fought for England well, and prospered accordingly. He married, first, Idonea, eldest daughter of Geoffrey, Lord Saye (by the daughter of Guy Beauchamp, Earl of Warwick), coheir to her brother William, Lord Saye, and cousin and heir of William de Saye, Baron of Sele; and on the death of her brother and his children without issue, Idonea, Lady Clinton, became eventually the eldest coheir of the noble family of Saye. On the death of this first wife, Lord Clinton made a match without the consent of the King with another heiress, Elizabeth, daughter and at length heir of William de la Plaunch, of Haversham, Bucks; and in the twentieth year of Richard II., on the attainder and banishment of Thomas Beauchamp, Earl of Warwick, Lord Clinton had the castle of Warwick, with all the manors and lands belonging thereto, committed to his custody. He died on the 8th of September 1399, during the session of the celebrated Parliament which dethroned Richard and raised Henry Bolingbroke to the throne, leaving by his first wife three sons, and a daughter married to Lord Berkeley. His second son was Sir Thomas de Clinton, whose seat was at Amington. He served in the Spanish and Portuguese wars with John of Gaunt; but the date of his death is uncertain. He left only a daughter, from whom are descended the Burdetts of modern political notoriety. The elder son, Sir William de Clinton, also died in his father's lifetime, but not till he had married a sister of Ralph Neville, first Earl

o

of Westmoreland, and left a son, William, who succeeded his grandfather as fourth Lord Clinton. This Baron was a soldier, and was engaged with credit in all the expeditions of Henry IV., Henry V., and the early years of Henry VI. In the fifth year of the last-named King he was called on to provide 25 men-at-arms and 78 archers, and four years afterwards to provide one knight, 38 men-at-arms, and 300 archers, for the French wars. In the sixth year of Henry IV., 1404, he did homage for and had livery of his proportion of the inheritance of his grandmother Idonea, as heir to William de Saye, and in the third of Henry V. he bore the title of Lord Saye ; but he seems to have had no legal right to it, as it was in abeyance between himself and the other coheirs of Geoffrey de Saye, his great-grandfather. In November 1448, Lord Clinton's son and successor executed a curious deed, by which he assigned all his right to the title of Saye to his cousin, James Fiennes, or Fynes (second son of Sir William Fiennes, the son of a younger sister of Idonea de Clinton), who had been summoned to Parliament in 1447 as Lord Saye and Sele ; Lord James in return releasing to Lord Clinton by another deed all right to all advowsons, knights' fees, wardships, rents, &c., incident to the barony of Saye *before* the execution of the preceding deed. The whole transaction is a very anomalous one, and seems to provoke the heralds and genealogists sadly. This James Fiennes is Shakespeare's Lord Say, executed by Jack Cade's mob in 1450.

William, fourth Lord Clinton, died July 30, 1432, having married a widow, Lady Fitzwavyn, and left by her, as his heir, John, fifth Lord Clinton, then twenty-two years of age. He was also a soldier in

the French wars, particularly under Richard, Duke of
York, Regent in that country. Less lucky than his
ancestors, however, he was taken prisoner in the nineteenth year of Henry VI., and continued in durance
for more than six years, and was then obliged to give
6000 marks for his ransom. The fine might have
injured his fortunes, but he was a man with courage for
other things than battle. To raise the money he took
to the occupation of a merchant, obtaining in the
twenty-sixth year of Henry VI. special licence to
employ his agents for the buying of 600 sacks of wool
in England, and to transport them from London or
Southampton into Lombardy, as also six hundred
woollen cloths, and to transport them to any foreign
country, "paying for every sack and cloth to the King
as any other denizen used to do." Perhaps his distressed circumstances urged him to give up his supposed right to the title of Saye, which he did on his
return to England in the following year. In the sixteenth year of this reign he had exchanged his castle
and manor of Maxstoke with Humphrey, Earl of
Stafford, for the manors of Whiston and Woodford, in
Northamptonshire. In 1459, Lord Clinton, induced
probably by his old connection with Richard of York,
took up arms against the house of Lancaster, and
was attainted in the Parliament held at Coventry in
that year; but in 1461, on the triumph of York, he
was restored to his lands and honours, and was joined
with the Earl of Kent, Lord Faulconbridge, and Sir
John Howard, in a commission for the safe keeping of
the seas ; and the four knights, landing in Brittany
with 10,000 men, won the town of Conquet and the
Isle of Rhée. He died on September 24, 1464, leav-

ing an only son by a daughter of Richard Fynes, Lord
Dacre of Hurstmonceaux. This son, John, sixth Lord
Clinton, has no history, and, to be brief, the same may
be said of the seventh and eighth Lords, though they
seem all to have been men of some mark, to have
married well, and to have steadily added to the family
property. Generations of brave and skilful soldiership
had brought them lands, and that credit in the eyes
of heiresses which in those days was as valuable as
royal favour, and the ninth Lord, Edward, was possessed, while still in his cradle, of possessions which
rivalled those of the greater barons. He succeeded
to the manors of Bolehall, Shustock, Pakington,
Amington Parva and Magna, Pericroft and Austrey
in Warwickshire, and, in the county of Kent, to the
manors of Folkestone-Clinton, Huntington, *alias* Hun-
ton, Bermsted, Golstane, *alias* Goddestanton, Lees,
alias Elmes, *alias* Selmes, Polre, *alias* Poldrex, and
lands in Poldrex called Eastdown and Rushin Marsh,
also lands in Wingham and Woodenesburgh, Ashe-
juxta-Sandwich, and lands in the parish of St Clem-
ents, Sandwich. The family had battled their way
slowly though surely up, and though they had never
commanded in battle or become King's favourites, the
" good service " of four hundred years had borne them
at last into the position which was immediately to
be recognised by the Crown. The baby heir of the
favourite whose birth Ordericus Vitalis had stigma-
tised was the recognised equal in rank and possessions
of the few nobles who had survived that great feudal
strife, the Wars of the Roses.

With Henry VIII. the Clintons commenced their
second career. They had been influential before, they

were now to become great nobles. Edward, the ninth
Lord Clinton by writ of summons, and thirteenth of
his branch in the baronial dignity, was carefully educated under the eye of King Henry in all the accomplishments and learning of the age. His creed, therefore, was that of every successive Tudor, and he was
present at the passing of the Act for the dissolution
of the monasteries, on May 23, 1539, though he escaped his share of the misfortunes which, according to
Sir Henry Spelman—from whom Cardinal Wiseman
borrowed the idea (a very erroneous one)—befell most
of those who participated in that measure. Like his
ancestors, he was a soldier rather than a statesman,
and by land and sea he shed new lustre on the family
name. His choice of the sea for a field of action—
any brave man being then held to be equally competent on land and water, and the generation enjoying
apparently an exemption from sea-sickness—was decided by his friendship for John Dudley Viscount
Lisle, Lord High Admiral, and in 1544 he accompanied that nobleman in the fleet sent to assist the
Earl of Hertford in his expedition to Scotland, and
stormed the Canongate at Edinburgh, at the head of
the English forces, for which he was with others
knighted by the Earl. The Admiral and his friend
Lord Clinton then scoured the Scottish seas and coasts
until they were summoned to attend the King at the
siege of Boulogne. At the funeral of Henry VIII.,
Lord Clinton was one of the twelve principal peers
of England who were selected to act as chief mourn-
ers to the royal corpse; and on the accession of Edward VI., Somerset the Protector, who, as Earl of
Hertford, had been a witness of his gallantry, enlisted

his services again for an expedition to Scotland. He was appointed to the command of the fleet, fifty men-of-war and twelve galleys, and greatly contributed to the Protector's success by the galling fire which he kept up on the Scotch and their Irish allies, as they came within his range. On his return from the expedition his services were rewarded by grants of the manor of Brunston, Lincolnshire, part of the possessions of Lord Hussey, executed in 1537 for the Northern insurrection, and the manor of Folkingham, in the same county, part of the possessions of the Duke of Norfolk, then attainted of treason, and divers other manors, lands, and tenements in Lincolnshire, with the manor of Clifford, in Herefordshire. Lord Clinton was next sent by the Protector's council to defend Boulogne against the French, and he held it until ordered by the King to surrender it (April 25, 1550). On his return in May he was thanked for his services by the Council and King, appointed by the latter Lord High Admiral for life, and one of his Privy Council; and had also lands of the value of £200 a-year assigned to him; and in June following the King granted him the manors of Westenhanger, Stotewood, *alias* Saltwood, and other manors, lands, and tenements in Kent, Cornwall, Yorkshire, Lincolnshire, Devonshire, and Sussex, to the value of £246 5s. 1d.

Clinton entered fully into the measures of Edward's Council—was one of those who signed the incriminating letter to Stephen Gardiner, Bishop of Winchester, and was sent by the King with a menacing message to the Earl of Arundel. In the November of the same year in which he had his first grants, Lord Clinton obtained another, of the office of High Steward of the manor of Westborough, and four others in Lincolnshire, for life. He was not, however, content, and honours, lands, and appointments fell on him in a shower which is absolutely astounding to read. He was, in fact, the one general at the Council's disposal, and his friend Lisle now governed England. In the January following he had a licence to make a deer-park in the lands which he had enclosed for a park in Aslackby and Kirby Underwood, in the same county; and the next day the King granted him during life the reversion of the office of steward of the manor of Bolingbroke, in that county, and of all the manors, &c., in the parts of Kesteven, parcel of the Duchy of Lancaster, after the death of Sir William Hussey. In February he obtained a gift of all the lordships, manors, lands, &c., lying in the town of St Botolph, *alias* Boston, in Lincolnshire, belonging to the chantry of *Corpus Christi*, founded within the said town, to hold by fealty, and to take the profits from Easter in the 2d Edward VI. On the 7th of the next month he exchanged with the King his lordships and manors of Folkingham and Aslackby for the lordship and manor of Wye and the rectory of Wye, in Kent, with divers other lands of the yearly value of £358 1s. 8d.; and on the 20th Lord Clinton had the stewardship of the lordship of Newark-upon-Trent, and all the lands and tenements thereunto belonging, with the office of constable of the castle there during life. On the 25th the King granted him a lease for sixty years of the manors of Folkingham, Aslackby, and Temple Aslackby, in Lincolnshire, with divers other lands. On April 2, he was elected a Knight of the

Garter, along with Henry King of France. The King,
or the King's Council, seem not to have thought even
these honours and gifts enough. In the same year
Lord Clinton had a grant of the stewardship of all
the King's lordships and manors in Lincolnshire,
forming parcel of the possessions of the late monasteries of Valday, Newbol, Swineshed, &c., for life, with
several fees, amounting to a hundred marks, and had
the King's letter to the Bishop of Carlisle for the
grant of a lease for sixty years of the manor of Horn-
castle, in Lincolnshire. He was sent as one of the
Royal Commissioners for proroguing Parliament, and
on the first appointment of lord-lieutenants of counties, he and the Earl of Rutland had Lincolnshire
and Nottinghamshire committed to their custody. In
November 1551, he set out as Ambassador Extraordinary from King Edward, to act as his proxy as
godfather to the French King's son, afterwards the
wretched Henry III. Before starting, Lord Clinton
received 500 marks in French crown-pieces of six
shillings each towards his expenses, and carried with
him two flagons of gold and gold chains, weighing
105 ounces, which he was to present to Catherine de
Medicis, and a ring to be presented to the Princess
Elizabeth of France (between whom and King Edward there was then a treaty of marriage, and who
afterwards married Philip II. of Spain). Lord Clinton was ordered to negotiate this marriage. He
brought back what seemed satisfactory ratifications
under the Great Seal of France, and in return received new marks of the royal favour—two good
lordships—Kingston, in Somersetshire, and Chissel-
born in Dorsetshire, with the advowsons thereof, part

of the possessions of Sir Thomas Arundel, attainted. In 1552, when the great Lords raised a considerable body of men at their own expense, splendidly attired, who were reviewed by the King, Lord Clinton had a troop of fifty, clad in black (the rest being in colours), with the Cross of St George, a silver anchor (he being Lord Admiral), and white embroidery. In the same year he was constituted sole Lord-Lieutenant of Lincolnshire. He was also one of a commission to take account of all the lead, bell-metal, jewels, plate, &c., which had come into the King's hands from the dissolution of monasteries or the attainder or forfeiture of individuals. He was next employed in dismantling several fortifications and removing the powder to the Tower of London, of which he was appointed constable, and ordered to take the sole charge thereof. He was one of those entrapped by Northumberland—his old friend Lisle—on the 21st June 1553, into signing the letter of acquiescence in the new disposition of the Crown by Edward to Lady Jane Grey; but he was too wary to proceed any farther in the matter, and failed the Duke in the crisis of the revolution; and we next find him accompanying the Duke of Norfolk, in 1554, on his unsuccessful expedition against Sir Thomas Wyat. He now was in favour with Queen Mary as he had been with King Edward, and was one of those appointed to receive Philip of Spain when he came over to marry the Queen. On the breaking out of war with France in 1557 Clinton was again in his vocation, and he went over as Lieutenant-General with the Earl of Pembroke, to besiege St Quentin, and being re-appointed Lord High Admiral, commanded the somewhat inglorious expedition which failed to take Brest, but burnt Conquet and its adjacent villages. Elizabeth continued the royal favour to the lucky and competent Peer, confirmed him in his dignity of Lord High Admiral, made him one of the Commissioners to hear Murray's accusations against Mary of Scotland, and then appointed him to the command of the army which broke up the force raised by the Northern Earls, in the last war ever made by English nobles against an English sovereign. They fled in utter rout, and Lord Clinton, on May 4, 1572, was raised to the dignity of Earl of Lincoln, still the title borne by the eldest son of the house. He died on January 16, 1585, after a life of such adventure, excitement, and success as few men have ever enjoyed. He was married three times, and his third wife was Elizabeth, daughter of Gerald Fitzgerald, Earl of Kildare—Lord Surrey's Fair Geraldine, and still fair, though a widow, when she came to Lord Clinton. It may be added to his history that he sold Amington, so long the seat of his house, to the Repington family, who had for many years previously bought bits of the estate, which the Clintons, oddly enough, seem for generations to have regarded as a sort of bank to be drawn on whenever they wanted money. It is curious how very little of this man's *character* is perceptible among the voluminous notices of his deeds; but the latter prove him to have been a true Clinton, a man of weight and activity, always very prominent, always very trustworthy as far as work was concerned, and always as efficient as it is possible for a man without genius to be.

Henry, second Earl of Lincoln and tenth Lord Clinton, who succeeded his father in 1585, although he filled several important posts under Elizabeth and James I., reflected no credit on his family name. He fell into great pecuniary embarrassments, which, considering the wealth accumulated by his father, speaks volumes as to his spendthrift habits. He was sent on an embassy to the Landgrave of Hesse in 1596, and Sir Anthony Bacon arraigns his conduct to that Court in the most bitter terms. He is said to have been a great tyrant among the gentry of Lincolnshire, and Denzil Holles (not the patriot, of course, but a relative of an older generation, who seems to have much resembled him in spirit) used to confront Lord Lincoln on the bench, and " carry business against him in spite of his teeth." Lodge mentions Lord Lincoln's outrages against Roger Fullshaw, of Waddingworth, and observes that his conduct seems to have been strongly tinctured with insanity. He died September 29, 1616. He was twice married, and left four sons, from a younger son of the second of whom (Sir Edward Clinton) is descended the present Duke of Newcastle. The eldest son, Thomas, who succeeded as third Earl of Lincoln, and was forty-five years of age when his father died, inherited the following estates in Lincolnshire :—The manors of Aslackby and Temple Aslackby, the castle and manor of Tattershall, the house and site of the monastery of Sempringham, with the manor of Sempringham, and the advowson of the church, the manor of Billingborough, rectory of the church, and advowson of the vicarage, the manors of East and West Claughton, the honour, castle, and manor of Folkingham, and manor of Thirkingham, and advowson of the churches, the manors of Thorp and Kirby Byrne, Roughton, Marton - juxta - Thornton, Conisby,

Billingay, Walcot-juxta-Billingay, Burthorp, and Kirk-sted, *alias* Cristed. He sat in the House of Commons during the reign of Elizabeth for St Ives in Cornwall, and Grimsby in Lincolnshire; and in the 1st James I. was returned for the county of Lincoln, and was one of the Parliamentary Commissioners appointed to treat with the Scotch Parliament for the union of the two kingdoms. In 1610 he was called in his father's life to the Upper House as Baron Clinton and Saye, and dying January 15, 1619, his eldest surviving son, Theophilus, succeeded as fourth Earl of Lincoln, at the age of nineteen, having been made a Knight of the Bath, along with Prince Charles, in 1616. He became colonel of a regiment of foot and two troops of horse, which were part of 12,000 men raised by Count Mans-field in England to assist the Palatine in the 22d of James I.; but neither France, Holland, nor Brabant allowing the troops to land on their shores, they were decimated by pestilence, and scarce one-half reached Germany. His share in this expedition shows the political leanings of the Earl of Lincoln, the Puritans being deeply interested in the Palatine's enterprise; but these were displayed more decidedly when the rupture took place between the King and Parliament. He espoused warmly the Puritan side, attaching him-self to the Presbyterian party. He continued firm to the Parliament throughout the first civil war; but in the year 1647 he fell under suspicion with the army, and on the 8th September he was impeached by the Com-mons, with other Presbyterian peers. The impeach-ment, however, was afterwards dropped, and he was discharged from it. He took no prominent part during the Commonwealth, but acquiesced in it, petitioning, in 1649, for compensation for the demolition of his castle of Tattershall in the civil war. Like the other great Presbyterian peers, he joined in the Restoration, and was carver at the coronation of Charles II., and thenceforth, like them, he disappears from history, and died in 1667. He married twice, but had children only by his first wife, a daughter of William Fiennes, Viscount Saye and Sele, and a sister of Nathaniel Fiennes. His son, Edward, who sat for Kellington in the Long Parliament, and followed his father's line of political conduct, died before him, leaving by his wife, daughter of John Holles, Earl of Clare, a son Edward, who succeeded his grandfather as fifth Earl of Lincoln. This Edward, who was a political nonentity, died without issue, November 1692, and for the first time since the ennoblement of this branch of the Clintons in the reign of Henry II. the direct male line failed, and the Earldom reverted to a collateral, Sir Francis Clinton, eldest son of Francis, third son of Sir Edward Clinton, second son of Henry, second Earl of Lincoln. The Barony of Clinton fell into abeyance twice among the daughters of Earl Theophilus and their coheirs, until at length it came to the Trefusis family, who now enjoy it. Francis, the sixth Earl of Lincoln, died the year after his accession to the title, at the age of fifty-eight. His younger son, George, became a distinguished Admiral, and was Governor-General of New York. He was the father of the more celebrated Sir Henry Clinton, Commander-in-Chief of the royal forces during the American War of Independence.

Henry, who succeeded his father Francis in 1693, as seventh Earl of Lincoln, was one of the Gentlemen of the Bedchamber to Prince George of Denmark. He was a firm Whig, and strongly opposed the Harley Administration and the Peace of Utrecht, refusing every offer made to him to join the Tories. This conduct so delighted Arthur Herbert, Earl of Torrington, that on his death he left Lord Clinton the bulk of his property. The accession of the house of Hanover was, of course, a welcome event to the Earl. He carried the pointed sword at the coronation of George I., became Master of the Horse to the Prince of Wales, a Lord of the Bedchamber to the King, Paymaster-General of the Forces, one of the Privy Council, and a Knight of the Garter—Lord-Lieutenant of the Tower Hamlets and Constable of the Tower, and Cofferer of the King's Household. He again carried the pointed sword at the coronation of George II., was appointed Lord-Lieutenant of the county of Cambridge, a Gentleman of the Bedchamber, and a Privy Councillor. He married, in 1717, Lucy, daughter of Thomas Pelham, first Lord Pelham, and sister of Thomas (who had taken the name of Holles), the well-known Duke of Newcastle, of the reigns of George II. and III., and of Henry Pelham, the statesman of the same period. The Earl died September 7, 1728. His eldest son, George, who succeeded him as eighth Earl of Lincoln, died April 30, 1730, in the thirteenth year of his age, and was succeeded by his brother Henry, ninth Earl of Lincoln, who married, October 14, 1744, his cousin, Catherine Pelham, daughter of Henry Pelham. This Henry Pelham having died without male issue, his brother (the Duke of Newcastle-on-Tyne) obtained a new patent in 1756, by which he was created Duke of Newcastle-under-Lyne, with remainder to his nephew, the Earl of Lincoln, and his heirs male by Catherine

Pelham ; and, in accordance with this patent, Henry
Clinton, ninth Earl of Lincoln, became, November 17,
1768, Duke of Newcastle. He obtained, by this succession, Nottingham Castle (purchased by the loyal
Duke of Newcastle, after the Restoration) and CLUM-
BER PARK, in Nottinghamshire, which has become the
chief seat of the family. On succeeding to his new
dignity, Lord Lincoln prefixed the name of Pelham to
his own. He held various offices, but was of no political rank, and died February 22, 1794, as much of
a political nonentity as a duke can in England be.
He was succeeded by his son Thomas, also a nullity;
and he (in 1795) by his son Henry, the third Duke (of
the Clintons), who would have been a nullity but for
his superb Toryism, and a disposition which reminded
his tenants and family of the tinge of insanity ascribed
to his ancestor, the second Earl of Lincoln. He crippled his fortunes by the only form of private war now
allowed to English peers—fierce electioneering battles;
and is said, though we mention this with reserve,
to have never forgiven the Liberal principles of his
far abler son, Henry Pelham Fiennes, the fourth
Duke and the twenty-fourth noble of the family, who
succeeded in January 1851. This Duke, who died
October 18, 1864, held nearly all offices short of the
Premiership, and rejected the one British office which
affords larger scope than that—the immense Indian
Viceroyalty. A follower of Sir Robert Peel, and a
man who sacrificed much for his political convictions,
he fell during the Crimean war into a disrepute, which
those who had means of knowing the truth assert
to have been wholly undeserved ; but dukes survive
clamour, and the country will rejoice if the fortunes

of the house, of late years often threatened, should hereafter, as a consequence of the match made by the present and fifth Duke, Henry Pelham Alexander, be re-established on a solid material basis. It is really a great house, though strangely lacking in hold on the popular imagination, and for seven hundred years has poured out a scarcely intermitted succession of men who have spent their lives in the furtherance of England's greatness and policy. If it has never had a genius, it has also never produced a traitor; and if it has never risen to the lofty position of one or two of its rivals, it has not in its annals chapters which it would give estates to conceal.

The Stanhopes.

THE Stanhopes stand at the head of all the peers of the drawing-room. Modern society has given birth to a class of magnates who are neither "of the robe" nor "of the sword," seldom soldiers or statesmen, yet great and useful in their way—men in whom strong will and keen brain is half concealed by external polish, who make of culture a means of ascendancy, use repartees like duelling-pistols, and fight social campaigns as difficult as those of the field. They have a tendency to cosmopolitanism, display a singular aptitude for diplomacy of a practical kind—the diplomacy which really settles things, and are apt to exhibit in emergencies the iron will and unscrupulous audacity of their true exemplars, the princes of the early Italian states. The late Lord Elphinstone was a perfect specimen of the kind—a man who could purr *so* softly till it seemed to him necessary to act, and then strike so savagely hard. The modern French Legitimists all tend to this type, and though the class is limited in England, still it exists, and in it the Stanhopes are unquestionably the first. Their whole history is in the career of the forgotten Chesterfield, the strange

P

being whose wit, and insolence, and brutal amours,
and courtly gallantry, and life of perils from water,
and bandits, and outraged husbands, and jealous
women, make up so strange a chapter in the story of
that Carnival of Belial, the Stuart Restoration.

The family of Stanhope, or, as it used to be spelt,
Stanhop, which now possesses three Earldoms, sprang,
like the Cavendishes, from a man who grew rich on
the great Sequestration. Who he was by birth is
still, in some degree, uncertain. The heralds, of
course, have given him a long pedigree, stretching up
to a Stanhope who, in 1373, was Escheater (collector
for the legacy duty, as we should say) in Derbyshire
and Nottinghamshire, but the story must be dismissed
as probably forged, and certainly not proven. If Earl
Stanhope is anxious about it he had better rewrite it,
for at present the pedigree makes a father and son
marry the same woman, slurs over some heraldic im-
possibilities about arms, invents reasons to account
for dispositions of property inconsistent with itself,
and generally wears the appearance of a very clumsy
romance.

The real founder was one MICHAEL STANHOPE, probably a cadet of a decent house, certainly a land-
less man without arms, for he took those of the
Newcastle Stanhopes, being the best of his name.
He, " having served King Henry VIII. from his
tender years," obtained from that King by letters
patent, bearing date January 28, in the 29th year of
his reign, a grant of Eveshall forest, in the county
of Nottingham ; and on the 24th of November in the
same year the King granted the house and site of the
priory of Shelford, in the same county, and one hun-

dred and sixty-four acres of land, thirty of meadow
and sixty of pasture, with the appurtenances, to
Michael Stanhope, Esq., and Anne his wife, and the
heirs male of Michael. In a similar manner, on the
5th February, in the 31st year of this reign, Michael
Stanhope received a royal grant of the *manor* of
SHELFORD, and the rectories of the parish churches of
Shelford, Saxendale, Gedling, Burton-Joys, and North
Maskham, in Nottinghamshire; Ronceby and West-
burgh in Lincolnshire; and ELVASTON and Okbrook,
in Derbyshire; and all manors, messuages, lands, and
tenements, &c., in Shelford, Saxendale, Newton, Brig-
ford, Gunthorp, Loudham, Calthorpe, Horingham,
Balcote, Gedling, Carlton, Stoke, Lambecote, Flintham, Long-Collingham, Caunton, the town of Nottingham, Newark, Burton-Joys, and North Maskham,
in Nottinghamshire, late belonging to the monastery
of Shelford. In the 35th year of Henry VIII.,
February 25, Michael Stanhope was constituted the
King's steward of the great lordship of Holdeness, and
of Cottingham, in Yorkshire. Two years later he was
knighted by the King at Hampton Court. He had
been before that time appointed Governor of Hull.
We can account for the rapid rise and aggrandisement
of Sir Michael, if the statement be true of his connection with Edward Seymour, Earl of Hertford—brother
of Queen Jane Seymour, and afterwards Protector of
England, and Duke of Somerset—whose second wife
was Anne Stanhope, daughter of Sir Edward Stanhope, and, if the genealogists are right, sister of Sir
Michael. This lady, whose pride and insolent demeanour are said to have precipitated the fall of her
husband, was the ancestor of the first line of Sey-

mours, Dukes of Somerset, and Earls and Marquesses
of Hertford, which terminated in 1750.　Burnet
seems not to be aware of the connection between the
Duke and Stanhope ; but supposing it to be proved,
it is not to be wondered at that Sir Michael Stanhope's fortunes culminated under Somerset's protectorate, and came to a violent catastrophe along with
his brother-in-law's.　He was appointed chief gentleman of the Privy Chamber, and in the first year of
Edward VI. was returned as one of the knights for
the shire of Nottingham, and in the third year of this
reign was appointed with others a commissioner to
examine the state of the guild lands in the kingdom.
He involved himself deeply in the administrative
measures of Somerset, and when the latter's power
was undermined and subverted by Dudley, Lord Lisle
(Earl of Warwick and Duke of Northumberland),
" on the 13th of October (1549)," says Burnet, " Sir
Thomas Smith, Sir Michael Stanhope, Sir John
Thynne, and Edward Wolfe, called adherents of the
Duke of Somerset, and the principal instruments of
his ill-government, were sent to the Tower ; and on
the 14th he himself was sent thither."　In the follow-
ing year, after the fall of the Earl of Arundel, who
had been one great agent in their overthrow, the
adherents of Somerset were discharged, on the 22d of
February, on their own recognisances, Sir Michael
Stanhope " acknowledging he owed the King £3000."
Two years later, however, having engaged with
Somerset and some of his friends in plans to overturn
Northumberland, and being betrayed by Sir Thomas
Palmer, they were all, with the Duchess of Somerset,
thrown into prison.　The charges against them,

though based on facts, were exaggerated, and the trials were conducted with the gross unfairness characteristic of the time, and on 26th February 1552, Sir Michael was beheaded on Tower Hill. Burnet says he died unpitied, and hints that the unpopularity was, at least in part, deserved. He says, "Sir Michael Stanhope, Sir Thomas Arundel, Sir Ralph Vane, and Sir Miles Partridge, were next brought to their trials. The *first* and the last of these were little pitied. For as all great men have people about them who make use of their greatness only for their own ends, without regarding their master's honour or true interest, so they were the persons upon whom the ill things which had been done by the Duke of Somerset were chiefly cast."

Sir Michael had three daughters and four sons, Sir Thomas (of Shelford), Sir Edward (who was one of Elizabeth's Queen's Counsel on the York circuit, and died childless), Sir Michael of Sudbury, and Sir John, who fixed his seat at Harrington, in Northamptonshire. This last gentleman rose to Court favour under Elizabeth, was a Privy Councillor of James I., was one of the commissioners of the first treaty of union with Scotland, and on 4th May 1605 was created Baron Stanhope of Harrington. He died 9th March 1620, and was succeeded by his son Charles, who passed through the Civil War as a lukewarm supporter of the Parliament, and died in 1675 without issue, the peerage, the first gained by the house, thus becoming extinct. They had, however, in the interim, gained another, Sir Thomas Stanhope of Shelford, eldest son of the founder, having prospered as, *pace* Cardinal Wiseman, almost all the holders of abbey lands have done. He was knighted by Elizabeth on her visit to Kenilworth, purchased the manors of Whatton, Bingham, and Toveton, acquired by marriage with the coheiress of Sir John Post, Etwell, and Cubley, in Derbyshire, and bought of the Berkeleys the castle and manor of BRETBY in the same county, still the seat of his descendants, the Chesterfield family. He is the Stanhope alluded to in the distich attributed to the Queen upon the Nottinghamshire knights—

" Gervase the gentle, Stanhope the stout,
Markham the lion, and Sutton the lout."

Sir Thomas Stanhope died August 3, 1596, and his eldest son, Sir John, was knighted by James I., and resided usually at Elvaston, in Derbyshire, a property which he left to his second son, John, ancestor of the Earls of Harrington, who, again, the third son's family ending suddenly, inherited Linby from them. Sir John's eldest son, Philip, was knighted in 1605; on November 7, 1616, raised to the peerage as Baron Stanhope of Shelford; and on August 4, 1628, created Earl of Chesterfield. These honours bound him to the King, and from this time forward the Shelford Stanhopes were consistent and ardent royalists. The Earl and his sons were among the first in the field for King Charles, but their military career was unfortunate. One of his sons fortified Shelford and held it till October 27, 1645; but it was taken by storm, and the Earl's son slain in the attack. Another son, who was at Edgehill, was slain at Bridgeford in Nottinghamshire, and the Earl himself, with a third son and 300 dependents, was taken prisoner in Lichfield, and died a prisoner on parole, September 12, 1656. Several of his sons had preceded him to the grave,—one by his second

wife was, as we shall show, father of the first Earl
Stanhope,—and the Earldom of Chesterfield fell to a
grandson, Philip Stanhope.

This extraordinary person, whose life reads like a
Spanish comedy, is the "Milord Chesterfield" of
'Grammont's Memoirs,' and must have been one of
the strangest characters even of that strange age. The
materials for his biography are unusually ample; for
while Anthony Hamilton, the writer of 'Grammont's
Memoirs,' has devoted more pages to him than to any
man not royal or of his own family, he himself left
notes of the principal events in his own life, and correspondence of the most private character. The
drawback is that half these notes are visible exaggera-
tions, and there is an air of romance thrown over all
the remainder. To judge from these accounts, he was
the very representative man of the age — an able,
dissolute man, with strong political principle, who had
seen half the countries of Europe and almost every
phase of life, who was drowned half-a-dozen times and
robbed as many, who once begged his way to Paris
only to find himself a great Earl, and who, after wanting almost every woman he saw, and winning almost
every woman he wanted, fell in love with his own wife,
and commenced a new series of adventures to cure her
of her disgust. We must tell the story as we find it,
but it is with the reservation that we believe it nearly
as little as we believe Jean Jacques Rousseau.

Philip's father, who never came to the title, died
when his son was one year old, leaving a widow, who
was daughter and coheiress of Thomas Lord Wootton,
and governess to Princess Mary, eldest daughter of
Charles I., and mother of William of Orange. The

widow married a Dutch gentleman, and the lad was
brought up in Holland, where we find him, after being
dragged out of the water by his *shoestrings*—so he
says, at least—an attendant on the Princess. At fifteen
he was drowned again, fifteen vessels having sunk
around his own between Delft and Antwerp; and at
sixteen he and the "messenger" to Paris rescued a
coachful of ladies who had been set upon by fifteen
soldiers of fortune. Travelling to Paris, he put himself into an academy, but was compelled to leave in
consequence of a duel, in which he hurt and disarmed
his antagonist. In 1649 he went to Italy; on his
return through Germany he was robbed and nearly
killed, but got at length to Holland, and thence repaired to England, which country he had not seen since
he was seven years old. In 1650, according to his
own dates (the Peerage books differ by two years), he
married Lady Anne Percy, eldest daughter of Algernon
Earl of Northumberland, and lived in retirement at
Petworth for some time subsequently to this event.
After two supernatural incidents or warnings, which he
vouches for and evidently believes in, though he makes
a feint of reasoning them away, his wife died in 1654,
in childbed, and her infant son soon followed her. He
then tells us he left England, taking with him only a
little foot-boy, and intended to have gone "with pil-
grims to Jerusalem," but not finding this practicable,
went to Rome instead, having, of course, a fight with
the Majorcan pirates on the voyage. He stayed about
a year in Rome, and here again was nearly drowned
from an attack of cramp. "I sank down," he says,
"to the bottom, and not being able to rise again upon
the water, and feeling the bank under the water to slope,

I crept on all fours till I came out at the side, to the amazement of the Lord Lindsey and many more, who were standers-by "—as one can well believe ! A plague soon broke out, and five persons died in the house in which he lodged ; at the same time he heard from England that a decree in Chancery had been given against him, and that his uncle, Arthur Stanhope, youngest son of the first Earl by his first marriage, and ancestor of the present Earl of Chesterfield, had seized his estate, and there would be no more remittances of money. His uncle also claimed a debt from him of £10,000; and as Arthur Stanhope, he tells us, stood well with the Protector Cromwell, the young adventurer feared imprisonment if he returned home. He left Rome with £25 in his pocket for Paris, but fell ill, lost all his money, and, after a period of actual begging, was rescued by a Jesuit priest, who paid his way to the capital. There he found the news of his grandfather's death, and his own accession to the Earldom. He immediately compromised matters with his uncle, regained his estates, and was pressed by Cromwell to marry his daughter with a portion of £20,000, and a command by land or sea. He refused, and Cromwell's love immediately turned to hate—a story which will deceive no one acquainted with Cromwell's real mode of negotiating matches for his children. The truth in all probability is, that the Earl, with half the young nobility, was a suitor for one of Cromwell's daughters, and also for Fairfax's, and was rejected by both on account of his notorious licence, a licence so great that it produced his imprisonment. A gross act of indecency towards a lady involved him in a duel with Colonel Whalley, in which the Earl, being utterly in the wrong, was, of course, the victor, and Cromwell sent him to the Tower. Next year (1658) he was three times imprisoned, the Earl of Stamford accusing him of treason; but "at great charge and trouble he got off," only to kill a gentleman in a duel, and abscond to Holland. There he obtained the pardon of the "King of Scots," Charles II., and returned with him to England, in fair favour from a connection which now seems almost impossible. The Earl had years before formed an intimacy with Barbara Villiers, Charles's proud and dissolute mistress, better known as Lady Castlemaine, and Duchess of Cleveland. The intrigue had commenced when she was Miss Villiers, continued after her marriage with Mr Palmer, and lasted up to her desertion of her first lover for the restored King. Piqued at this desertion, Chesterfield paid his court to Lady Elizabeth Butler, daughter of the celebrated Duke of Ormond, and contrived, in spite of his character, to convince her of his devotion. She married him, and he neglected her, till she, enraged at his open contempt, began to intrigue in her turn. George Hamilton, the biographer's brother, became her lover, and when she threw him off for the Duke of York, betrayed her to her husband, who suddenly carried her off to Bretby. All London rang with the scandal, and all the mothers in England declared that their sons should not visit Italy, "lest they should bring back with them that infamous custom of laying restraint upon their wives." The upshot of the affair was curious. The Earl fell deeply in love with his wife, and, being one of the men who always succeed, won back her affection, and the mutual confidence became complete. He learnt George Hamilton's real relation to his wife, and she that George had betrayed her, and the two laid a plot which tempted the culprit down to Bretby. There the lady kept him for hours in the garden, nearly frozen to death, till, discovering the trick, he rode sharply back to London, only to find all town jeering at his expense, and to hear the King sarcastically compliment him on his journey. It was a delightful state of manners, and paradisiacal at any rate in the absence of shame.

In 1667, Charles II. gave the Earl a regiment, which he raised in ten days, and then stationed among the swamps till half the men died of ague, and the Archbishop gave the Earl himself his farewell blessing. Chesterfield recovered, however, and we gladly turn from scenes of intrigue to his more credit-able political character. The Earl was from first to last, except for one short period, a strong and consist-ent Tory. He opposed the Exclusion Bill, declined to give evidence in favour of Lord Russell without the King's consent, was excluded from the deathbed of Charles II. as too determined a Protestant, disap-proved all James's concessions to Roman Catholics, and when the Revolution broke out rose in arms, only, as he said, to protect the Princess Anne. William, who had been bred up with him as a boy, would have taken him into favour; but the Earl, though anxious always for his own personal fortunes, resisted his pre-tensions in every debate, and steadily refused every offer of office or emolument. He resided at Bretby, which he had rebuilt, and added to the family pro-perty by purchases such as Brisancoate and Hartshorn. He had, moreover, obtained by a third marriage with the heiress of the Dormers all their Buckinghamshire estates, Wing Park, Ascot, Eythorpe, and Ilmer, and he latterly nursed his affairs with some care. Despite his magnificent constitution, however, the penalty of a life like his overtook him in a complication of diseases, of which gout was, probably, the least formidable. He died at last in his 80th year, tormented by scurvy, at his house in Bloomsbury Square, on 28th January 1713. After all deductions for exaggeration, he had lived a life which in romance would be pronounced absurd. Roderick Random is true to nature, and so is Earl de Guest; but a man who was both at once would be pronounced a failure. Yet that was Lord Chesterfield, page and wanderer, beggar and earl, who asked the hand of a Cromwell, lived with Barbara Villiers, after a life of *roué* excitement fell in love with his own wife, and with a ruined reputation was still one of the few men whom Catherine of Braganza, Charles II.'s " swarthy Kate," dared ask to be her executor.

Of the son of this strange adventurer, also Philip, but little is known, save that he was a violent Tory, and suspected of being a secret Jacobite. The Bishop of Waterford says of him, " He was, as I have often heard, of a morose disposition, of violent passions, and often thought that people behaved ill to him when they did not in the least intend it." He died January 24, 1726, leaving four sons, the eldest of whom, Philip Dormer Stanhope, is the one Chesterfield whose name has became a household word—as the author of ' Chesterfield's Letters.' He was born in London, September 22, 1694. His father seems to have conceived almost an aversion to him from his earliest years. " My father was neither desirous nor able to advise me," he says himself; and as he lost his mother while a child, his education passed into the hands of

his grandmother, the Marchioness of Halifax, daughter
of William Pierrepont—the "wise William" of Charles
I.'s time—a lady distinguished for her accomplishments and amiable character. Young Stanhope was
carefully educated, and at the age of eighteen sent to
Trinity Hall, Cambridge, where he devoted himself to
books, and especially the classics, to such an extent
that he described himself afterwards as having become
a perfect pedant—quoting a Latin author on every
possible occasion, and believing in the classics as the
key to practical life. From the University he went
abroad to the Hague, where he contracted the habit
of gambling deeply. From Holland he repaired to
Paris, to learn the graces of society. He describes in
amusing terms his *gaucherie* at his introduction into
Parisian saloons, and how, having mustered up courage
at last to address a fashionable dame with the original
remark, "*Il fait chaud*," she rewarded his courage by
formally undertaking his social education on the footing of easy morals then prevalent in French circles,
and under her auspices young Stanhope soon forgot
any awkwardness or scruples he might have brought
from England. His pedantry, however, remained, but
took another form—that of doing everything by rule,
and endeavouring to acquire the gifts of nature by a
course of self-tuition. He resolved to be a great
statesman and a great orator, and he got himself up
for both parts with such creditable appearance of success, that not his contemporaries only, but posterity
have been puzzled to account for his ultimate failure
in one point, and the small results from his success in
the other. His great rule was to be guarded in everything he said or did, with the affectation of easy *non-*

chalance and perfect frankness. One of his biographers says truly enough, " he *finessed* too much." He took so much pains to do everything in the most suitable and unexceptionable manner, that rivals stepped in before him, and successfully anticipated him with their rough and ready stupidity. With a strong desire to please every one he met with—high or low—and a just conception of the true character of a gentleman in these respects, he had no real warmth of heart and no real sincerity of character. His virtues were cultivated on such an artificial principle, that even where they were *bonâ fide* they produced little of the impression attaching to reality. His eloquence, though finished to perfection, was so carefully studied according to the best models of the ancients, that, admirable and admired as it was in the select and polished assembly of English Peers, it never touched the *public* heart, and laid no solid foundation for a great *public* reputation. On his return to England from Paris, on the accession of George I., he was elected to the House of Commons, before he had quite completed his legal majority, for the Cornish borough of St Germans, under the auspices of his cousin, the first Earl Stanhope. Speaking ardently in favour of the impeachment of the Duke of Ormonde, he received a hint, couched in complimentary terms, from one of the political friends of the latter nobleman, that he had better stay away from Parliament till he had attained his legal majority. So he left the House without voting, and went to Paris again, where he remained till recalled at the instance of his cousin, who had become Secretary of State, and was appointed a Gentleman of the Bedchamber to the Prince of Wales. He returned with his character completely formed—a proud, haughty, self-willed man, striving always to influence by drawing-room arts, yet conscious of the ability to govern, and hungering morbidly for large excitement. He voted with the Ministry until the difference took place between the King and Prince, when he adhered to the latter, and withstood the utmost solicitations of the Court to abandon him, extending, it is said, to an offer of a dukedom to his father. The Earl (though a Tory, if not a Jacobite) was very angry, it is said, at his son refusing this offer. The young Lord was sufficiently conciliated, however, to vote with the Ministers on one or two critical occasions, and was rewarded by being appointed in 1723 Captain of the Yeomen of the Guard. He declined the Order of the Bath as below his dignity. But he never succeeded in the popular assembly, being afraid of rude ridicule, and particularly standing in awe of one member distinguished in that way. His father's death in 1726 placed him in the more appropriate sphere of the House of Lords. On the accession of George II. Chesterfield was not placed in any high office, but sent on an embassy to the Hague. It was probably intended thus to shelve him, but the post exactly suited his talents, and he added greatly to his reputation by his management of the mission. While there, in 1729, he joined in a secret intrigue with Lord Townshend to supplant the Duke of Newcastle; and though this failed, and Townshend fell from power in consequence, Sir Robert Walpole was so much impressed with the ability of Chesterfield that he endeavoured to gain him by making him High Steward and giving him the Garter.

He returned home in 1732, with impaired health, and then resumed his attendance in Parliament, soon quarrelling with Walpole, voting against him on the Excise Bill, asking his three brothers to do the same in the House of Commons, and being summarily dismissed from his office of High Steward, and violently assailed by the Ministerial papers. For two years he played the part of a leader of Opposition with great zeal—even, it is said, submitting to be bled by a noble amateur doctor in order to obtain his vote. On the fall of the Minister, however, Chesterfield was not included in the new Ministry, and continued in opposition, speaking very freely, and giving strong personal offence to George II. by an allusion to the battle of Dettingen. But in 1744 Carteret fell, and the "broad-bottom" party forced their way in, and with them Chesterfield. He was, however, at first only restored to his early embassy to the Hague, with a seat in the Cabinet, the King struggling hard but vainly against conceding the latter, or even giving him a personal interview on leaving for the Hague. As it was, when Chesterfield on parting asked his Majesty's commands, the King replied gruffly, "You have received your instructions, my Lord !" Towards the end of the year 1745, Chesterfield was transferred, at his own request, and much to the surprise of his friends, to the Lord-Lieutenancy of Ireland, then looked upon as an easy sinecure, the Viceroy receiving the money and the Secretary for Ireland doing all the work, and *managing* Ireland through the select "managing" families, as they were called, of the Orange connection. But Chesterfield had another idea of the office. He longed for an arena in which

he might act the affable sovereign and the impartial
governor, and he had found it. There was in him, as
in all the class to which the Stanhopes belong, a faint
and intermittent, but still real, sense of social justice,
and a covered but immovable will. He appointed
an agreeable and unbusinesslike young man as the
Secretary, and told him he was to take his salary but
leave the work to the Lord-Lieutenant himself. He
threw over the select Orange families, and had the
audacity to employ a Roman Catholic as his coachman,
while he kept quiet the Catholic Jacobites by telling
them in private that if they remained so they should
have impartial justice, but if they rose in rebellion he
would prove worse to them than Cromwell. He carried out fully this programme, and Ireland remained
under his rule more perfectly tranquil during the crisis
of "the '45" than it had been for many years before.
Chesterfield's administration was a great success, for
his government was firm, conciliatory, and upright,
he eschewing all jobs, and clearing the administration
of the jobbers. His theoretical notions of toleration,
however, were as narrow as those of the other Whig
statesmen of that age, for he thought that the best
way of converting the Irish was not merely to give
them the means of education, but to enforce the laws
which held out a bribe to one member of a Catholic
family to become a convert at the expense of the property of his kindred. In October 1746, he consented
to exchange the Lord-Lieutenancy for the Secretaryship of State in the English Government, being
tempted by an idea that he could manage the King
through Lady Yarmouth. He succeeded, indeed, in
conciliating the King thoroughly ; but he failed in

governing him, as the mistress was allowed no political influence ; and the clever, insinuating, and plastic Chesterfield had soon the hard fate to find he was out-manœuvred, and made a nonentity, so far as the patronage of the Government was concerned, by the man he so much despised—the Duke of Newcastle. At last, in January 1748, he could endure the mortification of his position no longer, and resigned, retiring to his books, and only occasionally re-appearing in Parliament. He did one great service more, however, to his country, by proposing and carrying, in 1751, the reform of the Calendar, against the most insane opposition out of doors. His retirement from public affairs was rendered permanent by his increasing deafness, and from this time Chesterfield may be said to disappear from the roll of public men. He had gone down to White's the very evening of his resignation of office, and resumed the deep gambling which he had been able to intermit during the larger excitements of his public career. He also devoted himself now to the education of his illegitimate son, to whom the celebrated Letters are addressed. Chesterfield had married a daughter of the Duchess of Kendal (George I.'s mistress), but had no children by her, and regarded her with indifference, holding matrimony itself in the light of a troublesome encumbrance. He was a man of pleasure, and his idea was to make his son not only a man of pleasure, but the model of a polished gentleman. All he succeeded in producing was a rather learned, heavy man, without an atom of grace or polish, who failed in the House of Commons, and only rose to be Envoy at Dresden. The son married secretly during his father's life, but preceded him to

the tomb, leaving him to drag out a dreary and
objectless old age.   He adopted and tried to feel an
interest in the next heir to the Earldom—a descendant of that Arthur Stanhope who was on such excellent terms with Cromwell—but the young man was
completely uncongenial to him, and all he could do
was to guard as far as he could against the possible
effects of his tastes by a curious proviso in his will.
The Earl had felt the mischief of gambling from his
own experience, and he had always detested "the turf"
as ungentlemanlike — so he provided as follows :—
"In case my godson, Philip Stanhope, shall at any
time hereinafter keep, or be concerned in the keeping
of any racehorses or pack of hounds, or reside one
night at Newmarket, that infamous seminary of ini-
quity and ill-manners, during the course of the races
there, or shall resort to the said races, or shall lose in
any one day, at any game or bet whatsoever, the sum
of £500, then, in any of the cases aforesaid, it is my
express wish that he, my said godson, shall forfeit
and pay out of my estate the sum of £5000, to and
for the use of the Dean and Chapter of Westminster."
He said that this contingent bequest to the Dean and
Chapter was occasioned by his having found them so
sharp and exacting in some transactions with them
respecting the land on which he had built Chesterfield
House, that he was sure they would take care to exact
any penalty incurred by his heir.   Before his death
his sight failed him as well as his hearing ; but he
retained his mind and memory unimpaired, and when
a Mr Dayrolles called to see him, only half an hour
before he died, the old Earl cried out from his bed, in
a polite, though faint tone, "Give Dayrolles a chair."

He died on the 24th of March 1773, in the 79th year of his age; and after his death, his son's widow collected all the letters the Earl had addressed to her husband in the strictest confidence, and sold them to the booksellers for £1575. They rose at once to the popularity they have scarcely yet lost, and the fame of the old statesman who had passed his life in training himself for greatness, who succeeded in governing Ireland, and who was, perhaps, of all peers of his time, the one most competent to govern England, rests on a correspondence which he never dreamed of giving to the world. That correspondence has been defined as the "recipe for going to hell gracefully;" but the letters are full, nevertheless, of a Rochefoucauldian wisdom, of deep knowledge of the world, and the few living thoughts they contain have, as living thoughts do, survived all the work their author thought important. *The* Chesterfield's successor, Philip, the fifth Earl, was the father of the present Earl, George, sixth of the name (who succeeded August 29, 1815)—a man chiefly known for his consistent Toryism, and his devotion to the amusement Lord Chesterfield prohibited in his will. The family retains its great properties almost unbroken, but not unencumbered, and exercises for the hour but little political influence.

The true epoch of the greatness of the Stanhopes is the reigns of the first Hanoverian sovereigns. Then, besides Philip Dormer, the head of the Chesterfield branch, two other remarkable men built up the fortunes of the younger branches of the Stanhope family. These were James Stanhope, first Earl Stanhope, and William, first Earl of Harrington. The former of these, as we have already said, was son of Alexander, youngest son of the first Earl of Chesterfield. Alexander was appointed, through his nephew's interest, ambassador to Spain during the reign of the imbecile Charles II., where, and at the Hague, he earned the character of a skilful and honourable representative. His son James was born in Paris, 1673, and after a short time passed at Oxford, where he made such use of his time as to be afterwards known for his classical learning—all the Stanhopes have an instinct for culture —joined his father in the embassy at Madrid. In 1691, after a tour to Rome and Naples, he entered the army of the Duke of Savoy, and then served at the siege of Namur, under William III.'s own eye, and attracted his especial attention for gallantry. After a brief service in Parliament, as member for Newport and then for Cockermouth, the War of Succession drew him to Spain, in command of the vanguard of the expedition. In this capacity (combined with the diplomatic) he remained, contributing greatly to the earlier victories, till the disastrous defeat of Brihuega left him a prisoner of war till 1712. Meanwhile, not satisfied with his achievements as a soldier and diplomatist, he had (with many other officers of the army) availed himself from time to time of the regular cessation of hostilities during the winter season to attend in his place in Parliament, and had acquired a leading position in the House as a debater and manager of the Whig party. "Your return," wrote Walpole to him, "is the only good effect that I ever hoped from our celebrated peace." He showed his own dislike to the peace by refusing Bolingbroke's offer of a personal introduction to Louis XIV., and his antagonism to the Tories was so marked that they got Shippen appointed to the head of a commission to inquire into Stanhope's accounts during his Spanish services. Instead, however, of the balance turning against him, it proved to be in his favour, and he ironically thanked Shippen in the House for assisting him to get repaid. On the accession of George I. his political position was superior to that of Walpole, and he was appointed one of the principal Secretaries of State, Walpole only becoming Paymaster, without a seat in the Cabinet. This relative position of the two, however, though it continued in the Court and Cabinet, was in the House of Commons soon changed—Stanhope, eloquent, vigorous, and clear-headed, was too impetuous, dictatorial, and, above all, indiscreet in his language. He boasted of deceiving the foreign ambassadors by telling them the truth; but the English House of Commons preferred the cautious sagacity of Walpole. In 1716 occurred a political transaction which severed him from Townshend, and soon after from Walpole, and has exposed his memory to some obloquy. This was his journey to Hanover along with the King, and his alleged treachery to Townshend in suffering the intriguing Earl of Sunderland to have access to the King at that city, and in suddenly, in the midst of professions of friendship, writing a letter to Townshend announcing his dismissal from the Premiership. The present Earl has defended his ancestor from the charge with some vigour, but with only partial success. Walpole, a man singularly free from rancour, never forgave him, and on Townshend's final dismissal the Ministry was reformed. With Stanhope as Premier, and Chancellor of the Exchequer, and life and soul of the government, the governing power of the

family and its cosmopolitan tendencies had at last
fair play. While governing England, Stanhope—who
on the 2d of July was created Viscount Stanhope of
Mahon (in Minorca), and Baron Stanhope of Elvaston,
and in April 1719 Earl Stanhope and Viscount
Mahon—kept flying over the Continent as supreme
diplomatist. No man so successful ever occupied
such a post. He broke up all European leagues hostile to his policy, compelled the King of Spain to dismiss Alberoni, and by cementing a firm alliance with
the Regent Orleans, reduced the hopes of the Jacobites
to zero. All this while he so ruled his party that
Walpole and Townshend felt it expedient to sink their
personal feud, and re-enter the Ministry under him as
Paymaster and President of the Council. In the
height of his success he was seized with a sudden
dizziness, and died after less than one day's illness,
on the 6th of February 1721. His success seems to
have been owing first to his genuine mental power,
and a certain arrogance of temper often found in successful English statesmen; secondly, to the excessive
prominence of foreign politics which he alone understood; and lastly, to a real contempt for money
unusual in that age. Of the landed possessions, says
his descendant, "which his representative now enjoys,
scarcely one-fifth is derived from him."

He purchased, however, from the heiresses of Len-
nard Lord Sussex, the manor of CHEVENING, in Kent,
still the chief seat of his family. His successor Philip,
second Earl, devoted his life to science, as did Earl
Charles, the third Earl (1786), the husband of Lady
Hester Pitt, and the Peer whose eccentricities and
democratic opinions fill so curious a chapter in the his-

tory of the reign of George III., and who died December 15, 1816. His son, Philip-Henry, the fourth and late Earl, was also distinguished by a character and a line in politics which attracted considerable attention, being a democrat under the guise of an ultra-Tory. His son, also Philip-Henry, the fifth Earl, who succeeded him on the 2d of March 1855, is the accomplished noble who has made the founder illustrious by his history, and whose 'War of the Succession' will probably live when the Stanhopes are forgotten. He is the one man of the aristocratic caste who writes like a peer—brings, that is to say, to his history the maturity of judgment, the *weight* of style and thought, which should belong to men trained to affairs from boyhood. Though a Tory in politics, his Toryism is rather royalism—a disposition to increase executive power— than that sullen resistance to all change sometimes defined by that nickname.

William Stanhope, the founder of the Harrington branch of the Stanhopes, was descended from Sir John Stanhope, half-brother of the first Earl of Chesterfield, who had Elvaston, in Derbyshire, as his portion. He was a younger son, but his elder brothers dying, he inherited the paternal estates, and led a career singularly like that of his fortunate cousin, the first Earl Stanhope. He was a diplomatist of high merit and a gallant soldier, and his field of action was chiefly Spain. His services forced him upwards, notwithstanding the dislike which Walpole cherished to the name of Stanhope in consequence of his quarrel with the Earl; and at last, after having concluded successfully the treaty of Seville, William Stanhope was raised to the peerage as Baron Harrington (November 9, 1729), and on the resignation of Lord Townshend succeeded him as Secretary of State. Here his knowledge of foreign affairs was of great service, as in the case of his cousin the Earl, but unlike him he was a silent member of Parliament. He attached himself particularly to the fortunes of the Duke of Newcastle, who had first brought him into favour with the King. He was a quiet, sagacious, observing man. The Portuguese Ambassador said of him, " Lord Harrington was not accustomed to interrupt those who spoke to him." He made no personal enemies, and he disarmed all political hostility by his conciliatory tact, so that he escaped wonderfully from the libels of the day. His integrity is highly spoken of ; and, indeed, Newcastle had the merit of securing disinterested colleagues, since he always appropriated the jobbing to himself. Lord Harrington served in some other posts of Government, and from the end of 1746 to 1751 he was Lord-Lieutenant of Ireland. He succeeded in this post his cousin, the Earl of Chesterfield—the exchange of offices being forwarded by the coolness of the King towards Harrington, who had seceded in February 1746, in order to gratify Newcastle, who, of course, in return only lent him a feeble support. His Irish administration has left no special mark in history, but on February 9, 1742, he was raised to the peerage as Viscount Petersham and Earl of Harrington, and died September 8, 1756. His son and grandson, William and Charles, second and third Earls of Harrington (1756 and 1779), require no special notice, except that the former, who took to a military career, distinguished himself at the battle of Fontenoy. The two succeeding Earls, Charles (September 15, 1829) and Leicester (March 3, 1851), fourth and fifth Earls, were brothers. The former was known in early life as a leader of fashion and the husband of Miss Foote; the latter as an eccentric man, of a shade of politics which it was difficult to define, except, perhaps, by saying that he held every opinion for exactly the opposite reason assigned by other persons, and his political career, neither Whig nor Tory, was regulated by some similar paradoxical rule. He died September 7, 1862, and his son, the sixth and present Earl—Seymour-Sydney-Hyde—is a minor.

Possessed of three Earldoms and great estates, with a history which is for four reigns that of Great Britain, the descendants of Somerset's henchman rank among the greatest families of the land, and their double history is, perhaps, best told in one curious fact. While they have governed Ireland and conquered Spain, distinguished themselves as diplomatists, *litterateurs*, and scholars, and furnished one great Premier, they are still known to the public chiefly by three contributions to social life—the Chesterfield coat, the Petersham hat, and the Stanhope carriage.

The Talbots.

E are again among Norman magnates, men of the blue-blood, descendants of those who really conquered the land, and then stood forward for successive ages in the front rank of its defenders; who helped to extort the Great Charter, and fought through the Wars of the Roses ; whose single opinions hurried or retarded the Reformation, and who could almost individually throw a casting vote for or against a revolution. Since William the Bastard died there has been no day when the adhesion of the head of the Talbots has not been distinctly important to the acting Government of England. They themselves, or the pedigree-makers whom new men reward so highly, claim a still greater antiquity, and it is almost with regret that we are compelled finally to reject the claim. Had it been correct, there would have been one family among the greatest peers whose lineal ancestors had been barons before the Norman invasion, and who could prove themselves possessed of lands held without interruption from before the Conquest. Private gentlemen *can* ;—like Mr Myddleton, of Denton, in Wharfdale, whose single claim to his lands is a grant, or confirmation of grant, from

the Confessor, and one or two peers of Welsh descent, possibly, as, for example, Lord Willoughby
d'Eresby, if his pedigree can be trusted. The Talbots, or Talebots, claim, on the authority of the
Herald's Visitation Book of 1584-85, to be descended
from Philip Talebot, Lord of Eccleswall, Credenham,
and Worksop, in the reign of Edward the Confessor;
but no such person is named in Domesday Book, while
therein, among the under-tenants, appears RICHARD
TALEBOT, holding nine hides of land in Bedfordshire
from Walter Giffard, Earl of Buckingham, and a
Geoffrey Talebot, holding lands in Essex. Richard
Talbot also appears as witness to some grants of land
which this Walter Giffard made to some monks in
Normandy. It is probable that he came over in some
very moderate position after Hastings, for his name
is not in Wace's Roll of the leading warriors in that
battle in his 'Chronicles of the Dukes of Normandy;'
but he was in England almost immediately afterwards.
Nothing is known of him, but he must have been one
of the strong men of earth, for, amidst that powerful
crowd, every man of whom was hustling his neighbour, he rose, either during the Conqueror's life or
immediately after his death, to baronial rank. He
married a sister of Hugh de Gournay, ancestor of the
existing Quaker family of Gurney, whose blood, though
they are now known chiefly in the money market, is
more ancient than that of most peers. His son Hugh
was castellan of Plessy, in 1118, for Hugh de Gournay,
against Henry I.; and died a monk in Normandy,
leaving a son, Richard, who received from Henry II.
a grant of the lordship of Eccleswall and Linton in
Herefordshire. His son Gilbert—we follow Dugdale,

and throw over the curious list of five barons sometimes inserted, as physiologically impossible—was present at the coronation of Richard I., and in the fifth
year of his reign had lands given him in Linton for
his custody of Ludlow Castle, and paid in King John's
reign soccage representing five knights' fees. Gilbert's
son Richard left two sons, the younger of whom became Bishop of London in the reign of Henry III.,
while the elder, Gilbert, succeeded in the barony. He
distinguished himself as a soldier, as soldiers went in
those days, curbing the turbulent Welsh within their
marches, and was the one noble who, when Llewellyn
rose in 1256, dared remain firm at his post. In the
44th year of Henry III., though then an old man, he
was made Governor of Grosmond, Skenfrith, and Blanc-
minster Castles, and the year after one of the Justices
Itinerant of Hereford, the gentlemen whose appointment was the first successful blow levelled at baronial
power. He was employed all his life in Welsh transactions, and married Gwendolen, a daughter of Rhys-
ap-Griffith, Prince of South Wales, wherefore his son
assumed his mother's arms—a lion rampant—instead
of his own. This son Richard, who succeeded in 1274,
inheriting Longhope and Redley, in Gloucestershire,
and Eccleswall and Linton, in Herefordshire, was also
a soldier of mark, who followed Edward I. in Wales,
Scotland, and France, everywhere with distinction,
and in 1301 was one of the great Barons who signed
the celebrated letter to the Pope vindicating the royal
authority against ultramontane pretensions. He died
in 1306, leaving three sons, of whom the eldest, Gilbert, succeeded to the principal estates, and, like the
rest of the descendants of the Conqueror's following,

resisted bitterly the new invasion of Angevin, Poitevin, and Fleming lords, with whom Edward II. tried to counterbalance his great nobility. He was present when Thomas Plantagenet, Earl of Lancaster, executed Piers Gaveston, but obtained a formal pardon for his share in that offence, which, however, Edward never forgave. Talbot was seized in 1322 by Hugh le Despenser, and compelled to enter into recognisances; but the Parliament held the same year released him from all penalties. He followed Edward III. in his great military enterprises, and received a grant of the castles and lordships of Blenlevenny and Bulkedinás, in lieu of some properties which belonged to him through his Welsh pedigree, and which had been united with the Crown. He died in 1353, leaving a son, Sir Richard Talbot, then about thirty-four years of age. He was a distinguished warrior, chiefly in Scotch expeditions, was one of Edward Baliol's most powerful allies, and married Elizabeth, daughter and subsequently coheiress of John Comyn, of Badenoch, with whom he obtained some Irish lands, and Goderich Castle in Herefordshire, which he made his principal seat. He followed Edward in every war, served in every Parliament of the reign, received grant after grant from the monarch—one being a private prison in Goderich Castle, "for the punishing of malefactors," and died October 23, 1356, seised of the manor of Bampton, Oxfordshire, of the inheritance of his wife, Farnham, in Berkshire, and Huntley, in Gloucesterhire; of the manor of Swanscombe, in Kent; and Credenhill, the park of Penyard, the manor of Wormlow, and hundred of Irchenfield; as also the manors of Goderich Castle and Eccleswall and

Linton, with the advowson of the church of Credenhill, in Herefordshire. Gilbert, his son and
heir, served, like his father, in the French wars,
and in the fleet, under Michael de la Pole. He
married, first, a daughter of Boteler (Butler), Earl of
Ormonde, and, secondly, a daughter of the Earl of
Stafford, and died April 24, 1387, leaving by his first
marriage a son, Sir Richard, then twenty-six years
of age. Sir Richard married the heiress of the Le
Stranges, of Blackmere, and obtained livery of his
wife's inheritance during his father's lifetime. He
was a Knight Banneret, served in the fleet under
the Earl of Arundel, and took part in the Castilian
expedition under John of Gaunt. In 1391, as one
of the heirs of the Valences and Marshalls, Earls
of Pembroke, through the marriage with Elizabeth
Comyn, he had awarded to him the county of Weysford, or Wexford, in Ireland, and was styled Earl of
Wexford. There was, however, no formal creation,
and the Greys de Ruthyn, as nearest heirs of the
Earls of Pembroke, assumed with the title of Hastings
that of Wexford. Oddly enough, that family seem to
have forgotten the meaning of their own title, and
now the Marquesses of Hastings use Weysford as if
it were a Christian name. Richard Lord Talbot died
on September 7, 1396, master, besides the great properties previously enumerated, of the manors of Great
Braxted, Haslingbury, and Waldbury, in Essex; a
moiety of the manor of Broughton, in Wilts; the
lordship of Leigh, in Gloucestershire; the manors of
Doddington, Wrockwardine, Blackmere, *alias* Whit-
church, in Shropshire; and Lidney and the castle of
Kilpeck, in Herefordshire. He left five sons and four

daughters. The third son became Archbishop of
Dublin; of the second, John, we shall treat presently;
aud the eldest, Gilbert, twelfth in succession from the
founder, succeeded to all the family estates. He was
made a Knight of the Garter by Henry IV., as heir of
the Pembrokes claimed to carry the great spurs at the
coronation of Henry· V., and was made Justice of
Chester by that King, being called on to bring as his
contingent to the French wars 120 men-at-arms and
240 archers. He was engaged to treat with Owen
Glendower, and was in the French wars appointed
Governor of Caen and Captain-General of the Marches
of Normandy, and with Gilbert d'Umfraville was
ordered to subdue all the forts and castles of that
province. He died October 19, 1419, leaving to the
guardianship of his brother John an infant daughter,
named Ankaret, who died in 1421, and John, the real
hero of the Talbot line, then became the head of the
family.

John Talbot had made a great match, marrying
Maud, the eldest of the daughters and coheirs of
Thomas Neville, Lord Furnivall; and in the 11th of
Henry IV. he was summoned to Parliament as Lord
Furnivall, and afterwards as John Talbot, of Hallam-
shire, *that* property—worth now Heaven knows what
number of millions !—with the castle of Sheffield, being
part of her inheritance. She brought him also the
castle and manor of Alveton, or Alton, in Staffordshire, now the chief seat of the Talbot house. In the
last year of Henry IV. he was appointed Lord-Lieutenant of Ireland; but the new reign opened un-
favourably for him. He fell under suspicion, and on
November 16, 1413, was committed to the Tower;

but was speedily released, and in February following was re-appointed Lord-Lieutenant, and held the office seven years. His eminent military abilities—he was unquestionably the greatest general of that age, perhaps the greatest of the whole feudal period—soon reduced Ireland to obedience, and so secure did the Pale become that the noblemen and gentlemen there resident addressed to the King a description of his services. In 1419 his elder brother's death recalled him to England, and leaving his brother, the Archbishop, as his deputy, he transported to England and imprisoned in the Tower a great Irish chieftain, Donald MacMurrogh, whom he had captured, and with whom he had the King's leave to make his own terms. He next crossed into France, accompanied Henry in his triumphal march to Paris in 1420, in 1425 was again appointed Lord Justice of Ireland, and then for the second time re-entered France. Here he was placed by the Regent, John of Bedford, in command of all the English forces, and was eminently successful till, in 1429, the Maid of Orleans gave him battle and took him prisoner. He remained a prisoner for three years, and was only released on promise to pay a large ransom, which he accomplished with the assistance of the Duke of Brittany, who gave him 2000 muves of salt, which he transported to England custom free. The instant he was released he flew back to England, raised new forces, rejoined Bedford, and became the terror of all France, and so prized by the English Government that, on the 20th of May 1442, he was created Earl of the County of Salop, or, as it was generally but most improperly called, Shrewsbury, which title his lineal descendant still enjoys. So clear is the object of the creation, that we have little doubt that the present Earl, if it were worth while, could enforce his right to the title derived from the county, and not from the town. In 1444 Talbot contrived to get £10,000 paid down, and departed again for France, carrying with him as his own contingent one baron, two knights, 96 men-at-arms, and 300 archers. In 1446 he was again, for the third time, appointed Lord-Lieutenant of Ireland, and on July the 17th in that year he was raised to the additional dignity of Earl of Waterford (being also styled Earl of Wexford) and Baron Dungarvan, while the city and county of Waterford, with the castles, lords, and barony of Dungarvan, were granted to him, with the *jura regalia* from Waterford to Youghal.

In 1451 Shrewsbury was again on his old field of fame, and the year after he was made commander of a fleet, having 4000 archers on board. But his career was now drawing to a close. In 1453 he had been appointed Lieutenant of Aquitaine, and, although eighty years of age, marching thither, took Bordeaux, and had reduced several other strongholds, when, hearing that Chastillon was besieged by the French, he advanced thither and gave them battle. Fortune once again deserted him, and on the 20th of July 1453, having his thigh shattered with a cannon-ball and his horse killed under him, John, Earl of Shrewsbury, remained dead on his last battle-field. His son, John Talbot, the eldest son by his second marriage with the eldest daughter and coheir of Richard Beauchamp, Earl of Warwick, was slain with him. This son had greatly distinguished himself in the wars, and had been created Lord Lisle, of Kingston Lisle, in Berkshire, in 1444, and Viscount Lisle in 1451. His father, when wounded, had earnestly entreated him to leave him, but he refused, and remained to share his death of glory. The great Earl, when he fell, had been the victor in forty-seven battles and dangerous skirmishes. When his dead body was found on the field by his herald, who had worn his coat of arms, "he kissed the body, and broke out into these compassionate and dutiful expressions :—'Alas ! it is you. I pray God pardon all your misdoings ; I have been your officer of arms forty years or more; it is time I should surrender it to you ;' and while the tears trickled plentifully down his face, he disrobed himself of his coat of arms, and flung it over his master's body." Thus, in the fulness of years, every one of which since he could bear arms had been marked by some stout action or skilful leadership in the service of his country, died the noblest warrior of the feudal period, whom Froissart would have worshipped, and whose name, even at this lapse of time, excites a proud sympathy in the breasts of Englishmen. He was the popular idol of his own age, and he has invested the name which he bore with a charm that generations of mediocrity could not destroy. We would gladly penetrate below the surface of his external actions, and learn what the man was in himself ; but the meagre facts and dry outlines of the chroniclers give us no assistance in conceiving what he really was who was a tower of strength to England as long as he lived, and whose death was hailed in France as the seal of emancipation.*

---

* We have been favoured with some curious extracts made by Mr Rawdon Brown from archives at Venice, illustrative of the history of the Talbots. One of these, taken from the diaries of Marin Sanuto, in

His eldest surviving son by his first marriage, Sir
John Talbot, was forty years old at his death, and
showed his sense of the benefits his family had received from the house of Lancaster by warmly espousing their cause. He perished with his brother at
Northampton, 10th July 1460. By his second wife,
a daughter of James Butler, Earl of Ormonde and
Wiltshire, he had five sons, the eldest of whom, John,
succeeded him as third Earl of Shrewsbury. This
Earl was made by Edward IV. Chief Justice of North
Wales, and was one of the Commissioners to treat
with James III. of Scotland on international grievances. He married a daughter of Humphrey Stafford,
Duke of Buckingham, and died June 28th, 1473.
George, his eldest son, and successor as fourth Earl of
Shrewsbury, was only five years of age at his father's
death, and thus escaped all the difficulties of maturer
nobles at the crisis which transferred the crown from
the house of York to the house of Tudor, his uncle,
however, leading his retainers to the aid of Richmond.
He was made one of Henry VII.'s Privy Council,

St Mark's Library, Venice, occurs in a letter from the Venetian ambassador in England, Andrea Badoer, to his son-in-law, dated from London, 25th and 26th July 1512. Speaking of an expedition about to
start for France under George Talbot, fourth Earl of Shrewsbury, the
writer says, " The Earl of Shrewsbury is captain, and writes that they
are accustomed to still the children in France with the name of Talbot,
threatening them, when they cry, that *the Talbot will come*."—(' Diaries
of Sanuto,' vol. xiv. fol. 488.) Most readers will call to mind Shakespeare's allusion to this, some eighty-eight years afterwards, in his
' Henry VI.,' act ii. scene 3,

> " Is this the Talbot so much feared abroad,
> That with his name the mothers still their babes ? "

And, scene 4,

> " Here, said they, is the terror of the French,
> The scarecrow that affrights our children so."

and distinguished himself in the King's service, at the
battle of Stoke, against Lambert Simnel. He was
made a Knight of the Garter, and sent as one of the
commanders of the forces in aid of Maximilian of
Germany against Charles VIII. of France. In 1509,
Henry VIII. appointed him one of his household and
Privy Council, and he accompanied him in most of
his French expeditions,* warlike and peaceful. He
seems to have attached himself personally to the King,
who made him Lieutenant-General of the North and
Constable of Radnor and Wigmore Castles. The
Reformation left him still an adherent of the Crown,
although he may have leant to the old doctrines; and
on the occasion of the dangerous "Pilgrimage of Grace,"
Mr Froude pronounces that Henry was, perhaps, indebted for his crown to Shrewsbury's resolution and
fidelity. He anticipated orders in raising his forces,
and overawed effectually the midland counties adjacent
to the revolted district. Shrewsbury, however, seems
to have been ill repaid for his great services to the
Crown, since, in the 28th year of Henry's reign, an
Act of Parliament was passed in Ireland, called the
Statute of Absentees, whereby the Duke of Norfolk,
the Earl of Shrewsbury, the Lord Berkeley, and the
heirs-general of the Earl of Ormonde, were obliged,
"for their absence and carelessness in defending their
rights" in that country, to surrender the same to the
Crown; and accordingly, the Earls of Shrewsbury were
not inserted in the Journals of the House as Irish Peers

---

* A Venetian merchant writes to his brothers from London, July the
14th, 1512, that Lord Shrewsbury, or, as he calls him, "Earl Talbot,"
was "well accustomed to beat the French."—('Sanuto's Diaries,' in St
Mark's Library, Venice, vol. xiv. fol. 474.)

till after the Restoration, when Charles II. restored
them to the titles of Earl of Waterford and Wexford.
Lord Shrewsbury died at his manor of Wingfield, in
Derbyshire, on the 20th of July 1541. He married
a daughter of George, Lord Hastings, and was succeeded by his son Francis, fifth Earl of Shrewsbury,
who was summoned to the Upper House in his father's
lifetime, and in the year of his father's death exchanged
with the King the manor of Farnham-Royal, in Buckinghamshire, for the inheritance of the site of the
priory of Worksop, in Nottinghamshire, with divers
other lands. Earl Francis had a share in Henry
VIII.'s expedition to Scotland, when every place was
desolated with fire and sword, and was appointed Lieutenant of the counties of York, Lancaster, Chester,
Derby, Stafford, Salop, and Nottingham, and Justice of
the Forests North of the Trent. In the second year
of Edward VI. he was sent again into Scotland, with
15,000 men, against the French. On the accession of
Mary he was made President of the Council of the
North. Earl Francis devoted his life almost entirely
to military services, and did not take any strong part
in the religious politics of the time. He was, however,
a firm though moderate Catholic. He was appointed
by Elizabeth, on her accession, one of her Privy Council, but was the only lay peer, except Browne, Lord
Montague, who had the courage and principle to oppose, in his place in Parliament, all the measures which
undid the work of Mary, and re-established Protestantism as the religion of the State. He died a few
months afterwards, September 21, 1560, at the age
of sixty.

His only surviving son, George, who then became

sixth Earl of Shrewsbury, was sent by his father, in October 1557, to the relief of the Earl of Northumberland, then pent up at Alnwick Castle by the Scots, and remained in service on the Borders for some months after. On the 24th April 1560, Elizabeth gave him the Garter, and in the summer of 1565 appointed him Lord-Lieutenant of the counties of York, Nottingham, and Derby. He was High Steward at the arraignment of the Duke of Norfolk, and succeeded him as Earl Marshal. In January 1569, the Queen of Scots was committed to his custody. From this period, for the next fifteen years of his life, the Earl was entirely absorbed in the guardianship of his dangerous prisoner. " In perpetual danger," says Lodge, in his introduction to the Earl's correspondence, "from the suspicions of one Princess and the hatred of another ; vexed by the jealousy and rapacity of an unreasonable wife, and by the excesses and quarrels of his sons, from whom he was obliged to withdraw that authoritative attention the whole of which was required by his charge, we shall view this nobleman, through the long space of fifteen years, relinquishing the splendour of public situation and those blandishments of domestic life which his exalted rank and vast wealth might have commanded." Such sacrifices did Elizabeth demand from her great subjects. How far the Earl really remained faithful in his allegiance to her under the assiduous wiles of Mary is still, perhaps, an undetermined point in history. Elizabeth, however, kept a keen eye on him, and on the whole found no safer or more trustworthy agent in securing this to her all-important end. The Earl was twice married—first to a daughter of Thomas Manners, first Earl of Rutland ;

and next, as we have already had occasion to notice, to
the widow of Sir William Cavendish, Elizabeth Hardwick,* and died November 18, 1590. Of his eldest
surviving son and successor, Gilbert, seventh Earl of
Shrewsbury, Lodge says he "came into public life
when the English nation was rapidly emerging from
that simplicity of manners to which it had so long
been confined by bigotry and war. We shall accordingly observe in his character certain amiable features
and certain faults which were equally unknown to his
ancestors. We shall find him the accomplished courtier and well-educated gentleman, occasionally relaps-
ing into the pomp and the ferocity of an ancient
baron. The story of his public life lies within a
narrow compass, for he was never called to any high
office of the State, though apparently better qualified
than any of his predecessors of whom we have been
treating. His case, in this respect, was peculiarly hard;
for though it should seem that Elizabeth passed him
over upon some suspicion of his disaffection to her,
yet in the next reign he appears to have been thrust
aside as one of the old followers of her Court." He
was summoned to Parliament as a baron a few weeks
before his father's death, and installed a Knight of
the Garter on the 20th of June 1592; in 1596 went
ambassador to France to ratify the treaty of alliance
with Henry the Great; and was appointed by James
at his accession Chief Justice of the Forests North of
Trent. His wife, Mary Cavendish (daughter of his

---

* Lodge, who has drawn a very unfavourable picture of this lady,
says of her: "She was a builder; a buyer and seller of estates; a
money-lender, a farmer, and merchant of lead, coals, and timber. When
disengaged from these employments, she intrigued alternately with
Elizabeth and Mary, always to the prejudice and terror of her husband."

step-mother), who seems to have much resembled her mother in character, was imprisoned in 1611 for two years as an accomplice in the flight of Lady Arabella Stuart. The Earl died at his house in Broad Street, London, May 8, 1616, and was succeeded by Edward Talbot, his only surviving brother, the eighth Earl of Shrewsbury, who had been on very bad terms with the last Earl, the latter not showing to advantage in the letters which passed between them. He only survived till the 8th of February 1618, and dying without issue, the Earldom devolved on the descendant of Sir Gilbert Talbot, third son of John, second Earl of Shrewsbury. The direct line had ended, but the estates and titles still reverted to a descendant of John the Warrior, the type man of the Talbots, whose function on earth, from William Rufus to William III., was always that of soldiers. The break, therefore, made no change either in the antiquity of the pedigree or the connection of the title with the hero who acquired it.

The recurrence to the old stock, however, did not alter the standard of the family, who, while they have never been quite unequal to their position, have produced a great man only at long intervals. The new stem, GILBERT, third grandson of the hero, had not been undistinguished under Henry VII., and had acquired the manors of Grafton, and Upton Warren, in Worcestershire, with interests in Hambury, Bromsgrove, King's-Norton, Kidderminster, Kenswick, and Estbury, forfeited by the attainder of Humphrey Stafford. His descendant, however, George, the ninth Earl, was an undistinguished man, as was his nephew John, the tenth Earl (1630), though he fought on the

royal side in the Civil War, and was besieged in
Alton, which was at the same time laid in ruins. He
died February 8, 1653, and (his eldest son, George,
the friend of the poet Habington, having died before
him) was succeeded by his second son, Francis, eleventh
Earl, best known as the husband of Anna Maria,
second daughter of the Earl of Cardigan, the "wan-
ton Shrewsbury" of Pope, who stood by Buckingham's
horse, disguised as a page, while the profligate peer
killed her husband in a duel, May 16, 1667, and
clasped her lover while her husband's blood left marks
on her dress.* CHARLES TALBOT, his son, the twelfth
Earl, was a man of more mark, though his character
still remains a puzzle to posterity—a man whose life
leaves on the mind an impression of intrinsic honesty
of purpose, and yet who acted the part of a dishonourable traitor. He was born July 24, 1660, and as
his parents were both rigidly Catholic in their views,
he was brought up strictly in those religious principles. "His person," says Macaulay, "was pleasing, his
temper singularly sweet, his parts such as, if he had
been born in a humble rank, might well have raised
him to the height of civil greatness ; all these advantages he had so improved, that before he was of age
he was allowed to be one of the finest gentlemen and
finest scholars of his time. His learning is proved by
notes, which are still extant in his handwriting, on
books in almost every department of literature. He
spoke French like a gentleman of Louis's bedchamber,
and Italian like a citizen of Florence." Having made

* Her second son, John Talbot, was also killed in a duel by Henry,
first Duke of Grafton, February 2, 1686, within a few days of his attaining the age of twenty-one.

the acquaintance of Tillotson, he resolved to fathom
the depths of the great controversy between Catholicism and Protestantism. He procured, through
his grandfather, the Earl of Cardigan, the most approved arguments of the Roman Catholic priests, and,
communicating them to Tillotson, received his answers
and transmitted them to his grandfather. This process continued for two years, and then Shrewsbury
declared himself a convert to Protestantism. His first
attendance on the worship of the Established Church
was at Lincoln's Inn Chapel, May 4, 1679. His
morals, however, partook of the libertinism of that
age, and his character generally was unsteady and im-
pulsive, though governed in the main by generous
instincts. He was early called the King of Hearts,
and his career is only explicable by some such reference to the heart rather than to the head. He had
carried the pointless sword at the coronation of James
II., held the command of the 6th Regiment of horse,
and was Lord-Lieutenant of Staffordshire, but, opposing the Court, he entered into communication with
the Prince of Orange, and as early as May 1687 offered him his services. He is even said to have mort-
gaged his estate for £40,000 to raise money for the
English expedition, the greatest direct service rendered
to the Revolution by any English peer. Certain it is
that on Russell sounding him as to his willingness to
take part in Orange's design, he at once frankly threw
himself into the affair, and agreed to stake everything
on the issue. In June 1688 he was one of the seven
who signed the "Association" inviting the Prince over,
and co-operated heartily in the Revolution which followed. He was one of those selected by William to

treat with James about removing from Whitehall, and accompanied the fallen King to the stairs on his embarkation, endeavouring to the best of his power to assuage the bitterness of the moment. On the accession of William he was appointed one of the Secretaries of State, at an earlier age than had been known in the case of any preceding Secretary. The Administration, however, was soon distracted by the bitter quarrels of the two Secretaries, Nottingham, the other, being at the head of the Tory interest, and denouncing every nominee of his rival's as a Roundhead and Republican, while Shrewsbury retaliated with the charge of Jacobitism. Shrewsbury, indeed, with all his talents, proved himself wholly unfitted for such an arduous post at such a difficult crisis. His nerves and his health alike gave way before the cares and anxieties of office. He was irritated with Nottingham and the Protestant Tories for endeavouring to secure a hold on the King's favour; he was irritated at William for lending an ear to them, and at his own party, the Whigs, for urging him on to press the King unfairly on his personal predilections. His religious belief had never recovered the terrible ordeal to a really earnest mind of a conversion from his inherited faith, and he had lost with the change that purity of principle which might have supported him in his present trying position. "For his own happiness," Macaulay observes, with great truth, " he should either have been much better or much worse. As it was, he never knew either that noble peace of mind which is the reward of rectitude, or that abject peace of mind which springs from impudence and insensibility. Few people who have had so little power to resist temptation have suffered so cruelly from remorse and shame." Before Shrewsbury had been six months in office he began to address to William letters full of earnest entreaties to be allowed to retire from office, and expressing in unmistakable terms the complete prostration of his mind and body. The letters, in fact, were those of a man stricken with nervous fever ; but William, who believed the Earl to be true, remonstrated against his resignation, and heaped new marks of favour on his head, only to have the seals of office conveyed again and again to himself, and to hear that Burnet had with difficulty restrained the Earl from an audience which would have ended in a personal altercation. Had he known the truth he would have been far more irritated than he at length became. The Earl's secret motive for his incessant repudiation of office was the command of James. Worked upon by his mother, an ardent Jacobite, Shrewsbury had opened communications with St Germains, and had been restored to favour with James, who, however, commanded him, as a test of sincerity, to resign the seals. The moment the arrangement was complete, Shrewsbury repented; and indecision, repentance, and the sense of a double treachery intensified the agitation of his nerves, and at last, obtaining his dismissal in June 1690, he shut himself up in misery at Epsom, to recover, with his health, his tone of moral character. The war with France awoke him. " The thought that by standing foremost in the defence of his country at so perilous a crisis he might repair his great fault, and regain his own esteem, gave new energy to his body and his mind. In a few hours he was at Whitehall, and had offered his purse and sword to the Queen," who was at the head of the Government in the absence of William. There had been some idea of placing a nobleman of high rank nominally at the head of the fleet, and Shrewsbury begged for the post ; but the fear of divided counsels prevailed, and the offer was declined. The danger passed, and the next prominent appearance of Shrewsbury was as the proposer in the House of Lords of the Triennial Bill, a measure most distasteful to King William. That king, however, still retained a greater feeling of personal liking for him than for any other of the great Whig lords, and at the close of 1693, on Nottingham's resignation of the seals, he made a great effort, through his mistress, Elizabeth Villiers, backed by Wharton and Russell, to induce the Earl to accept office again. Shrewsbury, however, declined on all sorts of pleas, the real cause, of course, being his entanglement with the Court of St Germains, and his aversion to the example of those statesmen who did not scruple at the same time to correspond with James and hold office under William. From November to March Shrewsbury stood firm in his refusal. Then his course was changed by a curious incident. Sir James Montgomery, who, from the representative of the Scotch nation in their offer of the crown to William had sunk to a disreputable and starving agent of the Jacobites, called on Shrewsbury and entered on a treasonable conversation with him. Shrewsbury, distrusting him, returned only cautious answers. Through some means the whole conversation reached the ears of William. He sent for Shrewsbury, and when he reiterated his excuses for not accepting the seals, observed, "There is another reason behind ; when did you see Montgo-

mery last?" Shrewsbury, remembering his cautious
answers, claimed the merit of having refused the offers
of the agent. The King, dwelling on the danger and
scandal of such communications with Jacobites, said
that the only way in which Shrewsbury could clear
his reputation with the nation and himself was to
accept the seals at once. "That," he said, "will put
me quite at ease. I know that you are a man of honour, and that, if you undertake to serve me, you will
serve me faithfully." Shrewsbury, seeing no alterna-
tive, accepted office March 4, 1694, and was rewarded
by being made a Knight of the Garter on the 25th of
April, and on the 30th was raised to the dignities of
Marquess of Alton and Duke of Shrewsbury.

The Duke continued to take a leading part in the
Government till the arrest of Sir John Fenwick, and
his confessions compromised him, along with Marlborough and several others in the King's employment.
Shrewsbury, in a state of great excitement, wrote to
the King, declaring, with a want of ingenuousness, that
his connection with Lord Middleton had resulted from
their relationship, and had not extended to any actual
offer of his services to James. William affected to
believe this. "Be assured," he wrote, "that these cal-
umnies have made no unfavourable impression on me.
Nay, you shall find that they have strengthened my
confidence in you." Shrewsbury was so overpowered
at this unmerited trust that he shrank from a personal
interview with the King on his return from the Continent, and hastened to the seclusion of a remote seat
of his, in the wolds of Gloucestershire, and availing
himself of the plea of a fall from his horse, declined
to come up to town or to face the Parliament. He

also again offered his resignation of the seals. But the King and all his friends so remonstrated that he gave way. A wretched Jacobite spy accused him of having been acquainted with the assassination plot, and not warning the King, but William declared he could himself prove the Duke's innocence, and Shrewsbury was again acquitted. But he never regained his peace of mind, though at this time apparently at the height of earthly prosperity. He continued to hold the seals of Secretary till May 14, 1699, though in a continual state of indecision and perplexity between the King, the Whig party, and the consciousness of his secret intrigue with St Germains. He acted frequently as a mediator between the King and the Whigs, and between the Whigs and the Earl of Sunderland, but with little success, being too easily moved himself. He was constantly importuning the King for permission to resign, and at last, in 1700, departed for Rome, where he married an Italian lady of high birth, and remained till the reign of Anne. On his return, in 1708, he was treated by his friends as a lukewarm supporter, and was persuaded by Harley and the Tories into the great attack on Marlborough and Godolphin. In 1713 he was sent to Ireland as Lord-Lieutenant, where, as one might have expected, with the best intentions he succeeded in raising the distrust of all parties, who united for once—Tories, Whigs, and Jacobites—in a chorus of satire on his government and person. On his return from Ireland he found the Tory Ministry in a state of decomposition, Harley and Bolingbroke contending for the mastery; and on Harley's discomfiture and resignation of the office of Lord High Treasurer, the Staff was

bestowed on Shrewsbury, who held both that office
and his Lord-Lieutenancy of Ireland at the death of
Queen Anne. At that crisis, for the last time, his
better spirit awoke, and, entering the Council Chamber
unsummoned, and followed by the other Whig peers
whose names remained on the list of the Privy Council,
the Duke carried into effect, with an energy which
completely discomfited the Jacobites, the plans which
placed the house of Hanover on the throne. He was
essentially a man who required great crises such as
these, and great pressing excitement, to call forth his
resolution, and enable him to do justice to his own
principles. On the accession of George I. he filled
several honorary offices; but his political career was
really at an end, and he doubtless felt the release from
necessary action as agreeable as it was, perhaps, salutary for his remaining reputation. He had purchased
an estate in Oxfordshire, near Woodstock, called Hey-
thorpe, Alton being still in a dilapidated condition.
Here, and at a house at Isleworth, he passed the
remainder of his life, being carried off by a fever
on the 1st February 1718. He was a man of a class
which only those who belong to it will ever understand—a man in whom high principle and great ability
were neutralised by a physical condition which, except
when overcome by a great crisis, rendered his powers
valueless. In a great crisis he was as effective and
decided as his ancestors; in little emergencies, irreso-
lute as a woman. As he left no children the Dukedom and Marquessate became extinct, but the Earldom
of Shrewsbury devolved on Gilbert, eldest surviving
son of Gilbert Talbot, fourth son of John, tenth Earl,
who succeeded as thirteenth Earl, but being in holy

orders of the Church of Rome died without issue in 1743.

It was probably with a view to his succession that the Duke obtained the Family Act, which entailed his estates for ever, so long as they should be in possession of a Catholic. The priest—the only one, we believe, who, since Queen Mary's death, has been a peer of the realm—was succeeded by his nephew George, fourteenth Earl;* he by his nephew Charles, fifteenth Earl (1787), and he again (April 6, 1827) by his nephew John, sixteenth Earl, who died November 9, 1852, having taken an active though moderate part in Catholic emancipation. Leaving only daughters, the title devolved on his cousin Bertram-Arthur, the seventeenth Earl (grandson of Francis Talbot, uncle of Charles, fifteenth Earl), a fanatic Catholic, who made a desperate attempt to upset the Duke's Family Act by bequeathing the Shrewsbury property to the Howards, his advisers telling him that as his Will only became operative after his death, the title had ceased to be held by a Catholic and the entail to exist. The Courts decided, however, that the Will was the act of a living man, and title and estates must therefore go together.

To find their possessor it is necessary to re-ascend the stream. Sir Gilbert Talbot, of Grafton, Worcestershire (third son of John, second Earl of Shrewsbury), who led the forces of his nephew the young Earl at the battle of Bosworth, had a son, Sir John

---

* We follow Sir Harris Nicolas, Burke, &c. A different succession is given in Collins's 'Peerage' (by Brydges)—viz., fourteenth Earl, George, *brother* of the thirteenth Earl (died December 12, 1733); fifteenth Earl, George, *son* of the fourteenth Earl (died July 1787); sixteenth Earl, Charles, nephew of fifteenth Earl.

Talbot of Albrighton, Shropshire, who is the common ancestor of the late and present Earls of Shrewsbury, his elder son (by his first marriage), Sir John Talbot of Grafton, being the ancestor of the line which has become lately extinct, and his younger son (by a second marriage), John Talbot of Salwarp, in Worcestershire, being the ancestor of Charles Lord Talbot, who founded the family which has now succeeded to the Shrewsbury title and estate. The father of CHARLES TALBOT, William Talbot, was the only son of William Talbot of Stourton Castle, Staffordshire, third son of Sherrington Talbot of Salwarp and Laycock, Worcestershire, eldest son of John Talbot of Salwarp. William Talbot went into the Church, and became successively Dean of Worcester, and Bishop of Oxford, Salisbury, and Durham. He died October 10, 1730, having been a stanch Whig, of considerable eloquence and ability, leaving a large family, the eldest of whom entered Oxford, was called to the Bar, and rose on the 29th of November 1733 to the Lord Chancellorship. He was then created Baron Talbot of Hensol, in Glamorganshire, an estate he had acquired with his wife, a daughter of Charles Mathews, Esq., of Castle-y-Menich, in that county. "As an equity judge," says Lord Campbell, "Lord Talbot exceeded all the high expectations which had been formed of him. In my long journey from the reign of Ethelred to that of George IV., I find this Chancellor alone without an accuser, without an enemy, without a detractor, without any one from malice or mistake to cavil at any part of his character, conduct, or demeanour. While in no respect deficient in judicial gravity and dignity, the flowing courtesy of his manners seems

to have won all hearts." " He was energetic and inde-
fatigable in business, punctual in his hours of sitting."
In the political arena Lord Talbot had little to bring
his talents into prominent play, the chief debates being
on foreign affairs. Still he showed his independence
by opposing his own Cabinet, along with his friend
Hardwicke, on the provisions of their "Smuggling
Bill," the enactments of which he considered dangerous to the liberty of the subject. While in the apparent enjoyment of perfect health, and with the prospect
of a long and brilliant career before him, Charles
Talbot was suddenly seized by a spasm in the heart,
which, from the first, was pronounced to be fatal, and
after a brief interval he expired on the 14th February
1737, in the fifty-third year of his age. His eldest
son, a youth of great promise, died before him, and
William, his next son, succeeded as second Lord Talbot. He seems to have been a man of some energy of
character, and in 1761 was raised to the Earldom of
Talbot, and in 1780 was made Baron Dynevor, with
special remainder in the latter peerage to his daughter,
who married into the family of Rice, who now, as
Lords Dynevor, represent the heirs-general of the
Chancellor Talbot. As Earl Talbot left no son, on his
death in 1782 the Earldom became extinct, and the
barony of Talbot devolved on his nephew, John Talbot,
who, in 1784, was created Earl Talbot of Hensol, and
Viscount Ingestre of Ingestre, in Staffordshire. He
assumed by royal licence, in 1786, the name of Chetwynd, in addition to that of Talbot, from his mother,
daughter of Viscount Chetwynd of Ireland. He died
in 1703, and was succeeded in the Earldom by his
son, Charles Chetwynd-Talbot, the father of the present

Earl, Henry John Chetwynd-Talbot, who became fifth Earl Talbot in 1849, and in 1856, on the death of his kinsman, the seventeenth Earl of Shrewsbury, succeeded in establishing his right to the succession of that older peerage, becoming eighteenth Earl of Shrewsbury.

The great legal battle with the Howards ended, as we have said, in the decision that the Duke's Act was operative, and the eighteenth Earl, who, be it remembered, is the direct lineal descendant of the man recorded in 'Domesday Book,' and of the great John Talbot of Shakespeare, stands possessed of all the properties of his house. He was in the navy, but has been known chiefly as a very decided Tory, and as Lord Ingestre was somewhat prominent in debates on naval affairs in the House of Commons. His son, Lord Ingestre, a moderate Conservative, is remarkable for his social leanings, and may yet take his place as one of the leaders in the next public crisis—the great fight with pauperism. As yet the Talbots, despite their splendid pedigree, their vast estates, and the two great men they have contributed to our annals, have not reached the historic eminence which belongs to most of their younger, but more efficient, rivals.*

* Richard Talbot, Earl and (titular) Duke of Tyrconnel, James II.'s favourite and Irish Deputy, the "lying Dick Talbot" of history, was the son of Sir William Talbot, of Carton, County Kildare, Baronet, nephew of William Talbot of Malahide, the ancestor of the present Lord Talbot of Malahide. This family trace their descent from Sir Richard Talbot, who, during the first settlement of the English in Ireland, received from Henry II. the barony of Malahide, which, they say, has continued for upwards of 650 years in his heirs male. They also say that this Sir Richard was descended from Richard Talbot of 'Domesday Book,' the ancestor of the Shrewsbury family ; but *how* they do not state. Possibly he was a son of another son of the Domesday Richard Talbot, and nephew, therefore, of Hugh Talbot, the son from whom the Shrewsbury Talbots descend.

The Leveson=Gowers.

HE Leveson-Gowers are the luckiest of the great English families. They have risen within two hundred and fifty years from simple country baronets into the greatest, though not the richest, territorialists in Great Britain, and their connection is at this moment perhaps the most powerful of the English political clans. They have been people of some mark and capacity in themselves, but the source of their dignity has been a succession of lucky alliances, they being, though Gowers in lineal male descent, Levesons and Sutherlands by the female side. The pedigree, though curiously uncertain, is by no means a bad one as English nobles go. SIR THOMAS GOWER, one of James I.'s baronets, was of Stittenham, in Yorkshire, and there certainly was a William Fitz-guhyer who held Stittenham in the time of Henry II., 1167. From that time Gowers owners of Sittenham are always turning up in more or less conspicuous positions, one having been Receiver-General of Berwick and Governor of Wark in 1543, and mentioned by Holinshed as a man of "too much forwardness" in battle. There was a Gower who stood by the Earl of Lancaster at the execution of Piers Gaveston, and

a Gower appears to have fought well in the battle of
Neville's Cross.　Another was one of the "forty-three
powerful persons" in Yorkshire who, in the 25th of
Henry VI., returned James Pickering and William
Normanville as Knights to serve in Parliament, and
was beheaded after the battle of Tewkesbury.　As
these Gowers dwelt at or owned Stittenham, or adjacent properties, and kept up the same family names,
there is little reasonable doubt that they were all of
one stock,—that, in fact, a Norman named Guhyer
obtained that manor and much land shortly after the
Conquest, and that his descendants maintained themselves as great squires and good soldiers until the first
English Stuart.　Then, as we have seen, they obtained
by favour and purchase a baronetcy.　Sir Thomas
Gower, first Baronet, commenced the series of alliances.　He married the daughter and coheir of John
Doyley, of Merton, Oxfordshire, and his son, the
second Baronet, was important enough to be twice
High Sheriff of Yorkshire, and one of the leading
partisans of Charles I.　He attended the King in his
unsuccessful attack on Hull, and raised an entire
regiment of dragoons at his own charge.　He married
first a daughter of Sir William Howard, of Naworth
Castle (ancestor of the Carlisle Howards), and then
Frances, one of the two daughters of Sir John Leveson, of Halling, in Kent, and Lillieshall, in Shropshire.　Edward, his eldest son by this lady, died before his father, leaving, however, a son Thomas, who
succeeded as third Baronet, and who died in the
King's camp at Dundalk, in Ireland, in 1689.　The
estates and baronetcy then devolved on his uncle, Sir
William, the fourth Baronet, who was adopted as heir

by his mother's uncle, Sir Richard Leveson, of TRENT-
HAM, in Staffordshire, since one of the principal seats
of the family. This Sir Richard Leveson was the
heir of a family which ranked in the reign of Edward
I. among the landed gentry of Staffordshire, and had
himself married Lady Catherine Dudley, daughter of
Alice, Duchess Dudley, the widow of Leicester's natural son, Sir Robert Dudley—a dukedom originally
German, and bestowed by the Emperor Ferdinand, but
in the person of Duchess Alice an English creation
for life—and with this lady received Trentham. The
adopted son received all and took the name of Leveson-Gower, which the family has retained. He was
one of the Duke of Monmouth's bail in 1683, sat
during his life for Newcastle-under-Lyne, and married
Jane, eldest daughter of John Granville, Earl of Bath.
This marriage did not at first appear a great one; but
the luck of the Gowers is a quality rather than an
accident, and the lady became coheir to her nephew,
William Henry, last Earl of Bath, of that family.
His son by this lady, Sir John Leveson-Gower, fifth
Baronet, sat for Newcastle-under-Lyne till, in 1703,
he was, after impeaching the Earl of Portland at the
bar of the House of Commons, raised to the peerage
by Queen Anne as Baron Gower of Stittenham, Yorkshire. Burnet says the motive of the creation was to
gain votes in the Upper House, where the most important measures were sometimes carried by only one
or two voices. The baronies of Finch, Granville, and
Germaine, were created at the same time and with
the same motive. Lord Gower was one of the Commissioners who concluded the union between England
and Scotland, and died in 1709. He married a

daughter of the Duke of Rutland with a portion of £15,000, and was succeeded by his son John, second Lord Gower.

This man was considered in his own time a turn-coat—so great a turncoat that Johnson said to Boswell, "When I came to the word 'renegado,' after telling that it meant one who deserts to the enemy, a revolter, I added, Sometimes we say 'a Gower.' Thus it went to the press, but the printer had more wit than I, and struck it out." The man, however, who thus escaped an unenviable immortality seems to have been merely one of those persons who, acquiring radically new convictions, are hampered for years by the ties created under the old. He was brought up a strong Jacobite, and was elected in 1742 President of the "Board," or Jacobite meeting, in the room of the Earl of Lichfield; but in the same year the Government appointed him Lord-Lieutenant of Stafford and Lord Privy Seal. It is said he held his Jacobite office still while serving in the Hanoverian Cabinet. He seems to have passed completely under the sway of John, the fourth Duke of Bedford, who, in 1737, had married his daughter Gertrude. On the breaking out of the rebellion of 1745, he raised a regiment of foot for King George, and, as a reward, was on the 8th July 1746 created Viscount Trentham and Earl Gower.

In 1750 his eldest son, Granville, Lord Trentham, stood a severe contested election for the city of Westminster, which attracted a curious amount of attention, and ended in establishing Lord Trentham's reputation as a competent and spirited speaker. In June 1751, a division of opinion took place between Lord

Gower and the Russells—who carried his sons with them. Lord Sandwich had procured the marriage of another of Gower's daughters, Lady Elizabeth Leveson-Gower, with Colonel Waldegrave, against the will of her father, even allowing the ceremony to be performed at his apartments in the Admiralty. The Pelhams, desirous of drawing off Gower from Bedford, who was a sworn friend to Sandwich, persuaded the Earl to complain of Sandwich to the King. The King took Gower's view, and Sandwich had notice of dismissal. Bedford hastened to persuade his father-in-law to resign along with him, and Lord Trentham accompanied him. "They found Lord Gower in no humour to resign; on the contrary, enraged at his son, who told him he could not serve under Lord Anson, the new head of the Admiralty. 'Sir,' said his father, 'he is your superior, he is a peer.' 'Who made him so?' replied Lord Trentham. Lord Gower told the Duke of Bedford that he had listed all his children against him; and threatened Lord Trentham to disinherit him of all that was in his power; who told him, in pretty plain terms, how much he was a dupe to the Pelhams, and, after many high words, they both left him." It ended in Lord Gower sticking to the Pelhams, and his sons going into opposition along with Bedford. Earl Gower was thrice married, his first wife, and the mother of his successor, being a daughter of Evelyn Pierrepont, Duke of Kingston. He continued to hold the office of Privy Seal till his death, December 25, 1754. Granville, the second Earl Gower, married, as his second wife, Lady Louisa Egerton, daughter of Scroop, first Duke of Bridgewater, great-grandson of Frances Stanley, a descend-

ant of Brandon, Duke of Suffolk, and Princess Mary
Tudor. This marriage entitles the Gowers to quarter
the royal arms, and brought eventually a large slice
out of the great Bridgewater property. In December
1755, the first Fox persuaded the Duke of Bedford to
ask for the office of Lord Privy Seal for Earl Gower;
"a great promotion," says Walpole, "for so young a
man." In January following there was a rumour of
coming invasion, and Lord Gower proposed that the
great lords should go to their counties and raise re-
cruits for the army—a plan which was adopted, and
succeeded, he himself raising 400 men. He continued
to act with the Bedford party, holding various offices
in the household until 1767, when he became President of the Council, and continued so under Lord
North, until in November 1779, disapproving of the
continued war with the Colonies, he resigned. "I
feel," said Lord Gower, "the greatest gratitude for the
many marks of royal goodness which I have received,
but I cannot think it the duty of a grateful servant
to endeavour to preserve a system which must end in
ruin to his Majesty and the country." His secession
was felt as a severe loss by the Government. Lord
North, writing to the King, says he had made every
attempt to retain him. But North himself adds in
the letter, "In the argument Lord North had certainly
one disadvantage, which is, that he holds in his
heart, and has held for three years past, the same
opinions with Lord Gower." Lord Gower remained
out of office till December 1783. On the resignation of North in 1782, the King, to avoid Rockingham, if possible, had solicited Lord Gower to
form a new Cabinet; but he declined. He was

again solicited by the King, in the spring of 1783, and again declined. But when William Pitt accepted the office of First Lord of the Treasury and Chancellor of the Exchequer, though not on any terms of political connection or intercourse with him, Lord Gower "sent through a friend a message to him. He stated that, desirous as he was of retirement for the remainder of his life, he could not be deemed a candidate for office ; but that in the present distressed state of his King and country he was willing to serve in any place where he could be useful. The offer was eagerly accepted, and on that same day, the 20th of December, Earl Gower was declared Lord President of the Council." In November of the following year he became Lord Privy Seal, and held this office till 1794. On February 28, 1786, he was raised, on the recommendation of Pitt, to the title of Marquess of the county of Stafford. He died October 26, 1803.

The family had now risen by four successive alliances to a Marquessate and a great territorial position; but George Granville, the second Marquess, succeeded in eclipsing the fortune of all his ancestors. On the 4th of September 1785, he married Elizabeth, Countess of Sutherland and Baroness of Strathmaver, in Scotland, only surviving daughter and heiress of William, seventeenth Earl of Sutherland, the oldest Earl of Great Britain, and lord of one-half of Sutherlandshire. She had been left an orphan by her father's and mother's early death when she was only a year old, the mother being worn out by twenty-one days of unbroken attendance on her husband. Her title was disputed by Sir Robert Gordon, Bart., of Gordontown, and George Sutherland, of Forse; but after various proceedings the

House of Lords, on March 21st, 1771, decided that the Earldom of Sutherland descended to her as lineal descendant of William, who was Earl of Sutherland in 1275. "The Countess's right," says Douglas, "was thus established to the most ancient title existing in Britain—a decision productive of the highest national satisfaction, the illustrious orphan having excited feelings of very lively interest, and public rejoicings took place in different parts of Scotland in consequence." The rejoicings might not have been so warm had it been known that the new English family were about to carry out steadily a system of clearing their Highland estates. These were almost completely ruined by the presence of great bodies of clansmen—men who would neither work, nor depart, nor let rentals rise. The new family, convinced that mercy had become cruelty, commenced and steadily carried through a process of eviction which was soon after extended to the rest of Sutherlandshire, purchased of Lord Reay, the head of the Mackays. The eviction, though causing great hardship to individuals, was kindly done, the old tenantry received grants in Canada, and Sutherlandshire, rescued from profitless tillage, was devoted to sheep-farming. The result, as shown in some recent reports, has been an increase of *population*, as well as rental and wealth, and the country has no ground of complaint. Whether the clansmen were not in some sense *owners* of the soil, tenants in common with their chief, is a moot question which the Courts decided one way and popular opinion another. The luck of the Gowers did not end here. Besides this immense accession of territory, the death of Francis, Duke of Bridgewater, in January

1803, brought a second. The great landed estates of that house in Lancashire, Shropshire, and Staffordshire, with the whole of the canal property, descended to the Marquess, and thence to his younger son, Lord Francis Leveson-Gower, who took the name of Egerton, and in 1846 was created Earl of Ellesmere. The second Marquess of Stafford continued to act with Pitt till the death of the latter, his motion in the House of Lords in 1804 precipitating the fall of the Addington Ministry. He afterwards attached himself to the fortunes of Lord Grenville, and made a motion on the fall of the Grenville Ministry stigmatising the pledges exacted by the King on the Catholic question as unconstitutional. From this time the Marquess gradually moved on to the Liberal party, and after the Reform crisis, on the 14th January 1833, was created Duke of Sutherland. He died in July following, and was succeeded by his eldest son, George Granville, second Duke, a man of consistent Whig politics, but owing to ill-health of very retired habits. He married, in 1823, Harriett Elizabeth Georgina, third daughter of George Howard, sixth Earl of Carlisle, who is still alive, and during her husband's life swayed the great power of the house—a power increased by her personal position as Mistress of the Robes. A large family of children were singularly fortunate in alliances, and the third and present Duke, George Granville William, who succeeded in February 1861, stands at the head of a family group which includes the Duke of Argyll, the future Duke of Leinster, the future Marquess of Westminster, the Earl of Ellesmere, and Earl Granville. The last is the son of Lord Granville Leveson-Gower, younger

son of the first Marquess of Stafford, who, in the
year 1815, was created Viscount Leveson for diplomatic services, and raised in May 1833 to an Earldom as Earl Granville, the family name of the old
Earls of Bath, whose property, with that of so many
other old families, now swells the great stream of the
luck of the Gowers. One more favour was still required to raise the stream to its bank, and this, too,
was accorded. The present Duke has been distinguished only for his interest in suppressing fires—a
useful but eccentric taste—and more recently as the
generous host of General Garibaldi during his visit to
London. But he married, in June 1849, Anne, heiress
of John Mackenzie, Esq., of Newhall and Cromartie,
and in October 1861 she was created Countess of
Cromartie, Viscountess Tarbat, and Baroness Macleod
and Castlehaven, with remainder to her second son,
Francis, by courtesy Viscount Tarbat. In less than
three hundred years the descendants of Sir Thomas
Gower, Bart., of Stittenham, will be in possession of
eight peerages—Sutherland, Argyll, Leinster, Westminster, Ellesmere, Granville, Cromartie, and Blan-
tyre—and an aggregate of influence scattered over the
three kingdoms such as no other cousinhood in the
land possesses. The direct descendants have been as
a race respectable and even useful; but their fortunes
have been beyond their deserts, and we must end as
we began, by pronouncing the Gowers the luckiest
among the great English houses.

The Pagets.

HE history of the Pagets, a family of successful men of the world, is a composite one. Strictly speaking they are not Pagets at all. They are BAYLEYS, a Scotch family with an Irish baronetcy, who settled in Wales, and married the heiress of the English Pagets. Being Scotch, the Bayleys have, of course, a pedigree, but the original Pagets have in the heraldic sense none, and with unusual modesty do not through the Peerages claim one. WILLIAM PAGET, the founder of the house, and beyond all dispute the ablest man it has ever produced, was the son of William Paget, a native of Wednesbury in Staffordshire, who, in the time of Henry VII., came up to London and became one of the "Sergeants at Mace" of the City. From the proceeds of this office, whatever they may have been, he managed to give his son William a good education under the famous Lilly, in St Paul's School, and afterwards to send him to Trinity Hall, Cambridge. From the University young Paget obtained admission into the family of Stephen Gardiner, the celebrated Bishop of Winchester, and attracted the attention of Henry VIII. by his remarkable capacity

for affairs. The King selected him in the twenty-first
year of his reign to proceed to France, and obtain from
the learned men of that kingdom an opinion in favour
of the divorce. He succeeded so well that Henry
thenceforward gave him his entire confidence, and his
rise was beyond all precedent rapid, the Tudors, with
their instinct of kingcraft, always preferring the men
whom *they* had built. Two years afterwards he obtained the custody of the castle of Maxstoke, in Warwickshire, during the minority of Peter Compton, Esq.,
and in the same year was made one of the Clerks of
the Signet. In 1537 he was sent (in disguise) on a
secret mission to Germany, to prevent the Protestant
German Princes from coming to a separate agreement
with the Emperor, and to persuade them to refer their
differences to Henry and the King of France. Here,
again, he gave such satisfaction, that in the 32d of
Henry he was made Clerk of the Privy Council,
one of the Clerks of the Signet *for life*, Clerk of the
Privy Seal, and soon after Clerk of the Parliament
for life. In the year following he was made Clerk of
the Privy Council *for life*, and sent ambassador to
France. Soon after he received the honour of knighthood, and on the 16th of January following the King
granted to him and his heirs the lordships of Bromley
and Hurst, in Staffordshire, and in the same year, 1543,
he was made one of the principal Secretaries of State.
In the following year he was joined in a commission
with the Chancellor Wriothesley and the Duke of
Suffolk to arrange the marriage between the Earl of
Lennox and the Lady Margaret Douglas, daughter of
Margaret Tudor and niece of the King, from which
marriage sprang the unfortunate Henry Lord Darnley.

T

In the following year Paget accompanied the King to the siege of Boulogne, and after its surrender had a grant (jointly with the diplomatist John Mason) of the office of Master of the Posts within or without the kingdom, and with the Earl of Hertford was commissioned to treat for a peace with France. In June following (1546) he, with Lord Lisle and Dr Wotton, concluded the peace. His own account to Henry of his management of this negotiation is characteristic, and probably tolerably correct. "Touching your Majesty, the Emperor, the French King, the Almayn, and every Prince's councillors, I have praised, dispraised, given hope, fear, mistrust, jealousy, suspicion respectively; I have lied, said truth, spoken fair, roughly, pleasantly, promised gifts, pensions, and done all that may be done or said for the advancement of this matter, and much more than I will abide, as Will Somers [the King's jester] saith, if I were asked the question. But all is in God's hands, and it is He that beyond all men's expectations directeth things at His pleasure to His glory." The year before he had been sent on a special mission to Brussels, as the man best able to cope with the Emperor Charles V., and if possible to fathom his intentions. "If ordinary inquiry was baffled," says Mr Froude, "Paget possessed an art of high-bred insolence which generally exasperated the best trained dissemblers into momentary openness. Charles knew him well;* and

* According to one account the Emperor said of Paget, "He deserved to *be* a king, as well as to represent one." And again, one day when Paget came to Court, "Yonder is the man I can deny nothing to;" and the Emperor is said to have once observed that three sorts of ambassadors were sent him from England : "The first was Wolsey, whose great train promised much, as his great design did nothing ; the second was Morisin, who promised and did much; the third Paget, who promised nothing and did all."

if he had chosen a Minister from the English Council whom he could have desired not to receive, it was Sir William Paget." Paget's favour with Henry continued unbroken till the latter's death. By letters-patent, dated October 26 (38 Henry VIII.), the King granted him the manors of Longdon, Heywood, and Barkeswiche parcel of the manor of Heywood, with their members and appurtenances situate and lying in Whittington, Fisherwick, Pype, Homerwiche, Wall, Morwhale, Strethay, and Brendwood, all in Staffordshire ; and in the following year (1547), 1st of Edward VI., the Bishop of Lichfield, to whom they had formerly belonged, confirmed the grants, and released all claim thereon. The manor of Longdon was of vast extent, above thirty other manors, townships, and villages, besides Cank, Heywood, and Rugeley, owing suit and service to the court-leet there. Longdon itself consisted of the manor of BEAUDESERT, with the appurtenances, including a mine of coal below the park, and of forty-eight messuages, with the appurtenances, and a mill called Longdon Mill. The King bequeathed Paget a legacy of £300, constituted him one of his executors, and appointed him one of the Council to the young Edward.

Paget had contracted a friendship with the Earl of Hertford, who, as Duke of Somerset, governed England during the first years of this reign, and he became at once one of the leading Councillors of England, had a seat in all the great " Commissions " appointed to carry out the Reformation, and was sent as ambassador to Charles V., receiving all the while ever increasing grants from the State. It has been estimated that he obtained at intervals £20,000 a-year from Church lands

—in those days a colossal fortune. "In 2d Edward VI., he obtained a grant of Exeter Place, without Temple Bar (formerly belonging to the bishop of that see), as also a certain parcel of ground lying within the garden of the Middle Temple, adjoining thereto. Which house he transformed into a new fabric for his own habitation, calling it Paget House." This is the Essex House of later years. When Somerset's power tottered, Paget urged him to energy with characteristic unscrupulousness. " The business," he wrote from Germany, " may, peradventure, at the worst, if resistance should be made, cost a thousand or two thousand men's lives. By St Mary, better so than mo ! And, therefore, Sir, go to it betimes. Send for all the Council that be remaining unsent abroad, and for because there are a good many of the best absent, call to your Grace to counsel for this matter six of the gravest and most experimentest men of the realm, and consider what is best to be done, and follow their advice. Send for your Almayn horsemen ; send for Lord Ferrys and Sir William Herbert to bring you as many horsemen of such as they dare trust out of Wales. Let the Earl of Shrewsbury bring the like out of Shropshire, Derbyshire, Nottinghamshire, Staffordshire, of his servants and keepers of forests and parks. Go yourself, accompanied with the said noblemen and their companies, and appoint the chief justices of England, three or four of them, to resort, with commission of Oyer and Terminer, to that good town which shall be next to the place where your Grace shall remain. Attach to the number of twenty or thirty of the rankest knaves of the shire. Let six be hanged of the ripest of them, the rest remain in prison. And thus, Sir, make a progress this hot

weather till you have perused all those shires that have
offended. Your Grace may say you shall lose the
hearts of the people ; of the good people you shall not,
of the ill it maketh no matter." Paget's advice, however, whether transmitted from abroad or delivered in
person after his return, was unable to nerve Somerset
to energy of action, or rather to keep his mind in a
balanced position between undue elation and despair.
Yet he adhered to him, along with Cranmer, till all
was lost, when he contrived to make tolerable terms
for the Duke, so as to break his fall, and himself was
treated with great consideration by the dominant
party. On the 3d of December 1550, he was summoned to the Upper House as Baron Paget, of Beaudesert, his principal seat in Staffordshire, holding at
the same time the offices of Controller of the Household and Chancellor of the Duchy of Lancaster. In the
early part of the following year he was appointed one
of the Commissioners to conclude a peace with France.
He disapproved, however, of much of the proceedings
of Warwick's government, and especially of the pressure put upon the Princess Mary in religious matters.
Paget, whose conscience was very easy and flexible on
such matters, was at heart, probably, a moderate Catholic, and his diplomatic associations induced him to lean
rather to the old Burgundian alliance (represented by the
Emperor and Spain) than to any new Protestant connections. Nor had he any sympathy with the enthusiasts
of Protestantism any more than with the Catholic fanatics. Somerset's later views were more in harmony
with this middle position, and Somerset beginning to
gather again his friends, Paget was induced to join in
an enterprise against Warwick, though too cautious to

commit himself to any great extent. When the plot exploded, Paget was sent to the Tower, but no complicity could be brought home to him ; yet, on the 22d of April 1552, he was deprived of the Order of the Garter, nominally for " defect of blood and arms for three generations," and was charged with selling the King's land and applying the proceeds to his own use. The same charge might have been brought against every rising man in that age of rapacious self-aggrandisement ; but the Star Chamber deprived him of his office and fined him £6000, reduced to £4000, on condition of payment within a year. He contrived, however, to obtain a full discharge on payment of £2000, and had his coat of arms restored to him, and after some opposition he ultimately signed the interpolated " device" for the succession of King Edward.

The Revolution which followed restored Paget to a high position, for Mary took him into favour, and made him several grants of lands, as the manor of Alcester, in Warwickshire, and other lands in the counties of Leicester and Derby ; also the marriage of Thomas Willoughby, and the reversion of the manor of Great Marlow, Buckinghamshire. However, he strongly recommended her to acknowledge her sister as her presumptive successor, and he was the author of the plan for marrying Elizabeth to Courtenay, in order that these two might be declared King and Queen, should Mary remain without issue. He also, though panicstruck at Wyat's rebellion, advised Mary to remain in London, advice which saved her throne. He helped in the Spanish match, and brought over Cardinal Pole ; but he was essentially a diplomatist, and though tired of conspiracies, disapproved the vio-

lent acts of Mary's reign, and remained quiet till the
accession of Elizabeth exposed his moderate susceptibilities to a trial in an opposite direction. He deemed
it more prudent to plead infirmities, and ask to be
allowed to retire from the Privy Council and public
employments, and Elizabeth allowed his plea, though
retaining to the close of his life a high opinion of his
judgment and sagacity. The change of times had
superseded Paget's diplomatic creed—his diplomacy
had become as superannuated as himself; but he was
too acute to be hidebound entirely by old ideas. He
had opposed the expedition to assist the Scotch Protestants against France, but he disappointed the expectations of the Court of Spain by opposing also the
Spanish alliance when coupled with the marriage with
Leicester, and he advised, in preference, an alliance
with the French Calvinists, which would bring Spain
to terms of itself. But, with these exceptions, his
public life was virtually at an end, though he did not
die till June 9, 1563, being then fifty-seven years of
age. He made his will three years before, and was
buried at West Drayton, Middlesex, where he possessed a house. His commonplace-book, which was
in the possession of Lord Boston, a descendant of the
family, " contains many particulars relative to the
Court, the navy, and foreign affairs, and concludes
with these [characteristic] maxims :—' Flye the
courte ; speke little ; care less ; devise nothing ; never
earnest ; in answere cold ; lerne to spare ; spend with
measure ; care for home ; pray often ; live better ;
and dye well.'" His character will be hardly judged
by men who value principle above adroitness ; but he
cared for England, and in one generation raised his

house from the lower class of society to an equality with the proudest.* His adhesion was a real support to a government like that of Elizabeth.

The founder married the daughter and heiress of Henry Preston, Esq., of Preston, in Yorkshire, by whom he left four sons and six daughters. His eldest son, Henry, second Lord Paget, at his death in 1568 left a baby heiress, who died in 1571, and the title and estates descended to his brother Thomas, who, as third Lord Paget, had a very unfortunate career. Being a strong Catholic, he engaged with his brother Charles Paget—a busy agent for the Catholics—in intrigues in Mary of Scotland's interest, along with the Earl of Northumberland and Francis Throgmorton, and some of their letters being intercepted, and Throgmorton arrested, Lord Paget thought it wise to quit England and fly to France. Thereupon he and his brother Charles were attainted in Parliament in the year 1587, and their lands and possessions confiscated. The Earl of Leicester then obtained Paget House—then rechristened Leicester House. The unfortunate nobleman died in exile at Brussels in 1589, "his death," Camden says, "proving a sad and universal loss to the commonwealth of learning." His son, William, was knighted in one of the Earl of Essex's expeditions, and in the first Parliament of James I. (1603) was restored to his paternal lands and honours as

---

* Mr Banks, in his 'Dormant and Extinct Baronage,' has drawn an excellent character of Paget. "His masterpiece," he says, "was an inward observation of other men, and an exact knowledge of himself. His apprehension was quick, and his mind ever ready and present, according to occasion and emergency." His manors, &c., will be found enumerated in Shaw's 'History of Staffordshire,' vol i. p. 215 ; Burton-on-Trent is the most notable.

fourth Lord Paget. His life was entirely uneventful.
He married Lettice, daughter and coheir of Henry
Knollys, of Kingsbury, Warwickshire, and died August
29, 1629. His son and successor, William, fifth Lord
Paget, was nineteen on the 13th September preceding his father's death, and was made a Knight of the
Bath at the coronation of Charles I. He was a man
of singularly uncertain character, changing from side to
side in the contests between the King and Parliament
with a suddenness which scandalised all parties. He
was a proud man, too, and once told Charles's Queen
that the country lords were "as strong as Samson,"
eliciting the stinging rejoinder, "Verily I believe it,
for ye lack not among ye the jawbone of an ass," an
allusion, says Lord Radnor, to his long lean physiog-
nomy. He survived till October 19, 1678, and married Lady Frances Rich, daughter of Henry Earl of
Holland, by whom he left, besides his son and heir, a
second son, who became the ancestor of the present
family. William, sixth Lord Paget, joined Lord
Russell, and voted in convention for declaring the
throne vacant. He had the diplomatic capacity of
his house, and in January 1699 contrived to conclude
a treaty between the Sultan and the Emperor of Germany, traversing the Turkish dominions himself from
Constantinople to Carlowitz, then a great feat. He
also arranged a treaty between "Muscovy," Venice,
and the Sultan, and quitted Turkey with many proofs
of the Sultan's high regard. He had married Frances,
daughter of Francis Pierrepont, a younger brother of
"Wise William," and was succeeded by her surviving
son, Henry, seventh Lord Paget, who, in December
1711, was, during his father's lifetime, raised to the

peerage as Lord Burton, of Burton, in Staffordshire ; and on October 19, 1714, created Earl of Uxbridge in the county of Middlesex. In September 1715, however, when the arrests of the English Jacobites were in full progress, the newly-made Earl resigned all his employments, and took no further part in public affairs, dying in August 1743. He was succeeded by his grandson, who dying unmarried, November 16, 1769, the Earldom became extinct; but the Barony of Paget devolved on Henry Bayley Paget, eldest son of Sir Nicholas Bayley, of Plas-Newydd, in the Isle of Anglesey, a baronet of Ireland, by Caroline, daughter of Brigadier-General Thomas Paget, grandson of the fifth Baron. These Bayleys, or Bailies, claim to have been bailiffs of Lanark; but their English head came to England with James I., was Chaplain to Henry Prince of Wales, and in 1616 was created Bishop of Bangor. He possessed, or acquired by marriage with a daughter of Sir Henry Bagenal, of Newry Castle, in Ireland, considerable estates which the Pagets still retain. The Bishop's eldest son narrowly escaped death for his share in Penruddock's royalist rising, and *his* son was created a baronet of Ireland in 1730, and left a son, Sir Nicholas, second Baronet, who by his marriage with the heiress of the Pagets brought to his son the honours of that family.

Henry Bayley Paget, son of Sir Nicholas Bayley, the inheritor of the barony of Paget, was created, May 19, 1784, Earl of Uxbridge, and died on the 13th of March 1812. His eldest son and successor, Henry William, had a more distinguished career. Having entered the army, first in the infantry and afterwards in the cavalry, he served under the Duke of York, Sir John Moore, and lastly Wellington, throughout the Peninsular War, distinguishing himself as a dashing cavalry officer. At the battle of Waterloo he headed the celebrated charge of the Household cavalry which, highly praised at the time, has been since so greatly censured as a brilliant act of folly, which disabled the English cavalry for the rest of the battle, without producing any favourable result in itself. Be this as it may, towards the close of the day the Earl, who had behaved with great daring, received a shot in his right knee which compelled the amputation of that leg. As a reward for his military services he was created, on the 4th July 1815, Marquess of Anglesey ; and on the 30th April 1827, he accepted the office of Master-General of the Ordnance, on the formation of the Cabinet under the Premiership of Canning. On the 1st March 1828, his personal attachment to his old comrade in arms, the Duke of Wellington, induced the Marquess to accept, in the Government which the Duke was reconstructing out of Tory materials, after the resignation of Huskisson and the Canningites on the East Retford Reform question, the Lord-Lieutenancy of Ireland. In this situation he fared like the Liberal Lord Fitzwilliam before him. The question of Catholic Emancipation agitating Ireland more and more towards the close of 1828, Dr Curtis, the Catholic Primate of Ireland, a Peninsular acquaintance of Wellington's, addressed a letter to the Premier on the state of Ireland. This elicited an answer, December 11, "in terms cautious, indeed, but indicating not obscurely an intention to concede emancipation." On receiving a copy of the Duke's letter, Anglesey (De-

cember 23) wrote to Dr Curtis, and openly spoke of
emancipation as the only means of pacifying Ireland.
This latter declaration went so far beyond the immediate views of the Cabinet, that the next post brought
the recall of the Marquess from the Lord-Lieutenancy,
and the appointment of the Duke of Northumberland.
On the formation of the Grey Ministry in 1830, the
Marquess was again sent to Ireland as a pledge of their
friendly feelings towards the Catholics; but O'Connell
at once organised a systematic opposition to him; he
was personally insulted, and his proclamations were
met with counter-meetings of defiance, while the repeal of the Union was loudly proclaimed as the pan-
acea. At length O'Connell and his colleagues were
proceeded against by the Government for such meetings. They pleaded guilty to the counts charging
them with holding them in defiance of Government
proclamations, and the Attorney-General then withdrew the other counts. It was soon rumoured that
there was some compromise between the Whigs and
the "Liberator," and that the "Irish Church" was to
be the peace-offering. Fresh misunderstandings, however, led to the introduction of coercion acts; and
Lord Grey and Lord Anglesey differing on some
points of Irish policy, the disruption in the Cabinet
followed which led to Lord Grey's retirement. During his administration of Ireland, Anglesey, though
not a man of remarkable talent, had the merit of
keeping his temper and assuming an appearance of
amusement rather than irritation when mobbed by
the Irish populace. He continued a supporter of the
successive Whig administrations, but did not assume
office again till 1846, on the formation of Lord John

Russell's Government, as Master-General of the Ordnance. He resigned with it in March 1852, and died
April 28, 1854. His domestic relations were unhappy
—his first wife he obtained a divorce from, and she
re-married the Duke of Argyll; and he himself married, secondly, the divorced wife of Lord Cowley. Of
his sons, the reputation of the present Marquess has
suffered from a similar domestic scandal, and the political credit of the family name is now supported by a
younger son of the first Marquess, Lord Clarence Paget,
Secretary to the Admiralty in the present Ministry.
The younger branches of the Pagets, however, are
numerous and active, if not always successful, in the
various branches of the public service, more particularly about the Court. They are a fairly competent
race, rarely making official blunders, and have been
throughout their career reasonably popular. Their
faculty is that of men of the world, and as such they
have met with a very full measure of success; but it
is doubtful whether, but for the founder, they would
ever have emerged from the ranks.

The Manners.

THE Manners have been gentlemen in character, in blood, and in English position for more than six hundred years. The founder of the house as a territorial power, was one of the earliest Yorkists, who, by a lucky alliance, obtained the estates of one of the oldest English baronies, but his own pedigree was one of very unusual clearness. Not to speak of Henry de Manners (or De Manneriis), who in the 25th of Henry II. paid eighty marks for livery of his father's lands in Northumberland, and whom Lord John Manners may, we believe, safely include in the next edition of the Manners pedigree, SIR ROBERT DE MANNERS was certainly extant in Henry III.'s time, and in 1272 held Hothal, now called Etal, of the Muscamp barony in that county, and his son Robert, in 1278, held so much land—two knights' fees in chief— that he was " constrained " to take on himself the honour and the responsibilities of knighthood. *His* grandson, Sir Robert, who succeeded in 1349, was a distinct historical figure, for in the 17th of Edward II. he was certified as a man entitled by ancestral descent to bear arms, and in the 1st of Edward III. he distinguished himself by his defence of Norham Castle against the

Scots. Edward, who had an idea apparently of creating a new Scotch aristocracy to back him, one of the
many ideas which threw back the Union, ordered him
to take seisin of Selkirkshire and the forest of Selkirk
and Ettrick, which, of course, he did not retain. He
had, however, his own lands and bits of new grants
in Northumberland, helped Lord Grey of Wark mate-
rially in his defeat of the Earls of March and Sutherland, and received in reward what in that age was
equivalent to a peerage, the right of fortifying his
house at Etal. He was subsequently one of the War-
dens of the Marches, fought at Neville's Cross, and
generally proved himself a stout and efficient feudal
gentleman. His son, Sir John, who married a widow,
daughter of Sir Henry de la Val, of Seton Delaval, was
dead before the 4th of Henry IV., and their son, Sir
John de Manners, was a regular Border chief, was
pursued and heavily fined for the murder of William
Heron and Robert Atkinson, but was, nevertheless,
knighted, and regarded apparently as a very decent
person. People had to be killed in those days, and
the killer's son, Sir Robert, not only was uninjured by
his father's crime, but in the 27th of Henry IV. obtained a joint grant with the Percy of the goods of
Sir Robert Ogle, outlawed. He married a daughter of
the despoiled gentleman, and their son, SIR ROBERT
MANNERS, was in the modern sense the true founder
—the man to whom we owe it that there is a Duke of
Rutland at Belvoir, and a Lord John Manners in the
Lower House. Sir Robert was an early Yorkist, and
Edward IV. gave him twenty marks out of some
Percy forfeitures, Locre, Newsham, Newslede, Shen-
how, and Elyngham ; together with the immensely

profitable Sheriffdom of Northumberland, an office
which was in all but name a most important viceroyalty. Neville, the king-maker, liked him too, and
gave him twenty marks a-year out of Barnard Castle;
and he managed so adroitly, or was personally a man
of such pleasant bearing, that after the Percies returned in 1469-70 they appointed him Master Fores-
ter. His crowning achievement was, however, his
marriage with ELEANOR, sister and coheir of Edmond
DE Roos, sixteenth Baron Roos, Norman of Normans,
of the real conquering blood, and owner of some of the
great slices of land carved by his ancestor out of the
Saxon kingdom. The real hold over England still remained with the few of these people who had survived
the Wars of the Roses, and Eleanor de Roos brought
into the new family vast lands in Leicestershire, and
Rutland, and Lincolnshire, among them the barony of
BELVOIR CASTLE, a splendid stronghold built by Robert
de Todenai, in the Conqueror's time. It descended
from him to the Albini, and Isabel d'Albini brought it
in Henry III.'s time to De Roos. The place has been
built and re-built, but a Belvoir Castle has been a
noble's house of the first rank in England since the
Conquest, a remark not true, we believe, of any other
house in the kingdom. Edmond de Roos dying without issue in 1508, the barony fell into abeyance between his sisters, but Isabel the second, dying also
childless—she was wife of Sir Thomas Lovell of Ryhall
—the barony devolved on Eleanor's son, George Manners, who thus inherited the baronies of De Roos,
Vaux, Trusbut, and Belvoir. So powerful did these
lordships make him, that he aspired to a semi-royal
alliance, and married Anne, sole daughter and heiress

of Sir Thomas St Leger, by Anne of York, eldest sister of Edward IV. His eldest son, Thomas Manners, inherited under his father's will the manors and lands of Pockley, Bindlowe, Howsom, Oswaldirk, and Anpleford, besides half the De Roos property, of the whole remainder of which he received livery in the 16th Henry VIII. The family had now risen to the grade of the greater barons, the blood royal flowed in its veins, and in consideration of that fact Thomas was, on the 18th of June 1525, created Earl of Rutland.

The new Earl was a courtier, conducted Anne Boleyn from Greenwich to her coronation, and sat as one of her judges, and fought with success against the insurgents in the Pilgrimage of Grace. In 1539 he was appointed Chamberlain to Anne of Cleves. In 1540 he was Chief Justice in Eyre of all places north of the Trent, and in the 33d year of Henry VIII. he received a magnificent slice of the Abbey lands. The King gave him the manor of Muston, Leicestershire, part of the possessions of the dissolved priory of Osulveston, and the manors of Waltham and Croxton, in the same county, as also the manors of Upwell, Outwell, Elme, and Ermithe, in Norfolk and Suffolk, belonging to the dissolved monastery of Nuneaton, in Warwickshire, also the manor of Branston, in Northamptonshire, belonging to the dissolved abbey of Lilleshall, in Shropshire, together with the manors of Bellesdale and Helmesley, and the rectory of the church of Helmesley, belonging to the dissolved monastery of Kirkham, in Yorkshire, with lands in Brandesdale, in the same county, belonging to the abbey of Riesvaulx. In 1542 he accompanied the Duke of

U

Norfolk into Scotland, and died on September 20, 1543, leaving, besides an estate to each younger son, and £60 a-year and £10,000 to each daughter, the following estates to his successor :—The manor of Melton Roos, Lincolnshire, and lands in Melton Roos, Becklesby, Kirton, Barnetby, Ulceby, Wrawby, Glanford Brigge, Elsham, and Wotton, Lincolnshire ; the manor of Orston, and the Stoke, and all the lands, &c., in Orston, Streton, Kneton, Scarrington, Carcolston, Thurverton, Staunton, and Dallington, in Nottinghamshire, as well as the manors of Belvoir and Wollestrop, and certain lands, tenements, and hereditaments in Belvoir, Wollestrop, Denton, Aubotn, Haddington, Wyvell, Aslackby, Cadby Magna, Uffington, Talington, Deeping, Stroxton, and Aslackton, in Lincolnshire ; and in Easton, Midleton, Melbourne, Blettesden, Barkby, South Croxton, Knipton, Muston, Bottesford, Stathern, Hardby, Howes, Lubbenham, and Redmilne, in Leicestershire ; in Dalton and Naborne, in Yorkshire ; in Carlton, Dingley, Brampton, Braddon, Sewell, Harpole, Stoke Aubeney, Wilarston, Rushton, Desborowe, and Cottingham, in Northamptonshire ; in Collesden, Oakley, and Richton, in Bedfordshire ; and in Clipston, in Buckinghamshire ; and in many other manors, &c., amounting to the clear yearly value of £1862, 1s. 8d., over and above the sum of £552, 1s. 5¾d., payable to the King for lands purchased or exchanged, and over and above all rents and deductions of bailiffs' and stewards' rents. To his wife he left several manors to the yearly value of £700.

The first Earl began the rebuilding of Belvoir Castle, which Henry, the second Earl, completed. The latter was a partisan of the Dudleys, and was flung, on

Mary's accession, into the Fleet; but he made his peace, and was appointed Captain-General of the forces intended to act against France. Elizabeth continued the royal favour, both to him and (after his death in 1563) to his son Edward, third Earl, who was sent, while still a royal ward, against the Northern Earls, grew up a "profound lawyer" and a man of singular accomplishments, and died in 1587, leaving an only child, Elizabeth, who became, as heir-general, Baroness de Roos, married William Cecil Lord Burghley, grandson of the statesman, and carried the De Roos barony for a moment into that new family.

The earldom, however, remained, falling to John Manners, brother of the last Earl, who died in a few months, and was succeeded by his son Roger, fifth Earl, and Essex's fast friend. When Essex made his mad attempt Rutland was by his side, and with the Earl of Southampton was thrown into prison. He was not, however, brought to trial, and was released on the accession of James I., with whom Essex's plot was intimately connected. After the accession of that King he was sent on a complimentary embassy to Denmark, and was appointed steward of the manor and soke of Grantham. He died June 26, 1612, having married Elizabeth, daughter and heir of the celebrated Sir Philip Sidney, but having no children by her, the earldom devolved on his brother, Francis, sixth Earl of Rutland. This Earl, also, had spent the early part of his life in foreign travel. On the accession of James he was made a Knight of the Bath, and, on his brother's death, Lord-Lieutenant of Lincolnshire, and Justice in Eyre of the forests, &c., north of the Trent; in 1616 he was made a Knight of the Garter, and accompanied the King to Scotland. In 1623 he had the command of a fleet of ships and pinnaces appointed to bring Prince Charles back from Spain, and died December 17, 1632.

In 1616 Earl Francis made a claim to the barony of Roos, as heir male of Henry, nineteenth Baron, William Cecil, the son of Elizabeth Manners, having died in the lifetime of his father without children. The ancient barony was, nevertheless, awarded to another, William Cecil, as heir-general. The Crown, however, at the same time, created, by patent, a *new* barony of Roos of Hanlake, Trusbut, and Belvoir, in the person of Earl Francis; and William Cecil dying in 1618 without issue, the ancient barony of Roos reverted to the Manners. Earl Francis, however, leaving only a daughter, Katherine, married to the first George Villiers, Duke of Buckingham, and afterwards to the Earl of Antrim, the barony of Roos became again separated from the earldom of Rutland. After the death of the second George Villiers it fell into abeyance between the heirs-general of the sisters of Earl Francis, till in 1806 this abeyance was terminated in favour of Charlotte Boyle Walsingham, the wife of Lord Henry Fitz-Gerald (fourth son of the first Duke of Leinster), as one of the coheirs of the barony, she and her descendants taking the name of "De Ros," in addition to Fitz-Gerald. Her second son is the present Lord de Ros—a mistake in the writ of summons to his brother and predecessor which seems now likely to be perpetuated.

Earl Francis was succeeded, in 1632, as seventh Earl of Rutland, by his brother George, who was knighted in the Irish wars in 1599 by the Earl of

Essex, married an aunt of *the* Lord Falkland, and
died in his house in the Savoy, in March 1641, leaving no children, when the earldom devolved on John
Manners, of Nether Haddon, Derbyshire (a property
obtained by this branch by marriage from Sir George
Vernon, called the "Knight of the Peak"), grandson
of Sir John Manners, second son of the first Earl.
John, eighth Earl of Rutland, had been Sheriff of
Derbyshire, and one of its representatives in the Parliament of April 1640. He had married in 1628 a
daughter of Edward, Lord Montagu of Boughten,
and, perhaps from coming freshly out of the ranks of
the gentry, he espoused the Puritan cause, becoming
a leading Presbyterian peer in the civil wars. He
retired from active political life after Colonel Pride's
"Purge," and after the Restoration occupied himself
in rebuilding Belvoir Castle, which had been nearly
demolished during the preceding revolutionary period.
He died September 29, 1679. His only surviving
son and successor, John, ninth Earl of Rutland, had
sat in the first Parliament after the Restoration for
the county of Leicester, and in the April preceding
his father's death had been called up to the House of
Peers as Lord Manners of Haddon. His opinions
were congenial with those of the "country party," but
he took no prominent part in politics during this
reign. His first marriage with one of the Pierrepont
family having proved unfortunate in its consequences,
he procured, in 1668, an Act of Divorce from her,
he then bearing the courtesy title of Lord Roos.
This Act was not carried through without warm
debates, all the bishops but two voting against it,
and the Duke of York strongly opposing it. The

King on the other hand as warmly supported it, and Burnet tells us it was looked upon as the prelude to the divorce of Charles himself. The Earl remarried twice, the last wife, by whom alone he left children, being Catherine, daughter of Baptist Noel, Viscount Campden. Rutland, who hated Court life, and London, staked his head in the Revolution, being one of the peers who at Nottingham associated themselves against the Government; but he lived thenceforward in retirement. He was, however, as the head of a family which had contributed greatly to the Revolution, created Marquess of Granby and Duke of Rutland on 29th March 1703, and survived his new honours eight years.

His son John, second Duke of Rutland, married the second daughter of the celebrated William Lord Russell, and so produced some of Lady Russell's best letters; but he was a man of no note whatever, and his son John, the third Duke, who succeeded him in 1721 and died in 1779, was little more distinguished. He held, however, high office in the Household, was singularly respected as a country gentleman, and married Bridget Sutton, heiress of the last Lord Lexington, whose great estate passed to the Duke's second son, who took that family name.

The Duke's eldest son, who died before him in October 1770, was the well-known Marquess of Granby, whose name is familiar to us on the signboards of old inns. He was a distinguished officer, who led the cavalry at the battle of Minden, and served with distinction in the subsequent campaigns on the Continent. His conduct on the trial of Lord George Sackville for cowardice was marked by great generosity. They had been on bad terms in the army, but, when summoned as a witness for the prosecution, Granby softened and extenuated the evidence against Sackville as much as possible consistently with truth. On May 14, 1763, on George Grenville succeeding Lord Bute, Granby was appointed Master-General of the Ordnance, and on August 13, 1766, was made Commander-in-Chief. He had been proposed for the office the year before—chiefly to spite the Duke of Cumberland; but the King then resisting, Grenville desisted at the express request of Granby himself. Lord Granby continued to hold this office and a seat in the Cabinet till January 1770, when, entirely disapproving of the proceedings in the case of John Wilkes's election, he both spoke and voted against the Ministry, and, notwithstanding the request of the King to the contrary, resigned all his employments, and went into strong opposition to Lord North's Government. His death in the autumn of the same year, in the prime of life, and of a great and increasing reputation and popularity, prevented him probably from redeeming the name of Rutland from the mediocrity which had for several generations attached to it. He had married a daughter of Charles, Duke of Somerset, and his eldest surviving son by her, Charles, succeeded his grandfather as fourth Duke of Rutland. Lord George Manners, his third son, became the heir of his brother Robert, and took the name of Sutton. Lord George's fourth son, Charles Manners-Sutton, became ultimately, in 1804, Archbishop of Canterbury. The Archbishop's eldest son, again, bearing the same name, was Speaker of the House of Commons from 1817 for seventeen years, and on March 10, 1835, was created Baron

Bottesford and Viscount Canterbury. Another peerage also was acquired for the Manners family by Thomas, fifth son of Lord George Manners-Sutton, who became successively Solicitor-General, a Baron of the Exchequer, and Lord Chancellor of Ireland, and Baron Manners, of Foston, Lincolnshire, in 1807.

The fourth Duke of Rutland was the early friend of the younger Pitt; the late Marquess of Granby, his father, having been a devoted follower of Lord Chatham. He had been one of the members for the University of Cambridge, at which University he sought and made the acquaintance of young Pitt, five years his junior. When they both came to live in London a close intimacy and fast friendship was formed between them, which continued to the close of the Duke's life, and determined the politics of the Manners family on the Tory side. It was through the interest of the Duke of Rutland with Sir James Lowther that Pitt first entered the House for one of the latter's boroughs. When Pitt formed his Ministry in 1783, Rutland entered the Cabinet as Lord Privy Seal, and at the commencement of 1784 the Duke was persuaded to accept the office of Lord-Lieutenant of Ireland. His post was not an easy one. "This city" [Dublin], he writes in the August of the following year, "is, in a great measure, under the dominion and tyranny of the mob. Persons are daily marked out for the operation of tarring and feathering: the magistrates neglect their duty; and none of the rioters—till to-day, when one man was seized in the fact—have been taken, while the corps of volunteers in the neighbourhood seem, as it were, to countenance these outrages. In short, the state of Dublin calls loudly for an immediate and vigorous interposition of Government." Pitt endeavoured to heal this state of things by stimulating Irish commerce, and some propositions of his extending the principles of free trade between the two countries were modified into "eleven resolutions" by the Duke, and passed in that shape through the Irish Legislature. However, they were rendered unpalatable to the Irish in the shape which they ultimately assumed after their passage through the English Legislature, and such was the outcry in Ireland that the bill introduced into the Irish Legislature to carry them into law was obliged to be withdrawn. But in other respects the Duke's Government was popular rather through his personal habits and character than any remarkable ability on his part. "Young," says Lord Stanhope, " of noble aspect, and of princely fortune, he was generous, frank, and amiable, as became the son of the gallant Granby. Fond of pleasure, he held a court of much magnificence; and the succession of various entertainments that he gave, splendid as they were in themselves, derived a greater lustre from his Duchess, a daughter of the house of Beaufort, and one of the most beautiful women of her day. But besides and beyond his outward accomplishments, the confidential letters of the Duke to Pitt show him to have possessed both ability and application in business." His Irish career, however, was cut short in October 1787, by a putrid fever, which carried him off at the early age of thirty-four. His son and successor, John Henry, fifth Duke of Rutland, passed through life without attaining any political prominence, remaining a constant Tory; and dying January 20,

1857, was succeeded by his eldest son, Charles Cecil
John, sixth and present Duke of Rutland, who, as
Marquess of Granby, was rather prominent in the
House of Commons as a Tory of the oldest type, a
stanch and unbending Protectionist, and in foreign
politics a disciple of the old Holy Alliance school.
He is unmarried, and his next brother, and heir pre-
sumptive, is Lord John Manners, who filled the office
of First Commissioner of Woods and Forests in the
Derby Cabinets, and is well known both as a politician,
an accomplished gentleman, and a partisan of High
Church principles.

For generations the family have been patricians,
kindly men enough, fond of country life, with fair
capacities and few conspicuous vices, but still patricians, doing something and enjoying much, without
much confidence in their own claims, and, therefore,
very apt to push forward those of their order. They
have produced at least one statesman of high ability,
but essentially they have been and are English gentlemen simply, and though that is a high service of its
kind, still Belvoir and its dependencies are an ample
recompense.

The Montagus.

HAT profound ignorance of their own history which distinguishes the English above every Continental people has given the Montagus a position which, with many other merits, they do not deserve. Their name, like that of the Howards, has become almost a synonym for aristocratic descent, the popular belief probably identifying them with Shakespeare's Montagues of Verona, and also making them heirs by blood of the great Earls of Salisbury—the Montacutes or Montagus—a pretension to which they themselves have always steadily adhered, choosing, as they rose, the titles borne by the great Yorkist, who was the heir of those Earls. The popular belief is as ill-founded as their own claim, unless, indeed, bastardy be descent, and the Montagus must be content to remain one of the most singularly active, accomplished, and successful of the houses founded upon the grand Sequestration. Lawyers, soldiers, statesmen, and all of the first class, the specialty of the race has been power of brain, tinged in some of the family with strong religious ideas, but, in the majority, with unscrupulousness of the kind seldom found except among the able. They themselves deduce their descent from a Simon Montagu, stated to have been a younger brother to John, third Earl of Salisbury, and uncle to Thomas, fourth and last Earl of Salisbury of that name, who died November 3, 1428. "Unfortunately," says Sir Egerton Brydges, "there is no proof of the existence of this Simon, or of any of the intermediate generations," before we come to the undoubted ancestor of the modern family. "The late Mr Thorpe (and it seems Mr Austin concurred in this opinion) suspected this family to have been descended from James Montagu, a natural son of Thomas, the last Earl of Salisbury, who lies buried in the church of Lansdowne, in Kent, of which place he derived the manor from his father. The bordure round the arms of the present family favours this idea."

The true founder of the present family of Montagu was SIR EDWARD MONTAGU, the younger son of Thomas Montagu, who lies buried in the church of Hemington, Northamptonshire. "Of your charite," says the brass tablet on his tomb, "pray for the soules of Thomas Montagu, gentleman, and Agnes, his wyff. Which Thomas deceased the 5 day of September, the year of our Lord 1517 : on whose soules Jesu have mercy." Beyond this Thomas Montagu we cannot go. His elder son, John, who succeeded to the property, such as it may have been, died without issue. Edward, the younger son, born at Brigstock, near Hemington, chose the law for his profession, entered at the Middle Temple, and became Autumn Reader to that society in the 16th Henry VIII., Double Reader in the year 1524, and a few years afterwards his legal reputation, by this time consider-

able, secured him a seat in the House of Commons.
There is a story that he was chosen Speaker, in which
capacity he found himself in a serious predicament
between the reluctance of the Commons to pass a
subsidy-bill and the King's displeased impatience for
it. Henry called Montagu to his presence, and said
to him, " Ho! will they not let my bill pass ? " and
laying his hand on the head of Montagu, who knelt
before him, he added, " Get my bill to pass by such a
time to-morrow, or else by such a time this head of
yours shall be off!" and, accordingly, Montagu *did*
procure the passing of the bill and retained his head.
Unfortunately Montagu never *was* Speaker at all, and
if there was any such scene, it must have related to
his conduct as a private member. But the whole
story sounds very incredible. In 1531 Montagu was
made a sergeant-at-law, and with his fellow-sergeants
kept high feast at Ely House for five days, honoured
with the presence of the King and Queen and the whole
Court. Six years afterwards, October 16, 1537, he was
appointed the King's Sergeant-at-Law; and, January
21, 1539, was made Chief Justice of the King's Bench,
and knighted. In the 31st of Henry VIII. he had
a grant of lands in Hemington, in Northamptonshire, belonging to Ramsay Abbey; and on November
6, 1545, he exchanged the Chief Justiceship of the
King's Bench for that of the Common Pleas—" a
descent in honour," says Fuller, " but an ascent in
profit." The reason he himself assigned for desiring
the change is, " I am now an old man, and love the
kitchen before the hall, the warmest place best suiting
with my age." Probably he had had enough of the
legal dirty work which he had been compelled in the

higher office to perform at the King's bidding. Besides having to commit both Catholics and Protestants under the statute of the *Six Articles,* he had to give legal opinions in conformity with the King's wishes in the cases of Anne of Cleves's divorce, Cromwell's alleged treason, and Catherine Howard's adultery. Once more, before the death of Henry, Montagu was called upon to exercise the unenviable office of keeper of the royal common-law conscience. When the Duke of Norfolk was called to account, nominally for quartering the royal arms without licence, the *two* Chief Justices were summoned to attend at his hearing before the Council, but Norfolk was persuaded to sign a declaration that he had committed an act of treason, and the Justices were only called upon to attest his confession, which but for Henry's own death would have consigned the Duke to the scaffold. On the accession of Edward, Montagu attached himself at first to the fortunes of Somerset, and we find him, in the fourth year of this reign, obtaining a licence to give liveries and badges to forty persons over and above his own menial servants. However, at the crisis with Dudley, Montagu deserted the Duke, and assisted his rival to ascend to the headship of the State. He paid for his desertion, however, for Northumberland fixed on him as the best person to give a legal sanction to the Jane Grey scheme of succession. He was summoned to the royal chamber, along with some other judges and law officers, and desired to draw up the required disposition of the Crown. They pointed out the illegality, and begged for time to consider the matter. The next day they repeated their objections, and stated that it would be high treason in those who

drew such a document and those who acted under it.
Northumberland, informed of what was passing, then
burst into the Council Chamber, and called the Chief
Justice a traitor, using threats of violence to him and
his legal associates. Two days afterwards this scene
was repeated, and Montagu being completely brow-
beaten, and the King commanding him on his allegiance to make quick despatch, he, as he himself says,
" being a weak old man, and without comfort," consented to draw the disposition, on receiving in writing
a commission under the Great Seal so to do, and a
general pardon for obeying the injunction. On the
proclamation of Queen Jane, Montagu had, of course,
to appear with Northumberland at her side ; but as
soon as it became evident that Mary would prevail,
the Chief Justice in great trepidation, as the Jane
Grey disposition was in his own handwriting, made
haste to join the winning side. This did not save
him from being committed by Mary to the Tower, and
placed on the list for trial. He drew up a narrative
in his defence, in which he denied having acted with
the Council after the act to which he had been forced
against his will, and claimed the credit of having, at
great cost, sent his son to join the Buckinghamshire
men in Mary's interest. As he really had been an
unwilling agent of Dudley's, after six weeks' imprisonment he was discharged, and pardoned on payment of
a fine of £1000, and the surrender of King Edward's
grant to him of lands called Eltington, of the yearly
value of £50. He was at the same time deprived of
his Chief Justiceship, and retired to shelter himself at
his house at Boughton, near Kettering, in Northamptonshire, where he passed the rest of his life in more

congenial quiet and hospitality, dying February 10, 1557. He had been, indeed, a large recipient of Church lands, and, notwithstanding the vicissitudes in his fortunes, had managed to retain his hold on most of them. In the 33d of Henry VIII., for instance, he had a grant from the Crown of the manor of Warkton, in Northamptonshire, belonging to the dissolved monastery of Bury St Edmunds, and the advowson of that church, with lands and messuages in Boughton, Scaldwell, Hanging-Houghton, Lamport, Maidwell, Clipston, Ardingworth, Farndon, and Hoothorpe, belonging to the same monastery, to be held by the service of the twentieth part of one knight's fee, and the yearly rent of sixty shillings. In the 2d of Edward VI. he purchased from the Kirkham family the manor of Barnwell-all-Saints, in Northamptonshire, which became one of the principal seats of his family.

By his will, made a few months before his death, he devises to his eldest son, Edward, manors and lands in no less than thirty-two places, in four counties, besides his leases, lands, and tenements in the parish of St Dunstan-in-the-West, London. These manors, &c., are Warkton, Brigstock, Houghton, Lamport or Langeport, Mellesley, Holwell, Guilsborough, Bringtonmagna, Brington-parva, Grafton, and the parsonage of Weekly; the manors, &c., of Weekly, Demford, Benefield, Sprotton, Luffick, and Eltington, in Northamptonshire; Colmworth, Shirenbrook, Souldrop, Felmersham, Luton Hoo, Pertenhall, Mechelborne, Swineshead, and Woodend, in Bedfordshire; Knighton, in Leicestershire; and Folksworth, Stilton, Little Styveclay, March Styveclay, and Alconbury, in Huntingdonshire. His third wife, and the mother of his surviving sons, was Helen, daughter of John Roper, of Eltham, in Kent, Attorney-General to Henry VIII.

Edward, his eldest surviving son and heir, was twenty-four years old at the death of his father, was one of the knights of the shire for Northampton in the first Parliament of Elizabeth, sheriff of that county in the twelfth year of her reign, and knighted by her in 1567. He bears the character of having been a man of great piety and private worth, but he has left no mark in history. He died at Boughton, January 26, 1602. Before his death he had settled all his manors on his six sons respectively, reserving only the manor of Colmworth to himself, which, by his will, he leaves to his eldest son Edward. He had married Elizabeth, daughter of Sir James Harrington of Exton, in Rutland, and from this marriage spring the different branches of the house of Montagu, which obtained severally the extinct Dukedom of Montagu and Earldom of Halifax, the Dukedom of Manchester and the Earldom of Sandwich.

The Dukedom of Montagu is extinct, but this branch played such a part in history that we must give it a few words. It sprang, as we said, from Edward Montagu of Boughton, the eldest son of the house, who, on the 29th of June 1621, was created Lord Montagu of Boughton.

Two panegyrical accounts of him exist, which, though bearing evident traces of fulsome adulation, give us one or two distinct points of character which are worth preserving. One of them, after speaking of his piety, says, " He was a patron of men of letters and merit, bestowing the livings in his gift to learned men

X

and such as he knew deserved them. But from his detestation to pluralities and non-residence (though he exacted no other covenant), he ever required, if they took any other living they should return his again." He is further spoken of as a tender father and good landlord, "easy of access, courteous to all, yet keeping the secrets of his heart to himself." And we are told that "the death of his second wife (Frances, sister of the famous Sir Robert Cotton, the antiquary) touched him the most sensibly of any." His "housekeeping" is described as "liberal and bountiful; that it is scarce credible what numbers (1200) were fed, cheered, comforted, and refreshed by his beneficence." In the other account he is described as a person of "a plain, downright English spirit, a steady courage, a devout heart, and though no Puritan, severe and regular in his life and manners; that he lived among his neighbours with great hospitality, was very knowing in country affairs, and exceedingly beloved in the town and county of Northampton; but he was no friend to changes, either in Church or State." He could not make up his mind to comply with the Militia Ordinance of the Parliament, and in 1642, though an old man, accepting the post of Commissioner of Array to the King, he was seized by a party of horse and carried up prisoner to London, where he was committed to the Tower, and remained in restraint until his death in 1644. He had three sons, the eldest of whom, Christopher, died before him; while the third, William, beame Chief Baron of the Exchequer in 1676, and in 1686 was dismissed by James II. for giving it as his opinion that "the Test and Penal laws could not be taken off without the consent of Parliament." He from this time lived in retirement, much respected for his integrity. The second, and eldest surviving son, Edward, second Lord Montagu of Boughton, sat in the House of Commons for the town of Huntingdon, but took sides against his father, adhering to the Parliament, and keeping aloof from the Stuarts, until the death of Cromwell, when, with most of the Presbyterian peers, he assisted in paving the way for the Restoration. He married Anne, daughter and ultimately heiress of Sir Ralph Winvood, of Ditton Park, principal Secretary of State to James I. Their eldest son, Edward—who had been dismissed from his post at Court for making love to Queen Catherine of Braganza—died at the siege of Bergen, in 1665, and the second, Ralph, was the most successful and the most unprincipled of the entire house. He was employed as Minister in France, and, as appears from Barillon's papers, received 50,000 French crowns from Louis to ruin Danby, who was dreaded and detested by France. This ruin he accomplished by reading in the House letters from Danby to the French Court asking for money in consideration of a treaty. Out of such disgraceful gains as these rose the pile of Montagu House, till lately occupied by the British Museum, which Lord Montagu built for his town house, intending to make of Boughton a miniature Versailles. Completely alienated from James II., Montagu supported the Revolution, and was made successively (April 9, 1689) Viscount Monthermer (Essex) and Earl of Montagu, (titles borne by the Neville of Edward IV.'s time, with whom he claimed connection), and (April 14, 1705) Marquess of Monthermer and Duke of Montagu. He died March 9, 1709, leaving a son, John, who was

Lord High Constable of England, and Grand-Master of the Bath, and received in the reign of George II. a patent creating him Lord Proprietor and Captain-General of St Lucia and St Vincent. He died without sons, in 1749, but one of his daughters having married George Brudenel, Earl of Cardigan, her husband was elevated in 1766 to the dignities of his father-in-law. He survived, however, his only son, John (who had been created Lord Montagu of Boughton, May 8, 1762), and on his death, in 1790, the higher titles which he derived from the Montagus became extinct ; but the barony of Montagu of Boughton (agreeably to a patent of August 21, 1786) devolved on Henry James Montagu-Scott, second son of his daughter, Elizabeth, by Henry Duke of Buccleuch. This peer dying without issue male, October 30, 1845, the barony also became extinct, and with it expired all the dignities of this branch of the Montagus.

Henry Montagu, *third* son of Sir Edward, the founder of the extinct Halifax branch, and of the existing ducal branch of the Montagus, was educated at Christ College, Cambridge, and entered the Middle Temple. He soon distinguished himself, like his grandfather, in the profession of the law. Entering Parliament at the close of the reign of Elizabeth for the borough of Higham Ferrers, he has left an honourable memento of himself on the records of its proceedings, by boldly asserting that there were no such precedents as one of the sergeants had stoutly quoted for the assertion that all the subjects' goods were the sovereign's. He told the House to examine all the preambles to subsidies, where they would see that they were free gifts. Unfortunately, Henry Montagu did not support,

in his after-career, these fair beginnings of public spirit.
He was Recorder of London at the accession of James,
and had been knighted before the coronation. As
Recorder, he was present at the opening of the New
River in 1613. In the first Parliament of that reign
he was elected for the City, and took an active part in
the discussions, particularly those relating to tenures.
As King's Sergeant, it fell to him to take part in the
trial of the poisoners of Sir Thomas Overbury, and
he had an action brought against him for libel as
counsel in a private case, which led to the rule of
the immunity of counsel for words spoken in the
name of their clients. On November 16, 1616, he
succeeded Sir Edward Coke as Chief Justice of the
King's Bench, having bought this place by consenting to give the Duke of Buckingham's nominee
the clerkship of the Court of King's Bench, worth
£4000 a-year, which Sir Edward Coke had refused to
part with. His judgments as Chief Justice are said
to have been respectable, though fulsome in their tone
of adulation of the King. He had the misfortune in
this capacity to have to award execution against Sir
Walter Raleigh, upon the sentence of death pronounced
against him fifteen years before, but he did it in a
decent and sympathising manner. He next offered the
Duke of Buckingham £10,000 for the place of Lord
Treasurer; but this offer was refused, and on December
14, 1620, he consented to pay £20,000 for it, and on
the 19th of the same month was created Baron Montagu
of Kimbolton, Huntingdonshire, and Viscount Mandeville. He had purchased KIMBOLTON CASTLE of the
Wingfield family, it having previously belonged to the
Staffords, the Bohuns, and the Magnavilles or Mande-

villes. The bargain for the treasurership having been concluded at Newmarket, one of the courtiers was audacious enough to ask him, with allusion to the white staff, whether *wood* was not very dear at that place. When Montagu was asked what the treasurership might be worth a-year, he replied, " Some thousands of pounds to him who after death would go instantly to heaven, twice as much to him who would go to purgatory, and a *nemo scit* to him who would venture to a worse place." As Treasurer he was one of the Commissioners of the Great Seal after Bacon's fall and before Williams's appointment. But Buckingham only allowed him to hold the Treasurer's staff till October in the year after his appointment, when he compelled him to resign it to Lionel Cranfield, Earl of Middlesex, and take in exchange the poor office of President of the Council. The sale of the treasurership to Montagu afterwards formed one of the counts of the impeachment brought against the Duke, but he alleged it was only a loan to the King, and that he himself had not ¦touched a penny of it. Mr Foss seems to think this defence, such as it is, supported by facts.

After the first three years of Charles's reign, Montagu exchanged his new office for that of Lord Privy Seal, in which he remained for the rest of his life, giving, it is said, great satisfaction in the " Court of Requests," over which he presided. On the 5th of February 1626, he had been raised to the title of Earl of Manchester, and he continued to do the King's pleasure in the most pliant manner to the close of his life. He died November 7, 1642, just in time to escape from the necessity of making up his mind between the King and Parliament in the Civil War. He wrote shortly before his death a little treatise of religious meditations; but his household at Kimbolton had the reputation of great licentiousness. He left five sons, the second of whom, Walter, became a Catholic priest, was made Abbot of St Martin's Abbey, near Pontoise, and was a busy intriguer, and in much trouble during the whole of his life, chiefly in connection with Queen Henrietta, till his death in 1670. James Montagu, the third son, was a Puritan member for Huntingdon, and is the ancestor of the Montagus of Wiltshire. Henry, the fourth son, was master of St Catherine's Hospital, and died without issue. George Montagu, the fifth son, was also a Puritan, and member for Huntingdon in the Long Parliament, and an Independent, who had some reputation in the House, and, though not an extreme man, sat on in the "Rump." He was M.P. for Dover in 1661, and died in 1681. His fourth son, Charles, rose to be Chancellor of the Exchequer in 1694; and on December 13, 1700, was created Baron Halifax, with reversion to his nephew, George Montagu. This Charles Montagu, Lord Halifax, first attracted notice by a satirical effusion, in combination with his college friend Prior, in answer to Dryden's 'Hind and Panther.' He soon distinguished himself among the younger Whigs, and entered the Convention Parliament to commence a brilliant career, in Macaulay's words, "as a statesman, an orator, and a munificent patron of learning and literature." He had been intended for the Church, but had been tempted at the Revolution by Dorset into the paths of politics. "At thirty," says Macaulay, "he would have gladly given all his chances in life for a comfortable vicarage and a chaplain's scarf ; at thirty-seven he was First Lord of the Treasury, Chancellor of the Exchequer, and a Regent of the Kingdom, and this elevation he owed not at all to favour, but solely to the unquestionable superiority of his talents for administration and debate." He was at college a diligent pupil of Newton's as well as a votary of the muses ; the latter pursuit he gave up after entering on politics. His great talents were subject to the drawback of arrogance and coldness to old friends as he rose above them, ostentation in the display of his new riches, and an inordinate desire for praise. These defects are not to be wondered at when we remember that he rose from a struggling younger son of a younger son, with barely £50 a-year, to an income of £12,000 and a magnificent villa on the Thames, furnished with every luxury. He was the great financier of the reign of William III.—the greatest the Whigs ever had—and was impeached along with Portland, but the accusation was dropped. The attack was renewed in Anne's reign, but the House of Lords protected him. He held no office during that reign, but was active in debate, particularly in favour of the union with Scotland. He was mainly instrumental in the creation of the British Museum by the purchase of the Cotton MSS., which formed the nucleus of the library. He survived to receive the reward of Court favour under the Hanoverian dynasty, and on October 19, 1714, he was made Viscount Sunbury (Middlesex) and Earl of Halifax. He died May 19, 1715, and his nephew succeeding to the barony, was raised to the higher titles, and left them to his son George (who assumed the name of Dunk), and was Lord-Lieutenant of Ireland in 1749, but died without male issue in 1772, when the Halifax honours became extinct. A brother of his, James Montagu, rose to be Chief Baron in 1722.

We now turn to the *existing* ducal branch. Edward, the *eldest* son of the evil lawyer who bribed and bowed himself into the ermine and a peerage, was a man of whom any family might be proud, for he is the Earl of Manchester of the great Civil contest. He was educated at Sidney Sussex College, Cambridge, attended Prince Charles on his expedition to Spain, and was made a Knight of the Bath on his coronation. He entered the House of Commons in the first Parliament of that reign for Huntingdonshire, and sat till, in May 1626, he was summoned to the Upper House in his father's barony of Montagu of Kimbolton. He was more generally known, however, by the courtesy title of Viscount Mandeville. He soon became a leader of the Puritan and popular party in the Upper House, and in 1640, was one of those peers who advised the King at York to call a new Parliament, and acted as a Commissioner to treat with the invading Scotch Covenanters. His name was one of those forged by Lord Savile to the letter of invitation to the Scots. In the Long Parliament Mandeville pursued the same popular career, being always in the van of the Puritan minority in the House of Lords. He was, as is well known, impeached of treason by the King along with the five members of the House of Commons in January 1642. Henceforth his career was determined still more decidedly on the Parliamentary side. He raised a regiment at the outbreak of hostili-

ties, and became their colonel. He next had a major-
generalship in some of the eastern counties, which was
extended, on the superseding of Lord Willoughby of
Parham, to the command of all the Eastern Association. Here, with Cromwell as his second in command,
he contrived to gain success after success, till their
return to the eastern counties after the battle of Marston Moor. Then differences sprang up between the
Earl, for such he had become by the death of his
father, and Cromwell, on questions respecting the
sectaries who formed so large a part of Cromwell's
regiments, and whose extreme opinions were distasteful
to Manchester, who was a Presbyterian. These differences were fostered if not created by the Scotchman
Crawford, the third in command, and we find both
Manchester and Cromwell in London busy in securing
support against each other. Manchester took counsel
with the Scotch Commissioners and Essex, while
Cromwell relied on the House of Commons, a great
majority of whom were weary of the existing conduct
of the war. Essex's defeat and surrender in the west
led to the consolidation of his army with Manchester's,
and the second battle of Newbury, in which Manchester had the command. The dissatisfation at the results of this battle led to inquiry into the causes, and
to counter-statements and charges by Manchester and
Cromwell. These led to the Self-denying and New
Model ordinances, which removed Manchester from
his command. He still remained, however, one of the
Committee of Government at Derby House. He had
been previously elected Chancellor of the University
of Cambridge, and became Speaker of the House of
Lords, and afterwards as such, in 1646, was appointed

along with William Lenthall to take charge of the new
Great Seal until regular Commissioners should be
appointed. He held it accordingly till 1648. Manchester's political course was now again tending towards the party of which Cromwell was a leader.
Crawford, the promoter of discord between them, had
been killed at the siege of Hereford; and when Danzil
Holles and the extreme Presbyterians carried matters
to such lengths in the July of 1647, and brought down
mobs to coerce the Houses of Parliament, Manchester
and Lenthall, with the Independent and Moderate
Presbyterian members of the Houses, withdrew, and
repaired to the army of Fairfax and Cromwell, by
whom they were soon restored to their seats. Manchester, however, resisted the trial of the King, and
after the establishment of the Commonwealth withdrew from public life. He never, however, quarrelled
with Cromwell, though the popular historians say he
did, and he was named by the Protector one of the
peers in his new Upper House. That House broke
down, Manchester, like the rest of his order, declining
to sit with the great country gentlemen and high
officers out of whom Cromwell hoped to manufacture
his new *noblesse*. With the rest of the Presbyterian
peers he promoted the Restoration, was appointed
Lord-Lieutenant of Huntingdonshire, was cajoled or
intimidated into sitting among the judges who tried
the "Regicides," and persuaded the City to advance
£100,000 for Charles II.'s mismanaged Dutch war;
but he never took any part in Stuart politics, and
died May 1, 1671, in the sixty-ninth year of his age.
He was called a "sweet meek man;" but though par-
donably amiable and very open to the influence of per-

sons about him, he had peculiarities of temper, and a
certain quiet obstinacy, which prevent us from looking
upon him as a tool in anybody's hands. He had
decided opinions, and took his own course certainly
more independently than most men of the time, and
though not a man of the highest ability, was possessed
of qualities which, had he not been eclipsed by greater
men, would have secured for him a higher reputation
than he actually achieved. His sitting in judgment
on the "Regicides,"—most of whom had been his
former companions in council or in arms,—has been
severely criticised ; but although a man of sterner stuff
might have declined the office, it must be remembered
that they were few, indeed, who at that epoch had the
moral courage to risk the loss of their fortunes, if not
their lives, by setting themselves up as opponents of
the wishes of the Crown. Robert, his eldest son and
successor, as second Earl of Manchester, was not a man
of any note, and died at Montpelier in March 1682.
His son and successor, Charles, fourth Earl of Manchester, was a man of greater energy of character.
Disapproving of James II.'s measures, he retired from
Court, and at the Revolution secured Huntingdonshire
for the Prince of Orange, raising a body of horse for
his service. He was present with William at the
battle of the Boyne, and was at the siege of Limerick.
In 1696 he was appointed Ambassador Extraordinary
to the Republic of Venice, and three years afterwards
went in the same capacity to Louis of France. In
1707 he was re-appointed Ambassador to Venice, but
had no further employments during the reign of Anne.
After the accession of George I. he was made one of
the Gentlemen of the Bedchamber, and in April 1719,

as head of a great Hanoverian house, was created Duke
of Manchester, April 28, 1719, and died in January 1722.
He was a man of some humour and penetration, a friend
of Addison and men of literature, and a great patron of
musicians and the opera. He was strongly anti-Jacobite
in his political opinions. The *Dukes* of Manchester,
however, have not been a distinguished line of peers.
William, the second Duke, was one of the Lords of
the Bedchamber to George I. and George II., and in
1737 was Captain of the Yeomen of the Guard, and
died October 21, 1739, being succeeded by his brother
Robert, third Duke, who sat in the House of Commons
for Huntingdonshire in 1734, and was Vice-Chamber-
lain to Queen Caroline, and afterwards a Lord of the
Bedchamber. After the accession of George III. he
was appointed Chamberlain to Queen Charlotte, and
died May 10, 1762. His younger son, Lord Charles
Montagu, was M.P. for Huntingdonshire and Governor
of South Carolina. George, his eldest son, and fourth
Duke of Manchester, was a Lord of the Bedchamber
in 1763, and in 1780 Master of the Horse. He was
sent as ambassador to Paris in 1783 by the Shelburne
Ministry, along with David Hartley, to conclude the
treaties of peace with America, and signed them at
that city on the memorable 3d of September. He
died September 2, 1788. William, his eldest surviving son, the fifth Duke, who married a daughter of
the Duke of Gordon, was Governor of Jamaica in
1808, and was also collector of the Customs for the
Port of London. He died March 18, 1843. His
eldest son and successor, George, sixth Duke, was a
commander in the Royal Navy. He married, first, the
daughter and heiress of General Sparrow, of Brampton

Park, Huntingdonshire, by Lady Olivia, daughter of
the Earl of Gosford—and this lady is the mother of
the present Duke, and of the present Lord Robert
Montagu, M.P.   The Duke married, secondly, a very
young Irish lady.   He was a strange man, of strong
Evangelical opinions, and author of some prophetic
commentaries.   His resemblance to the portraits of
the second Earl of Manchester, the Parliamentary
general, was very striking.   He died August 18, 1855,
and was succeeded by William Drogo Montagu, the
seventh and present Duke of Manchester, a man of
respectable but not remarkable abilities.   The family
for the last generation or two has belonged to the
Tory party, and now the younger brother of the Duke,
Lord Robert Montagu, holds a prominent place in
their ranks.

We turn to the second existing branch.   Sidney,
" of Barnwell," the *sixth* brother of the first and worst
Earl of Manchester, was Groom of the Bedchamber to
James I., and was knighted by that monarch ; he became afterwards one of the Masters of the Requests,
but his only notable act was connected with the rebellion.   He was sitting in the Long Parliament for
Huntingdonshire when the oath to live and die with
the Earl of Essex was tendered to the House, and not
only refused it, but produced the King's proclamation
declaring all who took it traitors.   He was expelled
the House on December 3, 1642, and committed for
thirteen days to the Tower, and on his release retired
from public life.   He had purchased from Sir Oliver
Cromwell, of HINCHINBROOK, the estate of that name
for £3060, and it has remained ever since the principal seat of this branch of the Montagus.   Edward,

his son, took the popular side, became Cromwell's right hand in the eastern counties, distinguished himself in the storm of Lincoln in May 1644, fought at Marston Moor, Naseby, and the storm of Bridgewater in 1645, commanded four regiments at the siege of Bristol, and was one of the officers who signed the capitulation when Prince Rupert surrendered the city. He entered the House of Commons as knight of the shire for Huntingdon, and down to the year 1648 acted with the Independents. In that year he retired, dreading the military encroachments; but the rise of Cromwell, his intimate personal friend, re-opened the path, and he was appointed in 1653 one of the Commissioners of the Treasury and Admiralty. He thenceforward turned his attention to the sea, and joined Blake in the direct command of the fleet. He was one of the sixty-two nominated by Cromwell to his " Other House "—an assembly not to exceed seventy in number, nor to be less than twenty-one, to be for life, and on the death of any member the vacancy not to be filled up except with the approbation of the existing members. It was intended, doubtless, as a step to an hereditary House, and was meant at the time as a check to the House of Commons, which had been proceeding against religious fanatics like Naylor and other persons with a severity which the Protector could not interfere personally to check without coming into direct collision with Parliamentary authority. The first nominations included a considerable sprinkling of the old peers, and their sons and relatives, joined with many of the leading gentry, officers of the army and navy, statesmen and members of Parliament, and the most active adherents of the Puritan party, Presby-

terians and Independents alike, including a certain
number of men who had risen from the lower ranks of
society. The House actually met and transacted business, though no regular record of their proceedings
remains. Their acts, however, were stultified by
the abstinence of most of the old nobility, and the
steady refusal of the House of Commons to recognise
their existence. At the downfall of Richard Cromwell, Montagu was at sea, " arbitrating " in a warlike
fashion between the Danes and Swedes ; but the restored " Rump " tried to conciliate him by naming
him jointly with Algernon Sidney and others to
negotiate a peace with Denmark, and afterwards
jointly with Monk to the command of the fleet.
Montagu's conduct at this crisis is the only blot on
his political reputation. He had been ardently attached to the Cromwell family, and hated those who
had overthrown it. Charles knew this, and at once
made overtures to him, and Montagu consented to
accept the command of the Commonwealth fleet, *with
the sanction* of the Stuart Prince, and the understanding that it was to be used in case of an opportunity
to forward the Restoration. In this matter he acted
independently of Monk and anticipated him, and the
latter never forgave this action, nor did, of course, the
Commonwealth men. He brought over the King to
England, and on the day after his landing at Dover,
Charles sent him the Order of the Garter, and on the
12th of July 1660, he was created Baron Montagu of
St Neots, Viscount Hinchinbrook and Earl of Sandwich,
Master of the Wardrobe, Admiral of the Narrow Seas,
and Lieutenant to the Duke of York, then Lord High
Admiral. The rest of his life was merely an uninter-

rupted series of naval services, in which he was generally eminently successful. He also gained great
popularity in the navy by opposing the promotion of
relatives of peers who had no other merit, and thereby
gave great offence to the Duke of York. In 1672, in
the war with the Dutch, lying in Solebay, off the
Suffolk coast, as second in command to the Duke, he
strongly warned him of the danger of their position;
but the Duke tauntingly replied that he said so because he had fear. The combined English and French
fleets were surprised by De Ruyter and entirely defeated. In the engagement which ensued, Sandwich's
own ship, the Royal James, took fire, and refusing to
leave it, in consequence of the Duke's taunt, he was
blown up in it, May 28, 1672, the Duke being greatly
blamed for not succouring him. Thus Montagu paid
with his life for his treachery to the Commonwealth
in behalf of the house of Stuart. Nor had his personal morality—if we may credit contemporary gossip-
mongers—at all improved with the advent of the
Restoration to which he had lent his aid. One of his
younger sons, Sidney, was, by the heiress of Sir
Francis Wortley, the father of Edward Wortley-Montagu, husband of the celebrated Lady Mary, and
father of the eccentric Edward Wortley-Montagu.
The Earl's eldest son, Edward, second Earl of Sandwich, was not a man of any note, and died in February
1689. His son and successor, also an Edward, third
Earl of Sandwich, was Master of the Horse to Prince
George of Denmark, and died October 20, 1729, being
succeeded by his grandson, John, fourth Earl, who was
a man of a very different intellectual stamp from his
immediate predecessors. Though not by any means

Y

remarkable for high ideas of public conduct, and of
the most licentious private character, he had great
administrative powers, great energy of mind, and some
decision of character, together with great application
to business. From his hour of rising, at six, till
dinnner-time, he was absorbed in public business.
When young he had visited Cairo and Constantinople,
as well as Italy and most of the Courts of Europe.
He attached himself to the Bedford party, and when
the Duke was appointed First Lord of the Admiralty
in December 1744, he was named one of the junior
Lords. In November 1746, he was appointed Minister
Plenipotentiary to the States of Holland, and afterwards to the Congress of Aix-la-Chapelle, being sent to
conduct the preliminaries to the treaty of peace there,
May 1748, nominally as assistant, but really as manager of the Duke of Cumberland. In February in the
same year he was appointed First Lord of the Admiralty and a Privy Councillor, and soon after a Lord
Justice, during the absence of the King in that year
and in 1750. In 1751 Pelham, finding the Opposition
weakened by the death of the Prince of Wales, and
the renewed friendship of his brother Newcastle, resolved to get rid of the Bedfords, and as a step to so
doing dismissed Sandwich. He remained out of office
till December 1755, when he was made Vice-Treasurer,
Receiver - General, and Paymaster of Ireland and
Treasurer of War there. In February 1763, he was
nominated Ambassador to Spain, but the legation was
not carried into effect, for on George Grenville succeeding Lord Bute at the head of the Government in
that year he appointed Sandwich to his old post of
First Lord of the Admiralty, instead of Charles

Townshend, for whom it had been originally designed.
In August of the same year he was appointed one of
the principal Secretaries of State, in which office he
continued till July 1765. During this period he
gained his celebrated *sobriquet* of " Jemmy Twitcher,"
from his violent attack on the blasphemous and ob-
scene poem of Wilkes, called ' An Essay on Woman,'
of which only eleven copies had been printed for presents to friends, of one of which the Government, in
a very discreditable manner, got possession. Being
written as a parody on Pope's ' Essay on Man,' it was
dedicated to Sandwich instead of Bolingbroke, and
began, " Awake, my Sandwich ! " instead of " Arise,
my St John ! " and there were notes professed to be
written by Bishop Warburton. Sandwich, in terms
of virtuous indignation, denounced the character of
the publication, and said it was a libel on a Bishop, a
member of that House, and the House ultimately
passed an address to the King to order a prosecution
of the author. It was publicly reported that Sandwich had been, only a fortnight before, one of a convivial meeting at the London Tavern along with Wilkes,
and had there joined him in lewd catches ; and the
Earl's private character being well known, the public
became greatly incensed at him. The ' Beggars'
Opera ' happened to be acting at the time at Covent
Garden Theatre, and when Macheath came to the
words, " That Jemmy Twitcher should peach I own
surprises me ! " a sudden burst of applause fixed the
name for the rest of his life on the Earl of Sandwich.
In 1764 he stood an unsuccessful contest for the High
Stewardship of the University of Cambridge, and the
poet Gray wrote a stinging pasquinade on him, in

which, alluding to the support he had obtained from the clergy, he makes *Divinity* address the Earl thus:—

"Never hang down your head, you poor penitent elf;
Come, kiss me, I'll be Mrs Twitcher myself!"

In December 1770, he resigned office as Secretary, and in January 1771, the Duke of Grafton appointed him First Lord of the Admiralty, greatly against the will of the King, who much disliked Sandwich. In this post, however, the Earl remained till the fall of the North Ministry, taking part warmly in all the measures of that Cabinet, and being himself as warmly attacked from time to time, getting into great disfavour with the public as the enemy of Admiral Keppel, and giving occasion for Erskine's first great burst of forensic eloquence, in a case brought on by Sandwich filling Greenwich Hospital with landsmen for electioneering purposes. He was, however, a great patron of Captain Cook, and instigated him to his last voyage, and when Admiral Rodney was made a Baron, Sandwich claimed for him an Earldom, observing that his own ancestor had been made an Earl and Master of the Wardrobe for three lives. In 1783, under the Coalition Cabinet, Sandwich took the office of Ranger of the Parks, and was dismissed from it with them. He then retired into private life, and died April 30, 1792. Among other romantic incidents of his life, his connection with Miss Reay, an actress, by whom he had nine children, terminated most tragically, she being shot by a clergyman who had fallen in love with her. One of her sons by the Earl, Basil Montagu, obtained considerable reputation as a barrister and as the editor of Bacon's works, and the first who attempted to vindicate that great man's moral character. The Earl was succeeded by his son John, fifth Earl, who with his son George John, sixth Earl (June 6, 1814), and his grandson John William, seventh and present Earl (May 21, 1818), present nothing calling for particular notice.

To sum up a narrative which must have struck our readers as unusually dislocated, the great house of Montagu possibly springs from a bastard of the great Norman family, obtained its first wealth from a Sequestrator, and has added to the history of the country five great men, of whom two at least were also unscrupulous profligates. These were the Edward Montagu who ruined Danby, but stood by the Revolution and became a Duke; the Charles Montagu who was William III.'s financier, one of Macaulay's Whig gods; Montagu, Earl of Manchester, and chief of the Presbyterian Puritans; Edward, first Earl of Sandwich; and Jemmy Twitcher, the statesman-scoundrel of the Wilkes faction fight. As a house they have, on the whole, deserved well of the people, having risked their heads and estates twice on the popular side, and even now, though both branches are distinctly Conservative, they neither profess nor favour bad immutable Toryism. Their specialty as a family has been unscrupulousness, but they have shown for centuries a high sense of the national weal, and from time to time have thrown off a man in whom great ability has been united with high public honour and exceptional private worth. Taking them as a whole, and setting the Puritan earl against the subservient judge, the stately admiral against Jemmy Twitcher, they have been no discredit to the English governing class.

The Osbornes.

E include the Osbornes, as we shall in-
clude the Fitzroys, among the govern-
ing families, partly on account of their
possessions, but chiefly because the
popular voice assigns them that position. They are, however, not of the
older nobility, have produced but one great man, and
for the last two centuries have been little more
conspicuous than all considerable landowners in
England are forced to become. Their pedigree is,
of course, made up in Peerages, and there was, no
doubt, a family named Osborne, in Kent, in the
time of Henry VI., but there is nothing to connect
that house with the present, and they bore different
arms. The real founder was EDWARD OSBORNE, who
may have been the son of Richard, the son of Richard
who married the heiress of the Broughtons, though it
is not probable, but who certainly was apprenticed in
Henry VIII.'s reign to Sir William Hewit, the cloth-
worker, a leading merchant of the City, said to have
had an estate of £6000 a-year. Edward's fortune
was made by a romantic incident. Sir W. Hewit had
a daughter, an only child, and the nurse, playing with
her in her father's house, one of the best on old

London Bridge, dropped her into the river. Edward
Osborne saw the accident, leaped into the water, and
won at the same moment a bride and an estate which
made his family historical. Miss Hewit brought him
lands in Barking, Essex, Wales (parish), and Harthill,
Yorkshire; and Osborne raised himself to the Lord
Mayoralty of London in 1582, when he was knighted.
In 1585 he became representative of the City in Parliament, and died in 1591, being succeeded by his son
Hewit Osborne, who served with distinction in Elizabeth's Irish wars, was knighted by Essex for gallantry
in the field, and died in 1614. He left, by his wife—a
Fleetwood, daughter of the Master of the Mint—a son,
and a daughter married to Christopher Wardesford,
Strafford's deputy in Ireland and devoted friend. The
son, Edward Osborne, of Kiveton, Yorkshire, consequently allied himself to Strafford, was created a
baronet on July 13, 1620, and was made Vice-Presi-
dent of the Council of the North, a machinery set
up, with Strafford as President, to exercise despotic
power.

He was highly esteemed by Strafford, who looked
upon him as one of his fastest friends. Writing to
him from Dublin, on the 10th of February 1639,
Wentworth says :—" I send you herewith my commission, which makes you my Deputy-Lieutenant-Gen-
eral, and gives you absolute power amongst them, as
if I were present in person ; nor do I only now give
notice to the rest of the Deputies the rank, esteem,
and power they must acknowledge in you, and conform
themselves to your orders accordingly, but have so
ordered the matter as, together with the commission,
you will receive his Majesty's gracious letters requir-

ing all the other Deputies to observe and obey your
person and orders for his Majesty's service, as is fit.
You see how much I have undertaken for you, and
what a field of honour you have before you; therefore,
I shall not need to incite you to take good heed to
yourself, and by your wakefulness and virtue in the
exercise of so great a trust to express yourself to his
Majesty's satisfaction and your own great advantage,
and, I trust, future preferment, always carrying in
mind that you are sure to be looked on with an evil
eye by such of the great ones as love me not, and to
hear of anything you chance to do amiss; and this
you get by being esteemed and avowed my friend.
But as this ought to awaken you to every good and
careful duty, so I trust their displeasure shall do you
as little hurt as hitherto, I praise God and thank the
King, it hath done me." This "field of honour," however, was closed to Sir Edward by the meeting of the
Long Parliament, to which he was returned as member for Berwick, having served for the same place in
the Parliament of April preceding. On petition, however, he was unseated, and thenceforth disappears in a
rather odd way out of history, even the date of his
death not being ascertained.

He married, first, the eldest daughter of Thomas
Viscount Fauconberg, and secondly, Anne, daughter
of Thomas Walmisley, of Lancashire, and coheiress,
through her mother, Eleanor Danvers, of the Nevilles,
Lords Latimer. His son by the first marriage was
killed by the fall of a chimney; but the elder son of
the second refounded the family, being the man
known to English history as the Earl of Danby.

THOMAS OSBORNE, born in 1631, was too young to

take any active part in the great civil contest; but
was brought up in the strictest Cavalier principles—
such as were held by his father, and taught in Strafford's school of statesmanship. Indeed, the ideas by
which he seems to have been guided in his subsequent
career as a minister are singularly in harmony with
the principles and feelings of the great Earl. Like
him, Thomas Osborne was bent on the aggrandisement
of the royal prerogative at the expense of the popular
liberties, and was a strong advocate of the doctrines of
right divine and passive obedience. Like him, he had
a certain regard for the dignity of his country, and
was desirous that the King, absolute at home, should
assume abroad an independent and leading position.
They both agreed in associating the untrammeled
government of the Crown at home with the dignity of
the nation in the eyes of Europe, quite as much as
with the gratification of the private wishes of the
King. They neither of them had any desire to see
the authority of the Crown dependent merely on the
support of a foreign government, and on this point
there was a fundamental difference between their
views and the grovelling notions of the Stuart princes.
Danby had the reverence for the Church of England and the dislike of Popery which so seriously
disturbed the unanimity of the Cavalier party during
the Civil War. He had, at the same time, the de-
ficiency in moral elevation of character and the profligate disregard of all principle, which detracts so much
from our admiration of nearly all that school and of
Strafford himself. Osborne was as audacious and
self-confident as his father's great patron, of whom he
was in some degree a feebler representative; but apart

from his undoubted inferiority in intellectual power, he had never undergone the early influences of a nobler political training, such as that to which the mind of Wentworth was subjected while he shared the counsels and friendship of Eliot, Pym, and Hampden. Osborne was a thoroughly unscrupulous man, bent on self-aggrandisement, and careless of the amount of personal degradation which he might incur in accumulating wealth and titles. He had succeeded to an estate seriously impaired by the Royalists' disasters in the Civil War, and he devoted himself to repairing these losses at the expense of all decency and honour. He was only redeemed from the common herd of profligate schemers of that age by his superior talents and sagacity, and his fixity of political ideas on two or three points. His versatility and plausible manners soon recommended him to the notice of the King, and the ascendancy of Clarendon was the only real obstacle to his immediate rise to power. He was one of the most vehement of the opponents of that statesman, whom the old Cavalier party always distrusted and disliked, and after his fall Osborne began his political ascent. In 1671 he was appointed Treasurer of the Navy, and in May 1672, one of the Privy Council. On June 19 in the following year, on the fall of the Cabal Ministry, Osborne was placed virtually at the head of public affairs by the immensely lucrative and important appointment of Lord High Treasurer. On the 15th of August in the same year (1673) he was raised to the Peerage as Baron Osborne of Kiveton, and Viscount Latimer of Danby, Yorkshire ; and on the 27th June 1674, he was created Earl of Danby— which last title had become extinct in the person of

Henry Danvers, brother of Eleanor Danvers. On July 19, 1675, he was created Viscount Dumblane, in Scotland, and on April 21, 1677, a Knight of the Garter. The administration of Danby must be judged with reference to what we have said above of his views and character. It is pronounced by Burnet to have been an attempt to revive the Cavalier party, and to govern England on their principles, and Macaulay adopts this view. At home Danby was a bigoted Protestant Tory of the exaggerated Cavalier type, who sacrificed everything to the royal prerogative, and detested and persecuted nonconformists to the Church of England. In this province he was shamelessly venal and covetous. Abroad, his policy was more creditable, owing to his higher ideas of national dignity. He wished to break off the subserviency to France, and he made Sir William Temple his political guide on foreign policy. Macaulay considers that he carried out this policy as well as he could consistently with the strong inclinations of the King for a French alliance and French money, and Danby's own determination to keep his place at any sacrifice. He contrived to bring about the match between the Princess Mary and William of Orange, which was deeply resented by Louis, and which was a master-stroke which stood Danby in good stead in future years. He was obliged, however, to be the agent of his royal master in his pecuniary transactions with Louis, and the latter, when he found Danby his implacable enemy, contrived, as we have seen, through Ralph Montagu, to convert this unwilling agency on the part of Danby into an engine of his ruin in England, as if he had himself been the hired servant of France. The fall of Danby—his impeachment in 1678

—the postponement of the proceedings from Parliament to Parliament through the rest of the reign of Charles without his ever being brought to trial—his imprisonment in the Tower for five years, until he was allowed to be bailed in 1684—the vote of the Lords, at the commencement of the new reign, that the impeachment had fallen through by the dissolution of Parliament, and his restoration thereupon to his seat in the House and to political life,—are matters of general history. Danby had always been a successful speaker, but his talents are said to have lain in practical action and decision of character rather than in oratory or theoretical speculation. Burnet says he was a plausible speaker, but too copious, so as to become wearisome. He soon perceived the tendency of James's measures towards Popery and the destruction of the Established Church, and entered into correspondence with the Dutch Ministers and William of Orange, on whom he had a great claim as the negotiator of his marriage. Having decided on his political course, there was no hesitation in Danby. He signed the letter of invitation to the Prince, and reconciled himself, as we have seen, to Devonshire and the Whigs, undertaking to secure York for the Revolution. This he managed in a very skilful manner, availing himself of a popular gathering to spread a panic-cry that the Papists were massacring the citizens, appealing to the militia, who had been called together to keep order, and, with their assistance, surprising and disarming Sir John Reresby, the governor, and the garrison. He then convoked the citizens and procured their cheerful adhesion to the Prince's cause. The Revolution accomplished, however, and King James a

fugitive abroad, Danby's Cavalier principles, which had
been rather rudely strained in the part he had just
taken in opposition to the Crown, began to revive, and
he endeavoured to accommodate theory and facts by
the specious doctrine of an "abdication" having taken
place by the flight of the King; and the Prince of
Wales's birth being held doubtful, and both unsub-
stantiated and unsubstantiable by the flight of the
only competent witnesses, he held that Mary had
become actually, according to the strict rules of
succession, Queen Regnant, and endeavoured to set
up her sovereignty in opposition alike to the Regency
scheme of some of the Tories, and the election of
William, which was advocated by the Whigs.   He
wrote to Mary herself, offering to support her pretensions, but her earnest and even angry repudiation
of any separate interest from her husband induced
Danby to retrace his steps, and by his influence the
House of Lords consented to invite William to ascend
the throne,—a service of inconceivable importance to
the country, and the one incident in the history of
the Osbornes which justifies their dukedom, and their
hold over the popular imagination.   In the new Government Danby became Lord President of the Council; William, much to his chagrin and disappointment,
putting the Treasuryship into commission, instead of
placing its enormous powers of jobbery and plunder
at the disposal of one individual.   After a sharp
struggle with Saville, Marquess of Halifax (towards
whom he had always entertained a strong hostility),
and Shrewsbury and the Whigs, Danby succeeded in
1690 in becoming the real head of the Government.
On the 9th of April 1689, he had been created Mar-

quess of Carmarthen. His administration was able,
but unscrupulous. He was, of course, entirely in
unison with the King's foreign policy, and at home,
at first against William's wish, he commenced again
on a great scale the system of Parliamentary corruption which he had carried to great lengths in his
ministry in Charles's reign. He was hated by the
Whigs, whose old feud against him had revived after
the Revolution; but though an attempt was made in
1690 to exclude him from power by a proposition
that no one should be admitted to any public employment who had been impeached in former reigns, he
held his ground for some time with the favour of the
King and Queen. When William went to Ireland, he
was nominated one of the Council of Nine, and Mary
was requested by her husband to be guided by him,
especially in case of any difference in the Council;
but a gradual divergence appeared between the King
and his Minister, and though, on the 4th May 1694,
he was created Duke of Leeds, he soon after fell hopelessly from power. The crave to build a great house
at any risk, which is the besetting sin of many prominent Englishmen, was never absent from his mind,
and his venality ruined him at last. A committee of
inquiry into the bribes said to have been received by
great men, soon led to the detection of the bribe of
five thousand five hundred guineas which Leeds had
received from the East India Company. Wharton
reported this to the House of Commons, and was ordered to impeach Leeds at the bar of the Lords in the
name of the Commons. Leeds had been addressing
the Lords in his defence, admitting that he had procured the money from the Company, but alleging it

was only for his friend Bates (the agent employed), and not for himself, and illustrating his peculiar ideas of public morality by quoting his conduct in a former case in Charles II.'s time, when he had told several falsehoods in order to obtain money for another friend. Hearing that he was about to be impeached by the Commons, he hastened thither, and obtained permission to address them at the bar of that House. But his speech was ill-judged in its tone, and he scarcely attempted to set up any defence on the point at issue, but boasted that had it not been for him there would have been no House of Commons at all to impeach him. On his withdrawal, the Commons sent up Wharton with the impeachment, and appointed managers to draw up articles and collect evidence. But one (legal) link in the evidence proved to be wanting, and the witness who it was believed could have supplied it fled to Holland. The proceedings were therefore suspended, and were never afterwards revived. Leeds had the effrontery to assume the bearing of an injured man, and even moved the Lords (but vainly) to declare the impeachment dismissed. The King, from respect to the memory of the Queen, allowed the name and emoluments of Lord President to remain with Leeds, who was, however, given to understand that he was not to appear in the Privy Council, or take part in the management of public affairs. He remained in this equivocal position four years, and only quitted it on receipt of very heavy grants of Crown lands. In Queen Anne's reign he took a prominent part in the defence of Sacheverel, with whom, of course, he sympathised strongly; and his excessive vitality—an attribute of almost all founders — kept his sickly body alive till July 26, 1712, when he died, eighty years old, and full, if not of honour, of dignities and wealth. His character, which has been the study of many English historians, may, we believe, be summed up in two words. He was a *bourgeois* Strafford.

The Duke married Lady Bridget Bertie, second daughter of the Earl of Lindsey, and was succeeded by his youngest son, Peregrine, a sailor, who, though of questionable discretion, distinguished himself by his courage and audacity, and died in June 1729, Vice-Admiral of the Red. He had married Bridget, daughter and heiress of Sir Thomas Hyde, Bart., of North Myms, Hertfordshire, and had two sons and two daughters, one of whom married afterwards Lord Dundonald. The elder son died before his father, but the second, Peregrine, succeeded him as third Duke of Leeds, and after an uneventful life he was followed by Thomas, the fourth Duke, remarkable only for a marriage which constituted him the heir of the Godolphins, and one of the heirs of the Churchills, marrying June 26, 1740, the Lady Mary, daughter of Francis, Earl Godolphin, son and successor of the remarkable statesman who took so ambiguous a course during the reigns of William and Anne, by the Lady Harriet or Henrietta Churchill, eldest daughter of the great Duke of Marlborough. By this marriage, agreeably to the patent granted to the Duke of Marlborough, the succeeding Osbornes as his descendants became Princes of the Holy Roman Empire, a dignity peerage-makers might take the trouble to specify, and ultimately inherited the Godolphin property, including the seat of GODOLPHIN, and the patronage of the borough of Helston, in Cornwall, and the GOG-MAGOG estate among the hills of Cambridgeshire, of that name. His surviving son, Francis Godolphin Osborne, fifth Duke, was Secretary of State for Foreign Affairs before his father's death, under Mr Pitt, and remained such till 1791. John Adams, the American Minister, says of him: "The Marquess of Carmarthen is a modest, amiable man; treats all men with civility, and is much esteemed by the Foreign Ministers as well as the nation, but is not an enterprising Minister;" and Wilberforce speaks of him in his diary as "the elegant Carmarthen." In 1787 he caused a great sensation by inviting, as Foreign Secretary, not only the Foreign Ministers, but Mr Fox and the leaders of the Opposition, to dine with him. In the 'Auckland Correspondence' it is told how Mr Fox was more noticed by the Foreign Ministers than the host himself, and was for once well dressed. The next year he caused equal surprise by inviting M. de Calonne to meet the French Ambassador at dinner, a lady having just been forbidden the French Court for visiting M. de Calonne. In 1791 he resigned, in consequence of Mr Pitt not persisting in his demands on Russia; but though he voted occasionally against the Government, he expressed strong aversion to the lengths to which some of Fox's Whig noblemen were going in foreign affairs. He died January 31, 1799. He had made a great match, marrying for his first wife (November 29, 1773) Lady Amelia Darcy, only daughter and heiress of Robert, last Earl of Holderness, Baron Conyers, in which last dignity she succeeded her father, and transmitted it to the Osbornes. This barony had been created in 1509 in the son of

z

Sir John Conyers by Margery, daughter of Philip, Lord Darcy. With this marriage Leeds obtained HORNBY CASTLE, in Yorkshire. The Conyers family were a branch from the parent stem at Stockton, in Durham, and rose to importance in Richmondshire by the patronage of the Scroopes of Bolton, about the time of Richard II. "Gul. Coniers," says Leland, "the first lord of that name, dyd great coste on Horneby Castle. It was before but a mene thing." By the Baroness Conyers (from whom he obtained a divorce in 1779) the Duke had two sons, the younger of whom, Lord Francis Godolphin Osborne, was the father of the present Duke of Leeds. The Duke married, secondly, a Miss Catherine Anguish, whose exquisite beauty is extolled by Lord Sheffield in the 'Auckland Correspondence.' His eldest son, George William Frederick, who succeeded him as sixth Duke of Leeds, was Lord-Lieutenant of the North Riding of Yorkshire, and Lord Proprietor and Governor of the Scilly Islands in right of the Godolphins. On the 4th of May 1827, he was appointed Master of the Horse in Canning's Ministry, and from this time the Osbornes, who had been rather Conservative-Whigs than Tories during Pitt's reign, moved forward with the Canningites to the Liberal party. The Duke died July 10, 1838, and was succeeded by his only son, Francis Godolphin D'Arcy D'Arcy Osborne (seventh Duke), who had been summoned to the Upper House as Lord Osborne the month before his father's death, and assumed, in 1849, the name of D'Arcy in addition to his own. He was married to an American lady, but died without children May 4, 1859, when all his titles, except the Barony of Conyers, devolved on his cousin, George Godolphin Osborne, second Baron Godolphin (of this family), son of Lord Francis Godolphin Osborne mentioned above, who had been created Lord Godolphin, of Farnham-Royal, Bucks, on the 14th May 1832, and died in 1850. This nobleman is the present and eighth Duke of Leeds, and a son and grandson promise a continuance of the dignity in the same line. The Barony of Conyers devolved on the nephew of the seventh Duke, Sackville-George-Lane-Fox, son of Sackville-Lane-Fox, Esq., M.P., by Lady Charlotte Osborne, only daughter of the sixth Duke of Leeds.

The descendants of the lucky apprentice have, therefore, acquired two peerages, and estates which raise them at least to the second rank. The family risked its fate on the Revolution, but it has otherwise not done much for England, and its most prominent member now is the present Duke's brother, Lord Sidney Godolphin Osborne, a Rector, who, as the "S. G. O." of the 'Times,' has so often and so ably pleaded the cause of the friendless and the poor.

The Fitzroys.

HE Fitzroys are the heirs of a bastard of Charles II. The illegitimate children of that King are popularly believed to be legion, but he acknowledged only James Stuart, son of a young lady in Jersey, who took holy orders and died a Catholic priest; James, Duke of Monmouth, son of Lucy Walters, executed for treason by his uncle's command; Mary, daughter of the same lady, married first to William Sarsfield, an Irish gentleman, and afterwards to William Fanshaw; Charles Fitzroy, Duke of Southampton, Henry Fitzroy, Duke of Grafton, George Fitzroy, Duke of Northumberland, and Anne, Countess of Sussex, all children of BARBARA VILLIERS, Duchess of Cleveland; Charles Beauclerk, Duke of St Albans, and James Beauclerk, sons of Nell Gwynne; Charles Lennox, Duke of Richmond, son of Louisa de Querouaille, Duchess of Portsmouth; Mary Tudor, married to the heir of Lord Derwentwater, daughter of Mary Davis; Charles Fitzcharles, and a girl who died young, children of Catherine Pegge; and Charlotte Boyle, *alias* Fitzroy, wife of Sir Robert Paston, Bart., afterwards Earl of Yarmouth, daughter of Elizabeth, Viscountess Shannon. Three of these founded dukedoms which still exist—Grafton, Richmond, and St Albans ; and other families trace their rise to connection with the children of the last popular Stuart.

BARBARA, DUCHESS OF CLEVELAND, ancestress of the Fitzroys, was one of the remarkable family of VILLIERS, she being daughter and coheiress of a half-brother of George Villiers, first Duke of Buckingham, of whom Felton rid England, cousin of Elizabeth Villiers, the mistress and counsellor of William of Orange, and niece of Sir Edward Villiers, ancestor of the Earls of Jersey and Clarendon. Her father died of his wounds, received in the royal cause, when she was only an infant. Her early connection with the eccentric Earl of Chesterfield has already been noticed.* Just before the Restoration she married Mr Roger Palmer—afterwards created Earl of Castlemaine—and on the King's return to England deserted Chesterfield for her royal lover. This connection lasted till about the year 1672, when she had a child, disavowed by the King, and generally attributed to Churchill. In 1670, she was created Baroness Nonsuch, in Surrey, Countess of Southampton, and Duchess of Cleveland, with remainder to Charles and George Fitzroy, her eldest and third sons. Her husband died in 1705, and she soon afterwards married an adventurer, who treated her with such brutality that she had to seek the protection of the law against him, and then discovered he had a previous wife still living. She died on the 9th of October 1709, of dropsy. Burnet says of her : " She was a woman of great beauty, but most enormously vicious and ravenous ; foolish, but imperious ; very uneasy to the King, and always carrying on in-

---

* *Vide antea*, under " the Stanhopes."

trigues with other men, while yet she pretended she
was jealous of him. His passion for her, and her
strange behaviour towards him, did so disorder him,
that often he was not master of himself, nor capable
of minding business."

Henry Fitzroy, the Duchess's second son by Charles
II., born September 20th, 1663, a man of "more spirit,"
Burnet says, " than any of the King's sons," was bred
to the profession of a sailor, and distinguished himself
in several expeditions. On the 16th of August 1672,
he was created Baron Sudbury, Viscount Ipswich, and
Earl of Euston, in the county of Suffolk, and on the
11th of September 1675, Duke of Grafton in Northamptonshire, and was appointed hereditary "Receiver-
General of the profits of the seals in the Courts of
King's Bench, and Common Pleas, and of the Prises of
Wines." This appointment was commuted in 1845
for a pension of £843 ; and a more valuable pension of
£9000, charged on the Post Office, was sold to the
nation in 1856 for £193,177. He received besides
the appointment of Hereditary Ranger of Whittlebury
Forest—WAKEFIELD LODGE in which became one of
his principal seats—and of Gamekeeper at Newmarket,
acted as Lord High Constable of England at the coronation of James II., commanded the advance-guard
against his own half-brother Monmouth, who beat him
at Philip's Norton, and indeed he seemed at first disposed to go all lengths with the Court. He played a
creditable part in the expedition to Tunis, but he had
fallen completely under the influence of Churchill, and
on the landing of the Prince of Orange, instead of
hastening as before to proffer his military services to
the King, he joined in the petition of the Bishops and

the Tory Protestants that James would call a Free Parliament. The King, when this address was presented to him, was greatly incensed with Grafton. "He was sure," James said, "*he* could not pretend to act upon principles of conscience; for he had been so ill-bred, that as he knew little of religion, so he regarded it less." But Grafton, unabashed, replied, that "though he had himself little conscience, yet he was of a *party* that had a great deal." He accompanied, however, the King and the royal army as far as Salisbury, but then, along with Churchill, took the lead in setting the example of desertion which was so generally followed. Grafton had been displaced from the command of the Foot Guards, but William replaced him, and intrusted him with the defence of Tilbury Fort. He voted for the Regency scheme, but took the oaths to William and Mary, bore the orb at their coronation, and in 1690 commanded William's land forces at the siege of Cork. On the 28th of September, while leading his men to the assault, he received a shot which broke two of his ribs, and he died of the wound on the 9th of October following. He had been married by his father on the 1st of August 1672, when he had barely completed his ninth year, to the Lady Isabella Bennet, only daughter and eventually heir to Henry Bennet, the Earl of Arlington of the Cabal Ministry, then a very beautiful child of five years of age. From this marriage the Grafton family derive their estate and seat of EUSTON HALL in Suffolk, which gives them their second title. By her he had an only child, Charles, born at Arlington House, October 25, 1683, who became, on his father's death, second Duke of Grafton, and in right of his mother, who died in February 1723, Earl of Arlington (Middlesex), Viscount Thetford (Norfolk)—the patronage of which borough is chiefly in the Duke of Grafton —and Baron Arlington.

This second Duke of Grafton was a man of fair, but moderate abilities, who rose in 1720 to the Lord-Lieutenancy of Ireland, which office he filled in an undistinguished, but decent manner. He was subsequently appointed a Lord-Justice several times, and died in 1757, a worthy but only half-trusted man. He married in 1713 the Lady Henrietta Somerset, granddaughter of the Duke of Beaufort, and by her had five sons and four daughters. Lady Hervey, writing, in September 1732, of a visit paid by her to the fair at Bury, a favourite festival then among the gentry of Suffolk, says, "The only things that pleased me there were the Duke of Grafton's daughters. The two youngest are the best behaved *children* I ever saw; but Lady Caroline is the best bred *woman*, the most agreeable dancer, the genteelest and the prettiest creature that ever lived. I envy the Duke that girl. You may guess what I think of any one's daughter whom I wish my own." This last-named young lady, "Lady Caroline Fitzroy, was afterwards too well known," says the editor of this correspondence, "as Lady Caroline Petersham and Lady Harrington. Contemporary writers are full of anecdotes of this lady's conduct and manners, which, if but half of them were true, would have made Lady Hervey repent the accomplishment of her wish." She was the wife of the second Earl of Harrington. The Duke of Grafton's three eldest sons died before him, the two eldest without leaving children, and he was succeeded by his grandson, Augustus Henry, eldest surviving son of Lord Augustus Fitzroy, third son of the second Duke. Lord Augustus had served with some distinction in the navy at the attack on Carthagena, and died at Jamaica in May 1741. His younger son, Charles Fitzroy, was created, October 17, 1780, Baron Southampton, and was the grandfather of the present Lord Southampton, and of the late Right Hon. Henry Fitzroy, who was an active member of the Peel party, and died in 1859.

Augustus Henry, third Duke of Grafton, was born in October 1735, and in November 1756 was appointed a Lord of the Bedchamber to George III., then Prince of Wales. In the same year he entered the House of Commons as member for Bury St Edmund's, for which place he sat till his grandfather's death. During the Bute Ministry he rendered himself so obnoxious to the ruling powers that in 1763 he was one of the noblemen whom Lord Bute removed from their Lord-Lieutenancies (Suffolk in Grafton's case). In the same year he showed his political feelings by visiting Wilkes in prison. But on the 10th of July 1765 he consented to take office under Lord Rockingham as one of the Secretaries of State. He held this post till May 1766, when he resigned, alleging as his reason the impotency of the administration. He declared that he knew but of one man—meaning the first Pitt—who could give them proper strength. Under that person he should be willing to serve in any capacity, not only as a general officer, but as a pioneer, and would take up a spade and mattock and dig in the trenches. On the 2d of August following he had the opportunity he desired, being appointed First Lord of the Treasury in Pitt's second administration. But he soon found himself in a very different position from what he calculated on. To begin with, Pitt's acceptance of a peerage and removal from the Lower House was a great and unexpected blow to his colleagues, and his subsequent illness threw the whole burden of government on the Duke. Until towards the middle of March 1767 Pitt had been effectually Prime Minister, but from that time Grafton really directed the course of events, with the disadvantage of having a censor of his actions who might revive at any time in the person of his secluded chief. He was compelled to act as he best could under these circumstances, and strengthen himself with the Bedford party, Lord North, and any others of the Opposition or outsiders whom he could secure. When Chatham's powers began to revive, he expressed great jealousy and distaste at some of these appointments, and in October 1768 he resigned his office of Privy Seal, which he had chosen as a cover to his intended Premiership, notwithstanding all Grafton's efforts to dissuade him. Thus Grafton was left to carry on the administration of public affairs alone. Lord Stanhope says of him: " He was upright and disinterested in his public conduct, sincere and zealous in his friendships, and by no means wanting in powers, either of business or debate. Unhappily, however, as his career proceeded, experience showed that these excellent qualities were dashed and alloyed with others of an opposite tenor. He was wanting in application, and when pressed by difficulties in his office, instead of seeking to overcome them, would rather speak of resigning it. Field sports, and, above all, his favourite pack of hounds at Wakefield Lodge, too much employed his thoughts, or, at least, his time. Newmarket also had great charms for him; nor could he resist a still more dangerous fascination. His frequent appearance in public with Nancy Parsons, a well-known courtesan, gave offence to the laxer age in which he lived. His contemporaries beheld with surprise that woman seated at the head of the ducal table, or handed from the Opera House by the First Lord of the Treasury in the presence of the Queen. Other circumstances, some owing to no fault whatever of his own, tended to lower the reputation and to limit the term of his official power. Still, however, in spite of every disadvantage and defect, he continued, through a long life, much respected by all who knew him for the uprightness and integrity of his public motives, and for a considerable period he exercised no mean influence upon parties." In 1769, when the resistance took place in America to the import-duties, Grafton, at a Cabinet Council, had the good sense to propose that at the commencement of the next session they should bring in a bill for the complete repeal of the obnoxious duties. Lord North opposed the including tea in the duties to be repealed, and carried the rejection of Grafton's proposal by one vote. Had Lord Chatham continued in the Cabinet, Grafton considered that America would have been saved. "But for that unhappy event," he says in his 'Memoirs,' "I must think that the separation from America might have been avoided. For in the following spring Lord Chatham was sufficiently recovered to have given his efficient support in the Cabinet to Lords Camden,

Granby, and General Conway, who, with myself,
were overruled in our best endeavours to include the
article of tea with the other duties intended to be
repealed." And he adds, that from this time he felt
himself ill at ease in his high post. He had better
for his reputation have quitted it before the proceedings against Wilkes, or, at any rate, have retired now,
when outvoted on so important a question as America. But he remained, and suffered during this year
from the violent invectives of "Junius," and at its
close was threatened by the formidable opposition of
Lord Chatham. A few weeks after the latter's resignation his mental condition began to mend, and his
malady found relief, and passed off in a violent fit of
gout. He appeared for the first time in public at the
King's levee, in July 1769, was most graciously received, and admitted to a private conference in the
royal closet; but he treated the Duke of Grafton at
the levee with cold politeness. No sooner had the
new session of Parliament commenced in January
1770 than Chatham appeared as the opponent of
Government, denouncing alike their Wilkes proceedings and the American policy. An explosion in the
Cabinet followed. Lord Camden, the Chancellor, rose
in his place, expressed his sorrow at having acquiesced
silently in measures he so much disapproved of, and
denounced the measures of the Government as much as
Chatham himself. Grafton defended himself stoutly,
and when Camden did not resign, sent for the seals,
and through the personal importunity of the King succeeded in persuading Charles Yorke to accept them,
though he was pledged to the Rockingham party.
The reproaches, however, with which Yorke was as-

sailed by his former friends so preyed on his sensitive mind, that he went home and destroyed himself. Grafton found it impossible to get any one to take the vacant post. Granby, the Commander-in-Chief, had resigned, the Solicitor-General intimated a similar purpose, and Grafton at last lost heart, and on the 28th of January retired from the Premiership. The Opposition, however, did not profit by the victory, for the King, who had a singular power of personal persuasion, induced Lord North, much against his wish, to take the command of the Cabinet, and the nation, under his guidance, was induced to involve itself in the disastrous civil contest with the American Colonies. A violent scene took place between the Duke and Chatham in the House of Lords almost immediately after his resignation of office, Chatham denouncing the supposed secret influence of Bute (although the latter was resident abroad), and Grafton declaring that this supposition could only be " the effect of a distempered mind brooding over its own discontents." Unfortunately for his fame, Grafton, though declining to enter the North Cabinet, accepted under them the office of Lord Privy Seal, June 12, 1771. He retained this office till November 1775. Then a petition for accommodation with the mother country from the Colonial Assembly having been rejected by the English Government, Grafton protested against this course in a letter to Lord North, and receiving in return only a copy of the King's intended speech from the throne, he came up to London and resigned, freely debating the matter with the King himself in the royal closet. At the beginning of 1779, the Ministry endeavoured to induce Grafton, Camden, Shelburne, and the Rockingham Whigs to enter the Cabinet; but they declined, and this offer, the Duke says, had the effect of consolidating the Opposition, and paving the way for the second Rockingham Ministry. When this was formed, in 1782, Grafton resumed his office of Privy Seal, and continued in the Shelburne Ministry after Fox's secession, though in so discontented a manner that he could hardly be said to support it. He opposed successfully, along with the younger Pitt, the cession of Gibraltar to the Spaniards, proposed by Shelburne, and his resignation seemed imminent when Shelburne himself abandoned office. In December 1783, when the younger Pitt was forming his Cabinet, Grafton was one of the first persons he applied to, and the offer was repeated in the following year, but both times declined, the latter time after some considerable hesitation, his friend Camden having accepted the office of President of the Council. But the subsequent measures of the Pitt Ministry, and especially the war with France, alienated Grafton entirely from this connection, and he fell back on his old Whig principles. He lived, however, almost wholly in the retirement of country life, devoting himself to farming and the care of a numerous family. In 1797 he made a rather striking speech in the House of Lords, seconding an address of the Duke of Bedford's condemnatory of the war. In this he also urged economy in the internal government, denouncing the financial and monetary plans of the Ministry, and pointing to the necessity of conciliating Ireland by granting Catholic emancipation if they would avoid an immediate catastrophe. The whole speech was in a tone of solemn warning, and, delivered as it was in the Duke's naturally impressive voice, produced considerable effect. He was equally opposed to the renewal of the war with France after the peace of Amiens. His *tastes*, at any rate in his later years, were more creditable than those already alluded to. He was a warm patron of the poet Bloomfield, who came from the immediate neighbourhood of Euston. He made a large collection of rare books, and read as well as bought them. He took considerable interest in theological questions, publishing anonymously two pamphlets on the reformation of the Liturgy and relaxation of subscription to the Articles, and on public worship and prayer. He also when in town habitually attended the Unitarian Chapel in Essex Street; and it was by his encouragement and under his patronage that Griesbach published the second edition of his Greek New Testament, the Duke supplying the paper at his own expense, and sending it abroad to the editor. His manners are spoken of by some as agreeable, by others as somewhat reserved and haughty. His saturnine cast of countenance strongly resembled that of his royal ancestor. His dress was very peculiar. He wore a coat of the Quaker cut and colour, and a cocked hat. Having passed many years in this retirement, the Duke died March 14, 1811, at the age of seventy-six. On December 5, 1768, he had been elected Chancellor of the University of Cambridge, and September 20, 1769, a Knight of the Garter. He was also Governor of the Ports in Cornwall and Devon. He was divorced from his first wife, who remarried the Earl of Upper Ossory, the Duke himself marrying again, and having a large second family, the number of his children altogether being sixteen. His character was a good deal discussed in his lifetime, and has been much debated since; but we conceive that Charles II., born Peer instead of King, forced into collision with equals, and possessed of some ambition, would have acted precisely as Grafton did. He was a very favourable specimen of a Stuart in a private capacity, the only one of whom we have any complete record. His eldest son and successor, George Henry, fourth Duke of Grafton, till his elevation to the peerage represented the University of Cambridge in Parliament, for which he was returned in 1784, conjointly with Mr Pitt, with whom he had formed a strong friendship, against Lord John Townshend, the former member. He continued for some time to vote and act with Pitt, becoming a Lord of the Admiralty and Treasury in his administration; but he became discontented with the war with France, and his father's influence assisting in the change, he gradually adopted Whig principles, and became an opponent of Government, though he never was a violent one. After his accession to the dukedom he continued in the same line of politics—Whig, of a rather Conservative and independent character — and the remainder of his long life presents no features requiring special remark. He died September 28, 1844, in his eighty-fifth year, and was succeeded by his son Henry, fifth Duke, whose politics were of the same moderate cast, and whose life was passed in country retirement. He was, however, rather a warm Churchman, inquiring, it is said, whether a man was a communicant before he admitted him as a tenant. He devoted great attention to his estates, visiting the cottages

personally, and distributing blankets and other com-
forts where required, and, we need hardly add, was
greatly esteemed on his estates. He died March 26,
1863, and was succeeded by his son William Henry,
the sixth and present Duke of Grafton, who, as Earl
of Euston and representative of Thetford, pursued an
independent Whig line of politics, not always, but
generally, to be counted on by Whig Ministries. The
family, despite its origin, has been, on the whole, a
useful one; but the pension, which was a stock subject
of declamation with financial reformers, was exorbitant pay for a career like that of the third Duke. The
members of the house have been markedly popular
as landlords, and have been fairly free from that in-
herent faithlessness which was a prominent vice of
the Stuart blood.

The Spencers.

THE Spencers, who have now a dukedom, an earldom, and a barony, and who have possessed several peerages, are the descendants of one JOHN SPENCER, who was believed, by those who envied his family, to have been a great grazier in Warwickshire. He may have been a remote descendant of the great house of Le Despencer, now represented through the female line by an heiress of the Stapletons, who married into the Boscawen family, and by the Fanes, Earls of Westmoreland; but he did not claim this descent, and generations afterwards, during a celebrated quarrel, his heir admitted that the founder had "kept sheep." Whoever he was, he had considerable command of money, and was a great land-buyer, beginning with the great lordship of Wormleighton, in south Warwickshire, which he bought on the 3d of September 1506, the 22d year of Henry VII., from the Cope family. Here he began the structure of a "fair mansion," where he resided in some state, with a household of sixty persons. Two years after his Wormleighton purchase, he bought from the Catesby family the manor of ALTHORPE, in Northamptonshire, which became the principal seat of his successors; and

in the 3d year of Henry VIII. he purchased the manor
of Brington, in the immediate vicinity of Althorpe,
from Thomas Woodville, Marquess of Dorset.　With
this nobleman in the same year he exchanged some
lands at Bosworth, in Leicestershire, for the manor of
Wykedyve, in Northamptonshire, and purchased from
him the manor of Wyke Hamon, in the same county,
which the Spencers sold in 1716.　He acquired other
estates in the midland counties, rebuilt the churches
of Wormleighton, Brington, and Stanton, in Northamptonshire, and his will contains many bequests to
the religious houses.　He was knighted, and became
guardian to the heirs of the Catesby family, the
grandchildren of King Richard's favourite; and the
younger Sir Richard, who succeeded ultimately to the
Catesby estates at Legers Ashby and elsewhere, married Dorothy, youngest daughter of Sir John Spencer,
who by him was the great-grandmother of Robert
Catesby, the Gunpowder Plot conspirator.　Sir John
Spencer married Isabel, one of the daughters and coheirs of William Graun, Esq., of Smitterfeild, in Warwickshire, which place he obtained from this marriage,
and is first designated as " of " it.　He died April 14,
1522, and by his will, made two days previously, he
requires his executors to " recompense every one that
can lawfully prove, or will make oath, that he has hurt
him in anywise, so that they make their claim within
two years, though he had none in his remembrance ;
but he would rather charge their souls than his own
should be in danger."　He enjoined his executors to
cause proclamation to be made hereof once a-month
during the first year after his decease at Warwick,
Southampton, Coventry, Banbury, Daventry, and North-

ampton. Sir John, the founder, clearly a man of the true English type, with a taste for piety and accumulation, was succeeded by his son, Sir William, who died in two years, and his grandson, Sir John,* who was Sheriff of Nottinghamshire under Edward VI., Mary, and Elizabeth, but was undistinguished, save as a mighty grazier, who gave up even his parks to sheep and cattle. He died November 8, 1586, and left a great family—Sir John, who succeeded him in his principal estates; Thomas, of Claredon or Claverdon, in Warwickshire; Sir William, of Yarnton, Oxfordshire; Sir Richard, of Offley, Hertfordshire; Edward, who died without issue; and six daughters; who married into county or lordly families. Sir John Spencer, who succeeded to Althorpe and Wormleighton, was knighted in 1588, and married the daughter and heiress of Sir Robert Catelyn, Chief Justice of the King's Bench, by whom he left a son, Sir Robert, who, at the accession of King James, was believed to possess the largest amount of ready money of all persons in the kingdom. He was, therefore, created, without special services (July 21, 1603), Baron Spencer, of Wormleighton, but he seems to have been a most excellent person. Camden calls him a worthy encourager of virtue and learning; and Wilson, in his ' Life of King James,' says of him, "Spencer (like the old Roman, chosen dictator from his farm) made the country a virtuous court, where his fields and flocks brought him more calm and happy contentment than the various and unstable dispensations of a court can contribute, and when he was called to the senate was

---

* Spenser, the poet, claimed relationship with this family, and dedicated some of his poems to ladies belonging to it.

more vigilant to keep the people's liberties from being a prey to the encroaching power of monarchy than his harmless and tender lambs from foxes and ravenous creatures." His "ready money" had been made use of by King James at the commencement of his reign, he being sent, in 1603, to carry the insignia of the Garter to the Duke of Wurtemburg, one of the leading German Protestant princes. He was magnificently entertained by the Duke, and both the Duke and the ambassador were so richly attired, glittering with gold and jewels, that we are told they attracted the attention of all the spectators. Spencer held no post at Court, and in Parliament he appeared on the popular side, and once, in 1621, is said to have come into collision with the proud Earl of Arundel, the head of the Howards. Happening to appeal to the actions of their ancestors as an incentive to the Peers to take a free line of action, Arundel broke forth, " My Lord, when these things were doing, your ancestors were keeping sheep." Spencer, too proud also to put forward any spurious descent from an older family, replied, " When my ancestors were keeping sheep (as you say), your ancestors were plotting treason." A violent scene ensued, and Arundel, as the aggressor, was sent to the Tower, but after acknowledging his fault, and offering to make satisfaction, was discharged. Spencer, in the same year, with 32 other English peers, petitioned the King against being compelled to give rank of courtesy as to foreigners to Englishmen who had been raised to titles in Scotland and Ireland. The King was angry at this reflection on the lavish honours he was bestowing on his favourites, and rebuked Lord Spencer especially as the chief mover in the petition.

Lord Spencer died October 25, 1627, surviving by thirty years his wife, Margaret, daughter and coheir of Sir Francis Willoughby, of Woollaton, in Nottinghamshire, by whom he had four sons and three daughters. He was succeeded by his second son, William (the eldest having died without issue), second Lord Spencer, who was created a Knight of the Bath along with Prince Charles, in 1616, and represented the shire of Northampton in the Commons in three Parliaments of James I. and the two first of Charles I. He followed the same popular course in Parliament, and died in the 45th year of his age, December 19, 1636. He had married Lady Penelope Wriottesley, daughter of the Earl of Southampton, who survived him thirty-one years. He had by her six sons and seven daughters. The second son, Robert, was made Viscount Teviot, in Scotland, by James II., in 1686, but left no children.

Henry, the eldest son, third Lord Spencer, was born in November 1620, and educated at Magdalen College, Oxford. When he was only nineteen his guardians (his mother and the Earl of Southampton) married him to Lady Dorothy Sidney, daughter of Robert, Earl of Leicester, and sister of Algernon Sidney, the Saccharissa of Waller's poems, and he went after his wedding along with his father-in-law on his embassy to France, returned to England in October 1641, in the very crisis of the Parliamentary struggle, and took his seat immediately in the House of Lords. He at once chose his side with the party of Pym, and adhered to them actively until the complete breach with the King, and really in his heart to the end of his days. But he had an overstrained idea of the guilt of appearing in arms against the King, and as he himself says, he feared to abstain from fighting on one side or the other lest he should be accused of cowardice; so he took arms with the King, though confining himself to attendance on his person and fighting as a volunteer in the Royal Guard. He found nothing congenial in the Royal camp. He writes to his wife from Shrewsbury, September 21, 1642: "How much I am unsatisfied with the proceedings here I have at large expressed in several letters. Neither is there wanting handsome occasion to retire, were it not for gaining honour. If there could be an expedient found to solve the punctilio of honour, I would not continue here an hour. The discontent that I and many other honest men receive daily is beyond expression." On the 8th of June 1643, the King rewarded the romantic devotion of the young nobleman by raising him to the title of Earl of Sunderland. He was at the siege of Gloucester, which he predicts to his wife to be a great mistake in tactics, as they ought to have marched on London. Here he associated with Falkland and Chillingworth, and heard their dispute on the merits of Socinianism. When the siege was raised there, he obtained leave to go for a day or two to Oxford, where the Earl of Leicester was staying, delayed by the King's commands from going to his Lord-Lieutenancy in Ireland, and doing nothing but await the King's pleasure. From Oxford Sunderland addressed his wife again, only four days before the first battle of Newbury : "Since I came here I have seen no creature but your father and my uncle [Southampton], so that I am altogether ignorant of the intrigues of this place. I take the best care I can about my economical affairs.

I am afraid I shall not be able to get you a better house, everybody thinking me mad for speaking about it. Pray bless Poppet [his little daughter] for me, and tell her that I would have writ to her, but that upon mature deliberation I found it uncivil to return an answer to a lady in another character than her own, which I am not yet learned enough to do." In four days from the date of this letter (Sept. 20, 1643), Sunderland fell in a cavalry charge at Newbury. His body was carried to Brington and there buried. The Earl of Leicester wrote to his widowed daughter to condole with her on the event. "I know," he says, "you lived happily, and so as nobody but yourself could measure the contentment of it. I rejoiced at it, and did thank God for making me one of the means to procure it for you." He left a son, Robert, and a daughter, Dorothy,—the " Poppet " of his letter,—on whom he settled £10,000 as her marriage-portion, and who became the wife of Sir George Savile, afterwards Marquess of Halifax. Lady Sunderland lived for some years in retirement, giving shelter at her house, it is said, to the distressed Anglican clergy during the civil contest. In 1652 she married, secondly, Robert Smythe, son and heir of Sir John Smythe, a Kentish knight, first cousin of the first Viscount Strangford. Lady Sunderland survived her second husband also, and died in 1684. Her great-grandson from this second marriage, Sir Sidney Smythe, became Chief Baron of the Exchequer.

Hitherto the character of the Spencers has exhibited high moral qualities and abilities of a very respectable but not the highest grade. They are now to lose in moral stamp what they gain in intellectual calibre. Robert Spencer, second Earl of Sunderland, the only son of the high-spirited youth who fell at Newbury, passed the early part of his life in foreign travel, according to the customary practice at that period, and attracted, after his return to England, the notice of those high in power by the precocity of his talents and his keen appreciation of men and manners. In 1671 he was selected by the King to go as ambassador extraordinary to Spain, and in the succeeding year he was sent to Paris in the same capacity, and as one of the commissioners who proceeded to Cologne with the view of negotiating a general European peace. In 1678, when Ralph Montagu was recalled from the French Embassy, Sunderland took his place, and only left this post to enter the English Cabinet, after the fall of Danby, as Secretary of State. Here he was at first associated with Capel, Earl of Essex, his brother-in-law, Saville, then Viscount Halifax, and Sir William Temple. After the resignation of Essex and the withdrawal of Temple, Sunderland and Halifax continued, though hating each other, and anxious for an opportunity of escaping from their companionship. The Exclusion Bill was at first opposed by Sunderland; but when the debates came on he deserted the King and spoke and voted in its favour. The struggle which ensued is well known. When it had terminated in the discomfiture of the Whigs, Sunderland was dismissed by the King, as the punishment of his apostasy. His political character is described in a few words by Macaulay, by saying that he was quick-sighted but not far-sighted. He had been brought up in the dangerous school of diplomacy, and while he had a shrewd and keen perception of men and events immediately before his eyes, he looked at every passing event simply with reference to these, and forgot that there was a world without which might be regulated by very different impulses from such nice personal considerations. His powers of personal fascination were nearly unrivalled, and in private society he captivated or influenced nearly every one he encountered. But in Parliament he was a silent member, and he never appreciated the nature or importance of popular feeling. His principles, religious and moral, were of the lowest kind. He had held in his youth, and for some time ostentatiously paraded, the doctrines of republicanism. But he kept them quite apart from the world of men, with whom he was willing to deal on whatever basis best suited his own personal interests. Macaulay pronounces that his leading impulses were the greed of power and wealth and the fear of personal danger, and asserts that by the operation of these two impulses all his vagaries may be explained. His religious principles were as vague as his political. He defended atheism to the French envoy, while he adopted in turn either Protestantism or Catholicism as each seemed most advantageous to his interests. He had great administrative power in all the details and subordinate arrangements of government, and much tact and adroitness in the management of individuals, and special and ascertained situations. But he was continually discomfited by the greater events of the age, and with difficulty escaped from utter ruin by the exercise of a remarkable ingenuity when the crisis became apparent. He was neither addicted to women nor wine, but he was an inveterate gambler, and even if his natural disposition had not led in that direction,

the encumbrances on his estates which ensued from
this habit would have driven him to acquiring money
in any possible way, without shame or scruple. He
had no views of any kind to stand in his way, as was
the case with Danby, and his only drawback to action
was an almost morbid fear of personal consequences
to himself. His great patron at this time was the
Duchess of Portsmouth, and with her assistance, the
necessity for his versatile talents which was daily felt,
and the co-operation of Lawrence Hyde, better known
as " Rochester," the younger son of the Chancellor
Clarendon, who was now rising into power, Sunderland was recalled to his office in January 1682, and
held it for the remainder of the reign of Charles.
Nor was he dismissed at the accession of James. He
managed to ingratiate himself with the new King,
though he had voted for his exclusion from the
throne, and in the same year succeeded Halifax as
President of the Council, retaining his Secretaryship
of State. From this time Sunderland tried in every
possible way to secure his continuance in power by
lending himself to all the King's wishes. He willingly joined in all his illegal measures, sat in the High
Commission Court, attended the King publicly at
mass in the Palace, and at last professed an inclina-
tion to consider the doctrines of the Church of Rome,
professed himself in a state of suspense and afterwards
almost a convert to those views, joining himself to the
party of the Jesuits, and collecting the Roman clique
at his table every week to consult on the measures to
be adopted in their interest. The same religious test,
when applied to Rochester, it is said at Sunderland's
treacherous suggestion, produced opposite results and

his dismissal from office. Soon after his fall, Sunderland himself found the ground beginning to shake under him, for he not only disapproved of the proceedings in the case of Magdalen College, Oxford, his father's old college, but opposed the appointment of Tyrconnel to the Lord-Lieutenancy of Ireland, in place of Rochester's brother, Clarendon—Tyrconnel being pledged and devoted to the destruction of the English in Ireland. Tyrconnel blustered and cajoled, and finally Sunderland, fearing the disclosure of some expressions of his respecting the King, gave way on condition of receiving an annuity of £5000 from Ireland, redeemable on the payment of £50,000 down. He already enjoyed a pension of £5500 from the French King for promoting his interests, and he was making a gigantic fortune by the profits and peculations of office. To secure himself in the King's favour he made a public avowal of Roman Catholicism, and was admitted into that Church. But soon after this apostasy he became suddenly aware of the real state of feeling in the country ; he opposed the attack on the Bishops, and when he found that he was powerless in arresting the King's course, he entered into secret communications with William of Orange. The agency he chose was as disreputable as his course itself. His wife, a daughter of George Digby, second Earl of Bristol, the Lord Digby of the Civil Wars—and a woman with many of the peculiarities of her father— at once a devoted attendant on Protestant popular preachers, and a busy intriguer both in love and politics—had formed a love intrigue with her husband's relative Henry Sidney, and through her letters to him Sunderland conveyed his sentiments to William.

They were favourably received, and Sunderland, in the interval between August and October 1688, during which the correspondence went on, contrived to do essential service to the cause of William by preventing, through his influence in the French Embassy, a French army from invading Holland and a French fleet from covering the shores of England. One of Lady Sunderland's letters, however, fell into the hands of James, and Sunderland never recovered this shock to the King's confidence in him. He carried matters with a brazen front, and for the moment persuaded the King of his innocence; but fresh rumours of his treachery undermined his position, and in October he was dismissed from his office while petitioning Mary of Modena to take his part. In the confusion of the ensuing revolution he disappeared. He fled to Rotterdam, where he was arrested and thrown into prison by the magistrates, until released by an order of William's. Thence he repaired to Amsterdam, where he recanted his Roman Catholicism, and published a defence of his conduct, professing to have been always in favour of constitutional principles. He also studiously attended the Dutch Protestant Churches. He was excluded by name from the Act of Oblivion, but, after the dissolution of the Convention Parliament in 1690, ventured over to England, and had an interview with King William. He then retired for the time to his country house; but in the spring of 1691 re-appeared in London at the drawing-room, to the astonishment of every one, and was most graciously received by the King. He seems to have succeeded in fascinating William completely, and the King for the rest of his political life had constant

reference to him for advice. This is a great tribute
to his abilities, though it produced great scandal at
the time, and was one of the charges brought against
King William's character. Sunderland managed to
skulk down to the House of Lords on the occasion of
a formal prorogation, and took the oaths and his seat;
but he did not appear again as a regular attendant in
Parliament till 1692. In 1693 he took a house at
Whitehall, was habitually consulted by the King, and
by his advice William in that year called the Whigs
to his counsels. His eldest surviving son, Charles,
Lord Spencer, was now taking a position in political
life in the ranks of that party, and Sunderland had
made up his mind to act with them as the less hostile
to himself personally of the two parties. Still the
Whig leaders distrusted him, and the Whig rank and
file hated him as a Romanist apostate. In 1695 he
was the main instrument in bringing about a reconciliation between the King and the Princess Anne, who,
since the death of the Queen, had been more disposed
to reconciliation as the way was paved to her own
succession. In the same year William paid Sunderland a visit at Althorpe, on occasion of a Royal progress which he was making. "All Northamptonshire," says Macaulay, "crowded to kiss the Royal
hand in that fine gallery, which had been embellished
by the pencil of Vandyke and made classical by the
muse of Waller; and the Earl tried to conciliate his
neighbours by feasting them at eight tables, all blazing
with plate." Sunderland had, during this period of
restored favour, been on the whole faithful to William,
though he had made one or two faint overtures to St
Germains, very ungraciously received. His assistance

to the Government had also been very considerable, as even his enemies admit that affairs went on much more successfully after he attained this position. But he had the folly, in 1697, to accept the office of Lord Chamberlain, instead of contenting himself with ruling the country without an office. Immediately all his enemies attacked him, Whigs, Tories, and Jacobites, in one unanimous cry of reprobation. His Whig colleagues did not pretend to support him, and one of them described him as a fireship, more dangerous to his friends than his foes. Nothing could appease the hatred and distrust of politicians, and the whole nation echoed the cry. The King stood firmly by him, and his friends tried to persuade him to hold his ground ; but a threatened address of the Commons to the King to remove him from the Royal counsels for ever, frightened him so much that he insisted on resigning, and retired in the most hurried way into private life, from which he never again emerged, dying at Althorpe, September 28, 1702, leaving behind him the reputation of an evil Ahithophel.

He was succeeded by his younger son, Charles, who had entered Parliament in 1695 as member for Tiverton, and ran a remarkable career. His character is the subject of much dispute among historians. Macaulay is very severe in his remarks on him. " The precocious maturity of the young man's intellectual and moral character had created hopes," he says, " which were not destined to be realised. His knowledge of ancient literature and his skill in imitating the styles of the masters of Roman eloquence were applauded by veteran scholars. The sedateness of his deportment and the apparent regularity of his life

delighted austere moralists. He was known, indeed,
to have one expensive taste; but it was a taste of the
most respectable kind. He loved books, and was bent
on forming the most magnificent private library in England. While other heirs of noble houses were inspect-
ing patterns of steinkirks and sword-knots, dangling
after actresses, or betting on fighting-cocks, he was in
pursuit of the Mentz editions of Tully's 'Offices,' of
the Parmesan 'Statius,' and of the inestimable 'Vir-
gil' of Zarottus. It was natural that high expectations should be formed of the virtue and wisdom of a
youth whose very luxury and prodigality had a grave
and erudite air; and that even discerning men should
be unable to detect the vices which were hidden under that show of premature sobriety. Spencer was a
Whig, unhappily for the Whig party, which before
the unhonoured and unlamented close of his life was
more than once brought to the verge of ruin by his
violent temper and his crooked politics." On the
other hand, Lord Stanhope, who may have been somewhat influenced by the friendship between his great
ancestor and Sunderland, observes: "The character of
Earl Charles has, in my opinion, been unjustly depre-
ciated; he has been confounded with his predecessor,
and the perfidy of the parent has cast its blighting
shade over the fame of the son. The father was a
subtle, pliant, and unscrupulous candidate for royal
favour; the son carried his love of popular rights to
the very verge of republican doctrines. If he be
sometimes open to charges of secret cabals, we find
him much more frequently accused of imprudent
vehemence and bluntness. . . . He was, undoubtedly, a man of great quickness, discernment, and skill,

of persevering ambition, of a ready eloquence. Under
the show of a cold and reserved exterior there glowed
the volcano of an ardent and fiery spirit, a warm
attachment to his friends, and an unsparing rancour
against his opponents. His learning is not denied,
even by the enmity of Swift, and his activity in business seems to be equally unquestionable. In private
life he might be accused of extravagance and love of
play, and his conduct in more than one public transaction appears to me either equivocal or blamable ;
but I may observe that several points for which he
was condemned by his contemporaries would, on the
contrary, deserve the approbation of more enlightened
times." On the whole, perhaps, we may say that the
cloud which overshadowed his father's fame gave a
deeper colouring, in the popular mind, to Sunderland's
moral delinquencies than the truth warranted ; but, on
the other hand, that there was just enough resemblance in his character to some parts of his father's to
support the belief that the hereditary taint existed,
though it may have been far less engrained than in
the father's case. His father also had an affected frankness of manner, though no man was really less frank.
In early life Charles Spencer put forward strong republican opinions, refusing to be called " Lord," and
saying that he hoped to see the end of that order.
Macaulay treats his republicanism as of the narrowest
oligarchical and Venetian character, based on the aristocratic types of Pompey and Cicero. But the reason
he gives for this opinion, the measure brought forward
at a later period by Sunderland to restrict the number
of the Peers, is not conclusive on the point. He certainly throughout life professed strong Whig opinions,

and in the Parliaments of 1695, 1698, and 1701, he advocated these principles so eloquently in the House of Commons, and, after his accession to the Peerage, in the House of Lords, that he soon rose to distinction in the ranks of the Whig party. In Parliamentary eloquence he much excelled his father. He had first married, in 1695, a daughter of Henry Cavendish, Duke of Newcastle; but on her death (leaving only a daughter, married to the heir of the Earl of Carlisle) he made a second and more important match with Lady Anne Churchill, Marlborough's second daughter and coheiress, and through his father-in-law's influence, probably, he was sent in the summer of 1705 as ambassador to Vienna, to compliment the Emperor Joseph on his accession, and on the 10th of April 1706, was appointed one of the Commissioners for the Union with Scotland. These were only introductory steps to the more important post of Secretary of State, which the Whigs obtained for him in December 1706. Marlborough is said to have opposed the appointment at first, distrusting his son-in-law's rashness; but the all-potent Sarah decided that it should be so. The Cabinet soon became entirely Whig by the removal of Harley, the other Secretary, and from this time down to the year 1710 Sunderland continued to act in this post with considerable ability, though historians differ as to his discretion as a politician and a political leader. According to Lord Dartmouth, " Queen Anne said Lord Sunderland always treated her with great rudeness and neglect, and chose to reflect in a very injurious manner upon all princes before her as a proper entertainment for her." But the Duchess of Marlborough's influence having then given way to

another's, Sunderland, as her son-in-law, got naturally
out of the Queen's good graces, and in June 1710, the
first public intimation of the approaching downfall of
the Whigs was given by the Earl's sudden dismissal
from his Secretaryship. As soon as Sunderland's intended dismissal began to be rumoured, Marlborough,
his wife tells us, wrote a very moving letter to the
Queen against the step, and the Duchess herself was
persuaded to condescend to similar appeals. But all
was vain, and Sunderland remained out of office for the
rest of that reign. When the house of Hanover was
proclaimed, he naturally looked for a high appointment
in the Cabinet. But first of all both he and his father-
in-law were passed over in the appointments of Lords
Justices before the King's arrival, and when the new
Cabinet was formed Townshend was preferred to him,
and he had merely the appointment of Lord-Lieutenant
of Ireland. Incensed at this slight, Sunderland never
repaired to his post, but consoled himself with annoy-
ing the Government by giving all the Irish appointments to " natives," to the horror of the " English "
party there. He is also accused of intrigues with the
Pretender, and it is certain he coquetted with the
Jacobites as well as the Tories to induce them to join
him against the Government, drawing off also some of
the Whigs. He alarmed the Government sufficiently
to induce them, in August 1715, to make him Privy
Seal with a seat in the Cabinet, and in February 1716,
Vice-Treasurer of Ireland. But as this gave him no
real power, he continued to maintain a sulky silence
in the House of Lords, and to intrigue against his
colleagues. In July 1716, he had an opportunity of
revenging himself on them. The King's journey to

Hanover, as we have said in our account of the first Earl Stanhope, gave Sunderland, who was at Aix-la-Chapelle, the means of personal access to the King. Of this he availed himself with such effect that he captivated George as completely as his father had Charles, James, and William. He also made a friend of Stanhope, and together they contrived to get Townshend dismissed, and in April 1717, Walpole and Pulteney shared the same fate, and Sunderland and Stanhope became the heads of a new Government—the former as Secretary of State. This post he subsequently exchanged with Stanhope for that of First Lord of the Treasury, and he also took for the time the post of President of the Council, and, on his resigning the latter office in February 1719, the King, as a sort of special favour, made him Groom of the Stole and First Gentleman of the Bedchamber. Sunderland now ruled the home policy of the Government as Stanhope did its foreign. In March 1719, the former introduced his Peerage Bill, restricting the number of creations—intended, it is said, by Sunderland, as an act of protection to himself and his colleagues against the Prince of Wales in case of the King's death. After passing through the House of Lords without a division, it was at last thrown out in the Commons, through the exertions of Walpole, by a large majority. Sunderland is accused of having vainly attempted to secure a pliant House of Commons by the exercise of the grossest bribery and jobbery. But, perhaps, here also we must allow something for party exaggeration and recollections of his father's conduct. He now found it necessary to conciliate Walpole, and the latter and Townshend also, despairing of overthrowing the

Cabinet, consented to enter it in June 1720. The Cabinet was scarcely re-formed when the South Sea Bubble crash occurred, and among the revelations which came forth was an accusation against several of the Ministers of corruption. Sunderland especially was accused of taking £50,000 of stock without paying for it. Lord Stanhope discredits the charge; other historians consider it proved. The public, however, at the time, from the recollection of his father's corrupt dealings, had no doubts, and the accusation, it is said, would have been declared established if it had not been for the great exertions of Walpole. The public still continued to believe in his guilt and to clamour against him, and Sunderland, like his father, thought it prudent to beat a retreat, and in April 1721 resigned all his appointments. He continued, however, to exercise a great influence on public affairs, and retained such favour with the King that he really nominated to the important offices, and among these appointments was that of Lord Carteret, who gratefully defends his memory. He is accused of intriguing without cessation to remove Walpole from power and procure his own reinstatement; and, again, of correspondence with the Pretender; but it appears, on the authority of the Chevalier himself, that he merely made vague professions of goodwill to some of the Jacobites, most probably, as before, to gain them over, and it would also seem that he did so with the knowledge and approval of King George. In the midst, however, of his intrigues and hopes, Sunderland died suddenly, on the 19th of April 1722—so suddenly that poison was hinted at; but on his body being opened it was found that he died from disease of the heart. Besides his patronage of books and learning, he was an active member of the Kit-Kat Club. He had married a third time ; but his sons who succeeded to the property were all by his second wife, eventually the heiress of the Churchills. Of his four sons, the eldest, Robert, succeeded as fourth Earl of Sunderland, but died unmarried November 27, 1729 ; the second, Charles, succeeded his brother as fifth Earl of Sunderland, and on the death of his aunt Henrietta, Duchess of Marlborough (the wife of Earl Godolphin), in 1733, became Duke of Marlborough. John, the third son of the third Earl of Sunderland, in 1744, succeeded to the *Spencer* property, with Althorpe, and was the father of the first Earl Spencer.

We shall first pursue the fortunes of the elder branch, who, as Dukes of Marlborough, still hold a high position in English political and social life. Charles Spencer, fifth Earl of Sunderland and seventh Lord Spencer, on the death of his cousin, the Marquess of Blandford, only son of Henrietta, Duchess of Marlborough, and Earl Godolphin, succeeded to an annual rent-charge of £8000, and on the decease of the Duchess without male issue, October 24, 1733, succeeded as Duke of Marlborough to the honours of the Churchills—a family claiming a descent from Roger de Courcill, who held lands in Somersetshire, Dorsetshire, and Devonshire in the time of the Doomsday survey; but which will be only remembered in history as the family of the "Great Duke." The new Duke chose the career of a soldier, and became Colonel of the 1st Regiment of Dragoons, commanded the Foot Guards at Dettingen, and the great but fruitless expedition of 1758 against St Malo.

He had scarcely returned when he was placed in command of an expedition to Embden, where he died, men said, of dysentery, but others suspected foul play—a gentleman having shortly before been prosecuted for threatening, if the Duke did not supply his wants, to avenge himself " by means which no physic would remedy." His successor, George, third Duke, was a man of very retired habits, of whom Lord Loughborough said that he would have been an excellent head for a coalition Cabinet if only he could have overcome his aversion to business. In 1789, in the 'Auckland Correspondence,' regret is expressed at his being too nervous to second the Address to the Throne. He was a Conservative-Whig in his opinions, and a general supporter of Mr Pitt's Government, but he scarcely took any part in politics, having a great aversion to the heartburnings and animosities often consequent on that career. He lived almost entirely at BLENHEIM, where he rendered himself an object of great affection to his tenants and the neighbourhood by his amiable and charitable disposition. His private life is described as unblemished even by the faintest scandal, and in him we seem to have a revival of the old Spencer type of character exhibited by the predecessors of the two intriguing Earls. He married a daughter of John, Duke of Bedford, and was found dead in his bed without any previous indisposition, January 29, 1817, at the age of seventy-eight. The Duke's second son, Francis Almeric Spencer, was created, on the 11th of August 1815, Baron Churchill of Whichwood, Oxfordshire, and his son is the present Lord Churchill.

George, fourth Duke of Marlborough, was a singu-

lar man, whose career had a most promising commencement and a melancholy termination. He was
educated at Oxford, and entered Parliament for Oxfordshire in 1790, in room of his uncle, Lord Charles
Spencer, but relinquished the seat to him again in
1796. In July 1804 he was appointed one of the
Lords of the Admiralty, which office he filled till
February 1806, when he was called up to the House
of Peers in his father's Barony of Spencer. After his
father's death, when he became Duke of Marlborough,
he took by royal licence, in May 1817, the name and
arms of Churchill, in addition to those of Spencer.
He attached himself to the Whig party, and became
a strong partisan. Some scandal was created at an
election for Woodstock by the Duke's younger son
standing on his father's interest against the elder, the
Marquess of Blandford, who had adopted Conservative views. While he was Marquess of Blandford,
the Duke exhibited many of the tastes of his family,
and was distinguished by the magnificence and reck-
less expense with which he indulged in them. Especially his gardens and his library at White Knights,
near Reading, which place he had purchased in 1798,
attracted general attention. At the sale of the library
of the Duke of Roxburghe, in 1812, the Marquess
(as he then was) engaged in competition with his
cousin, Earl Spencer, for an edition of the 'Decame-
rone' of Boccaccio, printed at Venice in 1471, and
obtained it at the enormous price of £2260. An im-
perfect copy was already in the library at Blenheim.
The Roxburghe Club was formed on this occasion,
Earl Spencer becoming President, and the Marquess of
Blandford one of its members. In 1815 he bought
the celebrated Bedford Missal for the sum of £698, 5s.

Besides these expensive tastes the Duke had the family vice of gambling, and the two combined brought him down from his princely position to one of great poverty. His collections were all sold, and for the latter years of his life he lived in complete but not reputable seclusion in one corner of Blenheim Palace, and seldom quitted the spot, except for a short visit every year to a watering-place. He died March 5, 1840. His eldest son and successor, George Spencer-Churchill, fifth Duke, did nothing to redeem the family character, though in the first period of his succession to the dukedom he managed by rather close economy to retrieve in some measure the family property. He also quarrelled with his eldest son on the score of politics—the latter having adopted Peel principles. The Duke died July 1, 1857, and was succeeded by his eldest son, John Winston, sixth and present Duke, a man of far higher personal character and some ability, though (of late years) of rather narrow Church-Conservative principles. His younger brother, Lord Alfred Spencer-Churchill, M.P., has exhibited some talent as a politician, and is a very Liberal Conservative.

We must now hastily glance at the career of the younger Spencer branch, represented by the present Earl Spencer. John Spencer, the youngest son of Charles Spencer, third Earl of Sunderland, by Lady Anne Churchill, entered Parliament for Woodstock at the beginning of 1732, for which place he continued to sit for many years. In October 1744, on the death of Sarah, Duchess of Marlborough, he acquired a large property. In the first place his elder brother, in accordance with his grandfather's will, relinquished the Spencer patrimony in his favour on attaining to the

Churchill estates, and Althorpe became the chief seat of the new Spencer family. At the same time John Spencer acquired an immense property from the deceased Duchess, whose favourite grandson he was,—nearly all her large paternal (the Jennings') estates—among them the Wimbledon property—and nearly the whole of the Duchess's own accumulations of money during her long life. The new family, therefore, started on a scale of opulence more than equal to the elder branch. John Spencer also succeeded to the office of Ranger and Keeper of the Great Park at Windsor, which fell to him on the death of his grandmother, the Duchess, and was the only place he was allowed by her will to accept. He died June 20, 1746, and was succeeded by his only son, John, born December 18, 1734. He entered Parliament for Warwick in December 1757, and on April 3, 1761, was created Viscount Spencer and Baron Spencer of Althorpe, and on November 1, 1765, Viscount Althorpe, and Earl Spencer. He held no public office, and died October 31, 1783. His only son and successor, George John, second Earl Spencer, attached himself to the Whig party, and particularly that section headed by the Duke of Portland. Along with the Duke he took office, 1782, as a Lord of the Treasury, and again in July 1794, under Pitt, as Lord Privy Seal. This office he exchanged in the autumn of the same year for that of First Lord of the Admiralty, which he filled down to the year 1801. He was no debater, but had considerable administrative abilities, and it was under his guidance that the naval department of the Government remained during the greater part of the first revolutionary war with France, besides which he had to contend with the formidable mutiny at the

Nore. He disapproved of the terms of the peace of Amiens, and, attaching himself thenceforth to Lord Grenville, with him took office in 1806 along with Fox. After the death of that statesman Lord Spencer retired from public life, and at Althorpe revived the old fame of his family for hospitality and attention to their estates. He took great pains in establishing savings banks in the county, and was for many years Chairman of the Quarter Sessions. About fifteen years before his death his tenantry presented him with a silver vase as a testimonial of their attachment, at a meeting at Althorpe, at which one tenant was present whose ancestors had held from the Spencers uninterruptedly from the time of the founder, Sir John Spencer, in the reign of Henry VIII. The Earl also, as we have intimated, was a great collector of books, " and the splendid library at Althorpe is a monument of his taste and energy." He had the true Spencer love of private life, and maintained the family virtues. His death, November 10, 1834, gave William IV. the opportunity of dismissing the Whig Ministry, of which his eldest son, John Charles, was the leader in the House of Commons as Chancellor of the Exchequer. The character of this nobleman, the third Earl Spencer, is well known. His early leadership of the Liberal party in the first days of the Reform administration, his retirement into private life and assiduous patronage of agricultural pursuits, and his advocacy of freetrade principles, are matters of recent history. He died October 1, 1845, and was succeeded by his brother Frederick, fourth Earl, who died December 27, 1857, and was succeeded by his son John Poyntz, fifth and present Earl Spencer. Neither of the two last Earls has made any position in political life, though the "*estimable*" character of the family seems not to have been misrepresented in their persons.

We have abstained hitherto, contrary to custom, from giving any opinion on the character of this great house, chiefly for this reason. No narrative within our limits of space would prove what we believe to be the truth,—that the Spencers have, from first to last, belonged to a class, formerly very rare, now terribly common—men in whom great ability, sound judgment, and a positive passion for culture were always weakened, and frequently vitiated, by a febrile nervousness of organisation. Their love of private life proceeded mainly from a consciousness of this fact, and so did the strange union of daring ambition and moral timidity which distinguished the ablest among them. In *the* Sunderland this nervousness rose to the height of morbid timidity, and we believe that the motive of all his unscrupulousness and the governing principle of his conduct was the morbid dread of consequences to himself — not consequences in the sense of direct personal danger, but consequences in the way in which these organisations always picture the unknown to themselves. There has not been a Spencer without capacity, or one who might not have repeated as his own autobiography Southey's line,—

"But I all naked feeling and raw life."

END OF THE FIRST VOLUME.